Georgia Harkness

LIBRARY OF THEOLOGICAL ETHICS

General Editors

Robin W. Lovin, Southern Methodist University
Douglas F. Ottati, Davidson College
William Schweiker, The University of Chicago

Editorial Advisory Board Members

Katie Geneva Cannon, Union—PSCE
Robin Gill, The University of Kent
James M. Gustafson, Emory University
Peter J. Paris, Princeton Theological Seminary
Jean Porter, The University of Notre Dame
Timothy F. Sedgwick, Virginia Theological Seminary
Charles M. Swezey, Union—PSCE
Allen D. Verhey, Duke University Divinity School
D. M. Yeager, Georgetown University

Other Books in This Series

Basic Christian Ethics, by Paul Ramsey
Christ and the Moral Life, by James M. Gustafson
Christianity and the Social Crisis, by Walter Rauschenbusch
Conscience and Its Problems, by Kenneth E. Kirk
Economic Justice: Selections from Distributive Justice *and* A Living Wage, by John A. Ryan
Ethics in a Christian Context, by Paul L. Lehmann
Feminist Theological Ethics: A Reader, edited by Lois K. Daly
The Holy Spirit and the Christian Life: The Theological Basis of Ethics, by Karl Barth
Love and Justice: Selections from the Shorter Writings of Reinhold Niebuhr, edited by D. B. Robertson
The Meaning of Revelation, by H. Richard Niebuhr
Morality and Beyond, by Paul Tillich
Moral Man & Immoral Society, by Reinhold Niebuhr
The Nature and Destiny of Man: A Christian Interpretation (2 vols.), by Reinhold Niebuhr
Radical Monotheism and Western Culture: With Supplementary Essays, by H. Richard Niebuhr
Reconstructing Christian Ethics: Selected Writings, by F. D. Maurice
Religious Liberty: Catholic Struggles with Pluralism, by John Courtney Murray
The Responsible Self: An Essay in Christian Moral Philosophy, by H. Richard Niebuhr
"The Responsibility of the Church for Society" and Other Essays by H. Richard Niebuhr, edited and with an introduction by Kristine A. Culp
Situation Ethics: The New Morality, by Joseph Fletcher
The Social Teachings of the Christian Churches (2 vols.), by Ernst Troeltsch
The Structure of Christian Ethics, by Joseph Sittler
The Ten Commandments, by William P. Brown
A Theology for the Social Gospel, by Walter Rauschenbusch
Treasure in Earthen Vessels: The Church as a Human Community, by James M. Gustafson
War in the Twentieth Century: Sources in Theological Ethics, edited by Richard B. Miller

Georgia Harkness

The Remaking
of a Liberal Theologian

Edited by Rebekah Miles

WESTMINSTER
JOHN KNOX PRESS
LOUISVILLE • KENTUCKY

© 2010 Westminster John Knox Press

First edition
Published by Westminster John Knox Press
Louisville, Kentucky

10 11 12 13 14 15 16 17 18 19—10 9 8 7 6 5 4 3 2 1

Georgia Harkness's "Nature as the Vehicle of Grace," originally published in *Religion in Life* 9 (Winter 1940): 503–12, is used by permission.

The following writings of Georgia Harkness are used by permission of the World Council of Churches Publications: "The Theological Basis of the Missionary Message." *International Review of Missions.* Vol. 28. Geneva. WCC Publications, 1939, pp. 518–26. "The Abyss and the Given." *Christendom.* Vol. 3. Geneva: WCC Publications, 1939, pp. 508–26. "A Symposium on Reinhold Niebuhr's *Nature and Destiny of Man." Christendom.* Vol. 6. Geneva: WCC Publications, 1941, pp. 567–70. Founded in 1948, the **World Council of Churches** is now a fellowship of more than 340 Christian churches confessing together "the Lord Jesus Christ according to scriptures" and seeking "to fulfill together their common calling to the glory of the one God, Father, and Holy Spirit." Tracing its origins to international movements dedicated to world mission and evangelism, life and work, faith and order, Christian education, and church unity, the World Council is made up primarily of Protestant and Orthodox churches. The Roman Catholic Church is not a member but participates with the World Council of Churches and its member communions in a variety of activities and dialogues.

Copyright © 1939 by the *Christian Century:* "Spiritual Pilgrimage" by Georgia Harkness is reprinted with permission from the March 18, 1939, issue of the *Christian Century.* Copyright © 1941 by the *Christian Century:* "The Christian's Dilemma" by Georgia Harkness is reprinted with permission from the August 6, 1941, issue of the *Christian Century.* Copyright © 1942 by the *Christian Century:* "What Is God Doing in This War?" by Georgia Harkness is reprinted with permission from the November 4, 1942, issue of the *Christian Century.* Copyright © 1942 by the *Christian Century:* "The Churches in This War" by Georgia Harkness is reprinted with permission from the November 18, 1942, issue of the *Christian Century.*

The following writings by Georgia Harkness are used with the permission of Marguerite Overholt: "Shall We Walk by Faith?" "Personality, Human and Divine"; and "Is There a God?—Evidence for Belief" from *Conflicts in Religious Thought* (New York: Henry Holt and Company, 1929). "A Christian Society: Ends and Means" and "Our Enlightened Paganism" from *Resources of Religion* (New York: Henry Holt and Company, 1936). "The Place of Ideals in Human Nature," "Synoptic Supernatualism," "What God Is," and "How God Is Limited" from *The Recovery of Ideals* (New York: Charles Scribner's Sons, 1937). "A World Church in a World Crisis," "By What Authority," and "Retrospect and Credo" from *The Faith by Which the Church Lives* (New York: Abingdon Press, 1940).

Book design by Sharon Adams
Cover design by Lisa Buckley

Library of Congress Cataloging-in-Publication Data

Georgia Harkness : the remaking of a liberal theologian / edited by Rebekah Miles.—1st ed.
    p. cm.—(Library of theological ethics series)
  Includes bibliographical references and index.
  ISBN 978-0-664-22667-1 (alk. paper)
  1. Liberalism (Religion)—United States.   2. Harkness, Georgia Elma, 1891–1974.   I. Miles, Rebekah.
  BR517.G47 2010
  230'.046—dc22

2009033747

In memory and in honor of Georgia Harkness, JoAnn Ridgway Miles,
and the many other women of earlier generations who,
by treading a hard way, made the way easier for me
and for so many other women who came after them

Contents

Library of Theological Ethics

General Editors' Introduction

The field of theological ethics possesses in its literature an abundant inheritance concerning religious convictions and the moral life, critical issues, methods, and moral problems. The Library of Theological Ethics is designed to present a selection of important texts that would otherwise be unavailable for scholarly purposes and classroom use. The series engages the question of what it means to think theologically and ethically. It is offered in the conviction that sustained dialogue with our predecessors serves the interests of responsible contemporary reflection. Our more immediate aim in offering it, however, is to enable scholars and teachers to make more extensive use of classic texts as they train new generations of theologians, ethicists, and ministers.

The volumes included in the Library comprise a variety of types. Some make available English-language texts and translations that have fallen out of print; others present new translations of texts previously unavailable in English. Still others offer anthologies or collections of significant statements about problems and themes of special importance. We hope that each volume will encourage contemporary theological ethicists to remain in conversation with the rich and diverse heritage of their discipline.

ROBIN W. LOVIN
DOUGLAS F. OTTATI
WILLIAM SCHWEIKER

Preface and Acknowledgments

In a speech given in 1961 to mark her retirement from the Pacific School of Religion, Georgia Harkness recalled a conversation from the 1930s with the president of Union Theological Seminary in New York. "What has happened— as Henry Sloane Coffin once reminded me when I ventured to defend liberalism against a hostile climate at the Union Seminary chapel—is that those who have never had to battle for the liberal spirit of free inquiry, but have simply inherited it from the efforts of an earlier day, have no realization of its cost. It is not essential that all theology bear the label of liberalism, but it is essential that theology, whatever its brand name, preserve the spirit of inquiry."[1]

In her article "Spiritual Pilgrimage" (reading 1 of this book), Gerorgia Harkness describes herself as "a liberal unrepentant and unashamed" and then adds that her liberalism had been "chastened and deepened" by the world events and theological disagreements of her time. As a creedal or orthodox Christian "unrepentant and unashamed," I have often found myself disagreeing passionately with Harkness. I have thrown books to the floor and have sworn, more than once, that I would never write another word about Georgia Harkness.

But I was wrong, of course . . . about a lot of things. My own theology has been chastened, and I hope deepened, by living with Harkness over recent years. She has given me many gifts—chief among them a new appreciation for the liberal theological tradition and its dogged fight to preserve the "spirit of free inquiry." As one who has inherited this gift "from the efforts of an earlier day," I am grateful to Harkness and to many others who fought to win it.

As wonderful as the spirit of free inquiry is, authors need more than *just* that to finish their books. They may need the assistance of others to copy articles and proofread manuscripts, the provision of time and space for research and writing, and the support to keep a household running. I have received that and much more. I am grateful to a series of graduate student assistants who have helped with this project, including Julie Mavity Maddalena, Kevin Carnahan, Pam Rose Beeler, Melanie Moore Briscoe, Terri Inman Rodriguez, and Larraine Waughtal; to Carolyn Douglas who scanned all the documents and helped with the proofreading; and to Len Delony and Mitzi Ellington who read and provided comments on parts of the manuscript.

My thanks go to the editors at Westminster John Knox Press, particularly Jana Riess and the late Stephanie Egnotovich, and to the board of the Library of Theological Ethics Series for their help and patience. Special thanks are due to Mrs. Peggy Overholt, the niece of Georgia Harkness, for giving permission to use many of the texts in this collection.

Harkness was the most productive in her writing when she had the gift of both time away from teaching as well as places where she could write, like her cottage on Lake Champlain in New York. The same is true for many other scholars, including me. My gratitude goes to the Motz-Storey family who helped to turn our garage into a home office; to Sister Pascalene Coff and other sisters of the Osage Benedictine Ashram who shared with me their hermitage, meals, and prayers; and to Nancy and James Allen and John and JoAnn Miles who gave me use of their lake homes to write. Thanks go also to Dean William Lawrence and Provost Paul Ludden of Southern Methodist University who approved a research leave that allowed me to finish this collection. The United Methodist Sam Taylor Award and the Ford Research Fellowship at Southern Methodist University provided support for which I am grateful. The Luce and Louisville Foundations granted funds for extended research leaves during which I worked on this project and others. I give thanks for and to the staff, the board members, and the donors of these two foundations for giving time to me and so many other scholars.

Without the support and prayers of an extended network of friends and family, I would be done for. I give thanks to God for the women who regularly pray with and for me: Karen Baker-Fletcher, Mitzi Ellington, Elaine Heath, Linda McDermott, and Jeanne Stevenson-Moessner, and for Martha Brooks who offers spiritual direction. Thanks go to my extended family and especially to my husband, Len Delony, and our daughters, Anna and Katherine, who have given a lot so that I could work on this project and others. They have given me peace and quiet on occasion and encouragement all the time. On top of all that, when I am locked away in my study, Len keeps the children fed, clean laundry in the drawers, and the whole family covered in prayer.

My mother, JoAnn Ridgway Miles, died unexpectedly as this book was being prepared for publication. She was to the end a "a liberal unrepentant and unashamed." A laywoman in the United Methodist Church, she was widely praised for working to support clergywomen and to help elect women bishops.

This book is dedicated to women of earlier generations, including my mother and Georgia Harkness. By treading a hard way, these women made the way easier for me and for the many other women who came after them. I have grown irritated at times with Harkness's confidence about history. Even in her chastened form, she still believed that history, in spite of temporary setbacks, was moving on a generally upward trajectory, and that, over time, freedom and justice were increasing. I grow impatient, until I remember how extraordinary it is, in the larger sweep of history, that Harkness and many other women of her generation were able to break through barriers that for centuries, even millennia, had appeared impenetrable—and to do it *so thoroughly* that women like me, just a few generations ahead, could so easily forget how far we have come and how much easier the path because of what we have "inherited from the efforts of an earlier day."

The "freedom of open inquiry" that Harkness and Coffin so prized means nothing when groups of people are restricted from the conversation. Women today, along with many others from groups that have suffered discrimination in the past, have much greater access to scholarly engagement, official church debates, political leadership, and scores of other areas than did previous generations. That is another gift of the liberal tradition, a gift from which I have benefited and for which I am grateful.

I finished this book just as the 2008 United States presidential race came to a close. Barack Obama's election was made possible not simply by the support he received in the build-up to the elections, but also by the efforts of many people within the liberal theological tradition who worked in previous decades for greater justice and inclusion in U.S. political life. Among these was Martin Luther King Jr., who, like Harkness, was trained at Boston University in the personalist tradition.

President Obama himself is part of that progressive religious tradition—as was his Democratic opponent in the primaries, Senator Hillary Rodham Clinton, now secretary of state. Progressive ideas about government and society are, for the first time in many years, in ascendancy in U.S. political life. In light of this reinvigoration of religious and political progressivism, the time is right to take a new look at Georgia Harkness, a theologian with a liberal theology and a progressive political and social agenda whose thought took shape in a time remarkably similar to our own.

Reading about the world events that shaped Harkness's theology in the late 1920s and 1930s, I have had to fight to keep my mind on Harkness's day and not on my own day. The parallels are obvious. The Harding and Coolidge administrations of the 1920s are well known for wedding business interests with government policy; they deregulated businesses—including banks—and dramatically lowered taxes for wealthy individuals and corporations. The economic boom that followed produced prosperity for the top half of the population but not for the poor. Record stock market growth from early 1928 and into 1929 was fueled in part by the rising number of middle-income people who began to invest in the stock market and also by the many speculators who bought stock on margin. Buying on margin, along with bank deregulation and other problems in the economy, all contributed to the sudden stock market crash in October of 1929.[2] The obvious parallels between the economic crisis of late 1929 and late 2008 have been the subject of many articles and commentaries.[3]

Columnists have also noted parallels between the New Deal legislation passed during Franklin Delano Roosevelt's administration in response to the economic crisis of the 1930s and possible legislative plans of the Obama administration. In a commentary entitled "Franklin Delano Obama?" *New York Times* columnist and Nobel Prize–winning economist Paul Krugman observed, "Suddenly, everything old is New Deal again. Reagan is out; F.D.R. is in. . . . Progressives hope that the Obama administration, like the New Deal, will respond to the current economic and financial crisis by creating institutions, especially a universal health care system, that will change the shape of American society for generations to come. . . . Progressives can only hope that he has the necessary audacity."[4]

Harkness was convinced throughout the crises of the 1930s (and beyond) that doing theology was an act of social responsibility that could help create a more just world. And looking at movements for transformation since the 1930s, it is evident that many have been fueled by theological commitments. Even the very existence of the Obama presidency is possible because of earlier faith-based movements for transformation such as the civil rights movement. A reexamination of Harkness and her time within the context of our era prompts the question, how will religious leaders and scholars in coming years forge theologies that help create a more just world? The question is not just about the audacity of President Obama, but the audacity of religious leaders and scholars as well.

Introduction

Liberalism as "the Centrum of American Theology"

Though defenders of conservative evangelicalism, neo-orthodoxy and radical theology agree on very little, all would gladly dance on the grave of . . . liberal Protestantism.[1]

In 1938 theologian and ethicist Georgia Harkness predicted, in the face of massive evidence to the contrary, that liberal theology was, and would long continue to be, in good health.[2] "The centrum of American theology is liberalism. In spite of premature funeral obsequies, it is likely to remain the basic American theology for some time to come."[3]

How wrongheaded Harkness must have seemed to many at the time. By the late 1930s when Harkness was offering her spirited defense of liberalism and her predictions of its continued vitality, liberal theology appeared to be *in extremis* and sinking fast. A few years earlier, John Bennett had insisted, "The most important fact about contemporary American theology is the disintegration of liberalism."[4] Henry Van Dusen had put forward an equally bleak assessment: "There is no more significant feature of the contemporary religious mood than the increasing disillusion with liberal theology. Wherever thoughtful Christians gather, there are references to the sickness of liberal religion . . . to its patent inadequacy for a moment like the present. One detects mounting agreement that Liberalism has served its mission but is now outmoded."[5]

Harkness refused to back away from her liberal identification. Looking back over the 1930s, a decade in which liberal theology had been battered, she wrote,

1

"Ten years ago I was a liberal in theology. I am still a liberal, unrepentant and unashamed."[6] This statement alone reveals much about the context of theology in that era. When people feel compelled to proclaim themselves "unrepentant and unashamed," they are almost certainly surrounded by detractors who think repentance and shame are precisely what is in order.

For the remaining decades of the twentieth century, attacks on liberal theology continued to be a popular genre for theologians from diverse camps. Gary Dorrien, the author of the monumental three-volume series on American liberal theology, recently described the progression of theological liberalism this way: "In the nineteenth century it took root and flowered; in the early twentieth century it became the founding idea of a new theological establishment; in the 1930s it was marginalized by neo-orthodox theology; in the 1960s it was rejected by liberation theology; by the 1970s it was often taken for dead."[7]

The death knell for liberal theology was a welcome sound for theologians from diverse and contrasting perspectives. As one reviewer of Dorrien's work on liberalism wrote, "Though defenders of conservative evangelicalism, neo-orthodoxy and radical theology agree on very little, all would gladly dance on the grave of . . . liberal Protestantism."[8] Dorrien has argued persuasively, however, that the death celebrations were premature, and, moreover, that some of the very people who have criticized liberal theology the most fiercely and celebrated its demise the most exuberantly, were themselves closet liberal theologians and key heirs of the liberal tradition.

Georgia Harkness's 1938 prediction that liberalism would "remain the basic American theology" seemed wildly off the mark at the time and yet is growing more and more believable today. Indeed, Dorrien has argued that liberal theology is not only still alive but that it "has been and remains the most creative and influential tradition of theological reflection since the Reformation."[9]

For many of these years when liberal theology was alternately attacked and pronounced dead, Georgia Harkness kept up a lively defense. Following her insistence in the late 1930s that she was a "liberal, unrepentant and unafraid," she charged in the 1940s that the liberalism she and many others espoused "has never, as is sometimes charged, lost sight of the reality of sin or of man's need of salvation."[10] In the 1960s, soon after her retirement from the Pacific School of Religion, she was, once again, defending liberalism: "I have long considered myself an evangelical liberal, and still do. The kind of liberalism that has been castigated throughout the century by the fundamentalists, and since the 1930's by the neo-orthodox, I do not recognize as a true picture of the liberalism of those who did the most to mold my thought. Nor do I recognize it as the theology I have tried to teach, write, and live by."[11]

When Harkness wrote of the castigation of liberal theology, she was speaking from personal experience. Harkness was widely known as a liberal and was criticized, on many occasions, for this affiliation. According to just a few of her critics, her work revealed the "vestiges of a rather musty old liberalism,"[12] fell "into the clichés of an earlier liberalism,"[13] and rested "on the same confused premises which seem to make so much of the liberal Protestant witness vague and incoherent."[14]

Harkness may have been *unrepentant* in the face of the criticisms of liberal theology, but she was not *unmoved*. In the same retrospective 1939 essay where Harkness proclaimed herself a liberal, unrepentant and unashamed, she also noted frankly that she had "profited" by her encounters with neo-orthodox theology and that her liberalism had been "chastened and deepened."[15] Harkness not only defended liberalism, she also repeatedly looked for ways that liberal theology could be improved upon by attending to its critics. In this article and elsewhere, she expressed gratitude to neo-orthodoxy and other theological movements for prompting a correction in the excesses of liberalism by reminding liberals of the depth of human sin, the radical need for divine grace, and the centrality of the cross.[16]

Throughout her interactions with various theologians and theological movements, Harkness was constantly looking for ways she could learn from them. This is not just a peculiarity of Harkness but is, instead, a hallmark of many liberal theologies, which are predisposed to take into account changing circumstances and changing ideas from an array of sources in order to form a new synthesis. Many liberals were confident that open reflection on various perspectives would lead one nearer to the truth. This willingness to take into account and shift with changing ideas and circumstances is responsible in large part for the staying power of liberal theology.

Harkness was self-conscious about this way of doing theology. In her 1937 book *The Recovery of Ideals,* written while she was at Union Theological Seminary for a semester and in conversation with Paul Tillich, she describes her synoptic method that "sees things from all angles in a related whole." In order to come to the truest possible understanding of God, one "ought" to consider multiple authorities and perspectives out of which one forms a conclusion that is a coherent whole. The "synoptic method is a form of the criterion of coherence. . . . When we have got all the evidence available . . . we are able to draw a conclusion which is as near correct as we can get. We shall not have absolute truth. But we shall have knowledge enough to enable us to advance toward more, with certainty enough to undergird our living as we go."[17]

From the late 1920s into the 1940s, Harkness and other liberal theologians were given many opportunities to take into account new "evidence" from a changing world, and with it, a changing theological conversation. Living through and reflecting on the economic depression of the 1930s, the political crises that led to World War II, and the devastation and difficult choices that came with the war itself, few people—theologians or otherwise—were left unchanged.[18] At the same time, for Harkness, the pain of these world crises was matched by the joy she found in the strengthening bonds of a global church as she participated in and was theologically challenged by major ecumenical conferences in Madras, Amsterdam, Oxford, and Geneva.[19] These world events, as well as the theological debates that surrounded them, all went into shaping Harkness's theology, including her theological ethic.

This collection centers on Harkness's writings during this critical period from the late 1920s and into the 1940s. Although her theology and theological ethic continued to change over the subsequent decades, by the early 1940s the main outlines were set. The collection reflects not only the changes Harkness underwent but also the shifts in American liberal theology during that time—particularly the branch of liberal theology that many (including Harkness) called evangelical liberalism. Her writings offer one vivid example of the way American liberal theology—and evangelical liberalism in particular—worked itself out during this critical period.

So many theologies have been grouped under the broad banner of liberalism it is fair to ask what makes a theology liberal. Liberal theologies have been described as the product of two divergent movements—modernism and religious evangelicalism.[20] In the early 1960s, Henry Van Dusen turned to the language of human reproduction (and betrayed his own dated assumptions about gender) in describing the origins of liberal theology. The various liberal theologies are the children of two parents: modern thought and religious evangelicalism. Some of the children were more influenced by what Van Dusen called "the male parent"—modernism—with "its bravado, its critical mindedness, its self-confidence." Other children bore a greater resemblance to what Van Dusen called "the female parent"—evangelicalism—with "her" focus on the religious experience of the heart and "her gift of vital spiritual experience."[21] For Van Dusen, the differences among liberal theologies, like the differences among children in a family, depend upon the combination of qualities and characteristics they have inherited and embraced from each parent.

For all the differences among the liberal children of these two parents, a few resemblances are shared across the family. Liberal theologians share a commitment to open and free inquiry. Consequently, they are hesitant—even suspicious—of a sole or primary reliance on any external authorities such as Scripture, and they rely at least in part on internal authorities such as experience. This includes the individual's experience of God and the world and, more broadly, other fields of knowledge such as science and history. Because they see continuity between what is revealed by reason and by revelation, there is no necessary conflict between drawing, for example, both on what has been revealed by God in Christ and in creation, and what is revealed as scientists observe creation and as historians reflect on the patterns of human history.

Some of the children of this liberal family embraced ideas that came to be associated—wrongly—with the family as a whole. For example, at the end of the nineteenth century and the beginning of the twentieth, some liberal theologians, star-struck by recent advances in technology and medicine, inspired by the growth in democracy and freedom in some parts of the world, captivated by the idea of Darwinian biological evolution and its parallels in social life, and perhaps blinded to some of the horrors of the world around them, became confident—even overconfident—about human progress over history and about the possibilities that lay ahead. When these expectations were dashed by the brutality of World War I, a worldwide depression in the 1930s, World War II, and the Holocaust, some critics of liberalism objected not only to the optimism of one part of the liberal family but, at least for a time, to the family as a whole. Reinhold Niebuhr and some other "neo-orthodox" critics ridiculed liberal theologies as a general group, while still maintaining many of the family resemblances themselves. Van Dusen described it this way: the "rebellious children of Liberal Theology, while indicting and disavowing their parentage, continue to carry, far more than they are prepared to acknowledge, the imprint of their lineage."[22]

Niebuhr did acknowledge years later, however, that his attacks on liberal theology had been "indiscriminate" and confessed: "I am a liberal at heart."[23] And as early as 1943, in a letter to John Bennett, Niebuhr reflected on his differences with European continental theologians Karl Barth and Emil Brunner, writing, "I belong to the liberal tradition more than to theirs."[24] Dorrien is quick to point out that the liberal theological tradition is much broader than and cannot be collapsed into the optimistic progressive liberalism of the turn of the last century. By broadening the definition of liberalism he is able to argue, as Van Dusen and Rasmussen before him, that Niebuhr and others who were commonly called neo-orthodox were actually liberals, or "neo-liberals" as Dorrien calls them.

If the family of liberal theology is so broad, how can one distinguish among the various liberal theologies? Among the many typologies of liberal theology, the most common may be the distinction between evangelical liberalism and modernist liberalism.[25] There is a danger to this model: it could be taken to mean that liberals were *either* evangelical *or* modernist, when, to use Van Dusen's image, all liberal theologies have inherited some qualities from each parent. In that case, the evangelicals are not on one side of the liberal family and the modernists on the other; all the children bear a resemblance to both parents but in different measures. The evangelical liberals, then, bore a somewhat greater resemblance to certain qualities on the evangelical side than did the modernist liberals.

This idea of family resemblance provides a simple way to think about the changes in Harkness's thought from 1929 to 1942, the years represented in this collection. In the beginning of those years Harkness bore a greater resemblance to the modernist parent, but over time she began to reintegrate additional characteristics of the evangelical parent with whom she was already very familiar because of her Methodist upbringing.

By 1940, Harkness had begun to describe herself as an evangelical liberal, and she continued to use that label throughout her life.[26] For Harkness, as for other evangelical liberals, the idea was not to favor one side or the other of one's lineage but to find the right balance between the two. If one believed, as Harkness and other evangelical liberals did, that God's special revelation in Scripture and in Christ was in continuity with God's general revelation through all of creation, including human experience and human knowledge of the world, then finding a balance between the two parents is not as hard as it might seem, because the two parents are themselves more similar than different. Of course, seeing the continuity between God's general and special revelation is no new thing at all. That is why Harkness insisted that evangelical liberalism was a new name for a much older tradition in Christian theology.

I

Georgia Harkness
The Making and Remaking of a Liberal

In 1938 *Time* magazine dubbed Georgia Harkness "the famed woman theologian."[1] And, to be sure, in the middle four decades of the twentieth century Harkness was widely known in the fields of theology and theological ethics. By the late 1950s she was arguably the theologian—male or female—whose works were read most widely among mainline Protestant laity and clergy. Over the course of a career spanning more than five decades, Harkness wrote over three dozen books, many hymns and poems, and hundreds of articles covering most of the classical categories of systematic theology and ethics and many key issues in the life of the church.[2]

Harkness was a woman of many firsts. She was the first woman to hold a faculty position in theology at a major theological school, serving as professor of applied theology at Garrett Evangelical Theological Seminary (1940–50) and the Pacific School of Religion (1950–61). She was not only part of the founding of the World Council of Churches, but was also one of only a handful of female delegates to many of the major ecumenical conferences of the late 1930s—including the crucial early meetings in Oxford and Madras. She was the first woman member of the most prestigious and exclusive theological societies in the country, including both the Younger Theologians Group (1933) and the

American Theological Society (1937).[3] The latter had voted to accept women as members "in moderation" and proceeded, in "moderate fashion," to invite into membership only one woman—Georgia Harkness.

Harkness was widely known not only for her scholarly interest in social issues but also for her social activism. She was an advocate for women's ordination from early in her career and is often given credit for bringing the Methodist Church to its 1956 decision to grant women full clergy rights. Becoming a pacifist in 1924 on a tour of postwar Europe, she remained one throughout her life—even during World War II, when pacifism was itself under attack. She spoke out against the internment of Japanese Americans in World War II, ongoing discrimination against African Americans, and economic injustice in the United States and around the world. She was as critical of the excesses of capitalism as she was of the excesses of fascism and communism.

Georgia Harkness's writings and the events of her life are interesting not only on their own merits, but also because they offer a window—or a series of windows—overlooking theology, ethics, and the life of church and society during the first three quarters of the twentieth century. Harkness, who was born into a Methodist family in rural upstate New York near the end of the nineteenth century, prayed, served, taught, agitated, wrote, and preached her way through most of the twentieth century, shaping and being shaped by key movements. Among these were ecumenism, social movements and crises of the time, Wesleyan pietism, and theological liberalism of various kinds—including personalism and the social gospel movement as well as neo-orthodoxy, process theology, and the death of God movement.

Most important for the purposes of this volume, her work illustrates the ways that liberal theology—especially that of the evangelical liberal variety—shifted in the 1930s to take into account its critics as well as global economic and political crises, changes in the world church, and subsequent shifts across the theological spectrum. For Harkness, as for many others, theology is tied to biography. It is hard to understand her theology without knowing about her life; and it is impossible to understand her theology *or* her life without knowing about what was happening in the world around her. The readings included in this collection, and my introductions to each set of readings, are focused on the years 1929 to 1942. But to understand Harkness's work during that critical period, it is important to know about the earlier years of her life and the events that shaped her.

Harkness was born on April 21, 1891, twenty-six years to the day after President Lincoln's body left Washington, D.C., in a draped funeral train for a slow procession back to Springfield. Benjamin Harrison was president of the United States. The British Empire stretched across the globe, and the German, Austro-Hungarian, and Russian empires were still strong. Women had the vote in only one state—Wyoming—and Harkness would be twenty-six when her home state of New York followed suit.

Georgia Harkness grew up in a farmhouse in the small crossroads town of Harkness—named for her grandfather—on the far northeastern edge of New

York.[4] The fires of the holiness revival movement were still burning in northern and western New York, though more dimly than they had a generation earlier. Harkness and her family went to the Methodist church every Sunday and to the winter revival every year. In her 60s, she told stories from her childhood to colleagues on the West Coast: "As often as the revival came I got converted. Then I backslid during the summer, and was ready for conversion again the next winter." In high school she and a friend went to a revival meeting where she experienced what she later called her "definitive conversion." Before officially joining the church, Harkness read the *Methodist Book of Discipline* and a book about Methodist theology and holy living—the *Methodist Probationer's Handbook*.[5] Harkness was one of many liberal theologians who were shaped by the holiness movement.

Harkness's father was the chief lay leader of their Methodist church; he began to teach Sunday school when he was a teenager and kept it up until he was in his 80s. Harkness often talked of her Quaker great-grandparents, but her Quaker lineage went back even further than she knew. One of the first Quaker meetings in the Americas was held surreptitiously in the barn of Harkness's ancestors, Daniel and Hannah Wing.[6] Both the Wings were children of clergy fathers who, because of theological dissent, had been forced to leave the Church of England.[7] She was also the direct descendant of Lawrence and Cassandra Southwick, Quakers from Salem, who were imprisoned and then banished to New York for their beliefs. The courts ruled that their teenage children, Daniel and Provided, were to be sold into slavery in Barbados or Virginia in order to pay the family's fines for being Quaker, but no ship captain in the Boston harbor would agree to take them. The Southwicks later came to be known as the "Quaker martyrs," and, in the nineteenth century, John Greenleaf Whittier wrote a poem based on the story entitled "Cassandra Southwick."[8] In short, Harkness's lineage includes Calvinists who were persecuted by the Church of England; Quakers who were persecuted by the Calvinists; and Methodists who left the Quakers only under duress. This is part of Harkness's heritage and the legacy of New England Protestantism out of which liberal theology would grow.

As a girl, Harkness went to the local "country school," as she called it. At twelve, she transferred to a high school several miles away. Although she passed her high school New York Regents exams when she was fourteen, she stayed on in high school for several more years. She especially loved reading classic Latin and Greek texts. She later wrote, "A Greek class was started of which I was the only member, and I ate up my four years of Latin."[9]

In 1908 she took a statewide exam and, after scoring the highest in her county, was awarded a scholarship to Cornell University, where she enrolled in the fall. She felt out of place there and joked with friends many years later that in those Cornell years she was "shy, green and countrified . . . My clothes were queer; I had no social graces; and I did not come within gunshot of being asked to join a sorority." She learned nothing about sorority life, but she did learn a little about liberal theology and more about history and political science—her major area of study. She also became active in the Student Volunteer Band, a growing national movement at the time designed to recruit young people for the mission field. Its motto was "the evangelization of the world in this generation." Like thousands of other college students in this movement, Harkness signed the pledge: "It is my purpose, if God permits, to become a foreign missionary."[10]

When she graduated in 1912, she decided, instead, to become a teacher of Latin, German, and French in a high school in northern New York. Teaching was, after all, one of the few professions open to women, and northern New York was her home. When she learned in 1917 of a new profession for women in religious education and of a new school that had opened that year at Boston University—the School of Religious Education and Social Service—she felt called to make a change. "I decided forthwith that if I could not be a missionary, this was my calling."[11]

Boston's School of Religious Education and Social Service was founded and run by Walter Athearn and others committed to the social gospel. They designed the curriculum and the program as a whole with the goal of contributing to the health of democracy and the building of the kingdom of God. Harkness began her master's program there in 1918 and graduated with both an M.A. and an M.R.E. two years later.

The faculty and students at the School of Religious Education and Social Service were particularly interested in the plight of recent immigrants and how churches could respond; this became the focus of Harkness's thesis. The United States had seen changes in immigration patterns over the nineteenth century, so that by the time of Harkness's birth in 1891, the largest numbers of immigrants were coming from eastern and southern Europe. Many people in the United States who were descendants of the "old immigrants" from northern and western Europe were uncomfortable and often outright racist when it came to those "new immigrants" who were from very different cultures. Over the first thirty years of Harkness's life, a series of laws were passed restricting immigration by various means, for example, requiring that immigrants speak English before being naturalized. At the same time, the terrible living and working conditions of many of these new immigrants in large U.S. cities prompted some Christians to work toward social reform, providing services for the new immigrants and supporting legislation that would improve working conditions.

Harkness's master's thesis was a handbook for church leaders who were helping to "Americanize" the new immigrants. She recommended, for example, that churches provide child care for working parents, athletic facilities for young men, and a place where young women could safely receive gentlemen "callers." The aim of these church ministries was to make the immigrants "not simply members of one church nor citizens of America, but members of the Church universal and citizens in the Kingdom of God."[12] Her thesis, *The Church and the Immigrant*, was published in 1921, the same year laws were passed setting limits on the number of immigrants that would be allowed from different countries.

The quotas for countries of southern and eastern Europe were lower than those of western and northern Europe.[13]

In the second year of her master's program, Harkness began to take philosophy classes with Edgar Brightman, a philosopher at Boston University. She quickly fell, as she later wrote, "under the spell of Dr. Edgar S. Brightman's kindling mind."[14] On finishing her master's degree, she entered the Ph.D. program in philosophy at Boston, studying primarily with Brightman, who was the leading personalist philosopher of the time and taking a few courses from a newly arrived professor at Boston, personalist theologian Albert Knudson.

In 1877 Boston University had become the first U.S. institution to grant a Ph.D. to a woman. This milestone was made possible in part by the leadership of philosopher Bordon Parker Bowne, who was the dean at the Boston University's Graduate School of Arts and Science at the time. Bowne was best known for his writings in philosophy. In the last quarter of the nineteenth century, Bowne had made Boston University the center of a certain brand of personalist philosophy that became known as Boston personalism. Brightman and Knudson later took on Bowne's mantle and with it the legacy of Boston personalism. All three men were lifelong Methodists as were most of the Boston personalists—many of whom were raised by parents who were Methodist pastors or were active in the Wesleyan holiness movement.

The central claim of Boston personalism is that personality is not just the key to help understand reality—it *is* reality. Reality consists of divine personality and human personality. In reading 3 of this collection, Harkness describes personality in this way: "My personality consists then in the totality of my mental processes—my thoughts, feelings, purposes, desires, etc.—not isolated or disconnected but *bound together by an awareness of their belonging together as mine*. . . . [It] consists in the total complex of experience which we call our conscious life." Harkness lifts up two human capacities at the heart of personality—"man's creative intelligence and his power of pursuing moral ideals." "Rationality and goodness," Harkness insists, are not only the "most distinctive attributes of human personality, [they] are the very qualities which above all others God must possess if there be a God."[15]

The first sticking point for many critics of personalism (including Harkness many years later) was that according to Boston personalism, persons—human persons and the divine person—are the only things that are real. Other things around us that seem independently real are actually manifestations of the divine person or, as Harkness later put it, "the acts of God." The natural world, for example, the rocks and the trees and all the rest, are "an eternal system of divine activity; not something God has created, or still creates, but something God *causes* with consistent regularity. Human persons, being relatively independent real units of existence, are created; physical things are caused."[16]

The second sticking point logically follows from the first. If only persons are real, then how does one make sense of the reality of evil except as part of the divine person or human persons? Brightman understood the evil and suffering of the natural world to come from a recalcitrant factor—or "a given"—within the divine person. Harkness would ultimately break with Brightman on these two points. (See the preface to section V and readings 10 and 11.)

Although this way of looking at the world seems alien to most Christians today—including pastors and many others with theological educations—it was remarkably persuasive at the time. Henry Nelson Wieman and Bernard Eugene Meland suggested in 1936 that Bowne's personalist philosophy "has probably reached the minds of more professing Christian people than any other philosophy of religion in the United States."[17]

In 1922, while writing her dissertation on the British idealist philosopher and social reformer T. H. Green, Harkness joined the faculty of Elmira College, a women's college in western New York. She taught in the philosophy department at Elmira for fifteen years, longer than in any other institution. These years were formative for Harkness and shaped her later work.

For example, teaching philosophy, ethics, and philosophy of religion to undergraduates, Harkness gained a skill that would shape her writing and speaking. She learned to present difficult theoretical issues in simple and engaging prose, becoming a very popular teacher, and, later, a popular speaker and preacher in churches and universities across the United States.

Harkness may have felt called to the university instead of the mission field, but she always had the missionary outlook of a Methodist reformer. From her earliest book (*The Church and the Immigrant*) to her last (*The Biblical Background of the Middle East Conflict*),[18] most of the things Harkness wrote—even technical essays in philosophy—were linked, directly or indirectly, to social problems in the world around her. And those problems were directly linked to politics. The theological shifts that Harkness underwent from the late 1920s to the early 1940s were tied to larger political shifts in the world around her. In the introductions to many of the sections in this book, I refer to political events of the 1930s that helped to shape Harkness's writings. Those political events were rooted, of course, in earlier events from the late teens and the 1920s.

Harkness was almost thirty when she was first eligible to vote in a presidential election. New York had granted women the vote in 1917 when Harkness was twenty-six, and by the time the next presidential election rolled around in 1920, the Nineteenth Amendment had granted all women citizens in the United States the right to vote. Democrat Woodrow Wilson was ending his second term in office. The First World War had come to a close two years before and in its wake, Wilson, a progressive idealist who was confident about extending peace and democracy around the world, was one of the chief promoters of the League of Nations. Congress did not share Wilson's optimism and blocked U.S. entry into the League.

In her first presidential election, Harkness likely cast her vote for Democratic nominee James M. Cox and his running mate, Franklin Delano Roosevelt of New York. They were the progressive candidates with the motto: "Their election means

Peace, Progress, and Prosperity." Friends to the labor movement and supporters of the League of Nations, they were trounced by Warren Harding and running mate Calvin Coolidge by the biggest margin in a century.[19] Harding and, to a lesser extent, Coolidge were isolationists, calling for the United States to have much less of an international role than in the Wilson administration. In the wake of World War I, their pledge for a "return to normalcy" was for voters an alluring promise.

When historians are asked to name the "worst presidents ever," both the Harding administration (1921–23) and the subsequent Coolidge administration (1923–29) are among the contenders. A 2006 *Washington Post* article noted that "Harding and Coolidge are best remembered for the corruption of their years in office . . . and for channeling money and favors to big business. They slashed income and corporate taxes. . . . 'Never before, here or anywhere else,' declared the *Wall Street Journal,* 'has a government been so completely fused with business.'"[20] As Harding and Coolidge lowered taxes and let businesses have their way, the economy began to grow. By the last years of the Coolidge administration the stock market was experiencing an unprecedented boom.

These were prosperous years for the wealthiest half of the population. The prosperity of the 1920s, along with the political and business scandals and the widening gap between rich and poor, led to disillusionment among many young people of the time. Out of this context, Harkness wrote her 1929 book, *Conflicts in Religious Thought.* (See the preface of section III and readings 2, 3, and 4.) The corruption and excess of those years have been blamed for the ultimate stock market crash in October 1929 and the subsequent U.S. and worldwide economic depressions.

In 1924, the year after completing her dissertation and graduating from Boston University with her Ph.D. in philosophy, Harkness spent the summer in western Europe with the "Sherwood Eddy Party." Eddy, a YMCA executive, was a pacifist and progressive. He organized and led reform-minded summer tours of Europe for clergy leaders, scholars, and social reformers. The participants traveled across Europe, hearing lectures each day about the political and social issues confronting postwar Europe and having conversations with political leaders and social reformers. Harkness became a pacifist on this trip. When the group was in Germany, she saw the destruction that had been caused by World War I and the extreme poverty that had come in its wake, in part because of the severe reparations that had been placed on Germany. These experiences and impressions would come to shape her response to the European conflict in the 1930s and 1940s. Harkness also got to know other members of the Eddy tour with whom she would continue to work in the decades ahead: Harry Ward, a radical Methodist reformer who began the Methodist Federation for Social Action and was an ethics professor at Boston University and Union Theological Seminary; Charles Clayton Morrison, a Disciples pastor and editor of *The Christian Century*; and Reinhold Niebuhr, who was then a pastor in Detroit.

Harkness was also shaped by postdoctoral studies with leading scholars of the time. In the fall of 1926, she took a research leave at Harvard University where she studied with philosophers William E. Hocking and Alfred North

Whitehead. She and Hocking continued to work together in the coming years. He tried to get her a teaching position at Radcliffe, but women were not eligible at the time.

Harkness was at Yale two years later on a Sterling Fellowship, studying with D. C. Macintosh, Robert Calhoun, and Roland Bainton. She later wrote obliquely about a relationship formed while on leave at Yale, "an abortive love affair, from which I now profoundly thank God I was delivered."[21] The young man in question was probably historian Kenneth Scott Latourette, Yale's professor of missions at the time.[22]

She had received the Yale Sterling fellowship to work on a project concerning Calvin and capitalism that was later published in 1931 as *John Calvin: The Man and His Ethics.* Her primary work at Yale, though, was writing the book *Conflicts in Religious Thought*, from which readings 2–4 are taken. Harkness was still deeply committed at the time to personalist philosophy. In *Conflicts,* she drew on that tradition to make religion credible for a generation that had lost its way and needed the grounding and direction of religious faith. (See the preface and readings from section III.)

In 1933 Harkness was invited to join the "Younger Theologians Group." In her preface to *Resources of Religion,* she acknowledged the influence of this group: "A nameless Theological Discussion Group of about twenty-five younger Christian thinkers has been very invigorating."[23] At their twice-yearly meetings, she enjoyed the debates with some of the faculty of Union Theological Seminary including Henry Van Dusen, Paul Tillich, and Reinhold Niebuhr.

Harkness subsequently decided to spend her sabbatical in the fall of 1935 at Union and then ended up coming back the following fall on a year's leave of absence from Elmira. Over these three semesters, she attended lectures of Reinhold Niebuhr and Paul Tillich, talked with faculty members at Union, and worshiped at the liberal Riverside Church, where her friend Harry Emerson Fosdick was the pastor. Harkness wrote three books during these three semesters: *The Resources of Religion* in the fall of 1935 over a seven-week period; *The Recovery of Ideals* in the fall of 1936; and *Religious Living,* which was begun in the summer of 1936 and finished in January 1937. During this same period the world was in an economic depression that had begun in 1929, and Roosevelt's New Deal was in its infancy. Hitler had come to power and the world political situation was unstable. These world events had an impact on these books that Harkness wrote in the mid-1930s.

The readings from sections IV and V come from *Resources of Religion* and *Recovery of Ideals,* both of which show the early chastening of her liberalism and a move toward greater realism. In *Recovery of Ideals* she breaks with key tenets of personalism and describes herself as a "theistic realist." In all three of these books she is still strongly committed to central claims of liberal theology. (See the prefaces and readings in sections IV and V.)

Harkness was at Union and had just finished the book *Religious Living* in late January or February 1938 when she learned that her father was ill. Harkness, whose mother had died several years before, returned home to help care for him in the last months of his life. The time with her father proved to be a turning point for Harkness and her writing. Several decades after her father's death, she wrote about the power of those "two months of intimate fellowship with a great soul."

> I am well aware of the sentimentality attached to "last words." Neverthe-less, I cannot faithfully recount my spiritual autobiography without telling something which he said to me within an hour of his death, and which I took as a directive from an eternal realm. Asking me how many books I had written (by that time seven), he said, "I think they must be good books. Wise men say they are. But *I wish you would write more about Jesus Christ.*" This word, reinforced by the fact that after that I was mainly teaching the Bible or theology rather than philosophy, *marks a definite turn in my writing and thinking toward a more Christ-centered approach to religious truth.*[24]

This shift was "reinforced," to use Harkness's word, by her experiences of the worldwide church. The summer after her father's death, Harkness attended the first of a series of international ecumenical conferences that would also shape her theology and deepen her faith. At these ecumenical conferences she was in discussion, worship, and prayer with continental theologians, their neo-orthodox counterparts from the United States, other American liberals, and other Christians from around the world who were not embroiled in the internal theological debates that consumed European and U.S. Protestant theologians. (See especially readings 1, 14, and 16 as well as the prefaces to sections II and VII.)

At Oxford, the first of these ecumenical conferences, Harkness gave a short speech on the role of women in the church that served to propel her into greater prominence, particularly in the United States. She later wrote that the speech "caused quite a stir, and being cabled under the Atlantic in an AP [Associated Press] dispatch, gave me a good deal of publicity at home. This would not be worth mentioning except that it precipitated so many invitations to speak here and there that I ran myself ragged."[25]

That fall of 1937 she moved from the philosophy department at Elmira College to the religion department in Mount Holyoke, a women's college in Massachusetts where she would teach for two years before accepting a position as professor of applied theology at Garrett Biblical Institute (later Garrett Evangelical Theological Seminary). These changes of employment further "reinforced" the shift toward what she called a more "Christ-centered approach." The shift was not just about Christology, though. She began to use the traditional language of the church with greater ease; was more willing to draw on external authorities of Scripture and church tradition; and was considering more seriously, though not always agreeing with, some classical creedal claims of the church.

Another marker of this shift was her ordination in 1938 as a local elder in the Troy Conference of the Methodist Church in New York. She had been ordained a local deacon in 1926 and later wrote that her deacon's ordination "ranks . . . among my highest moments."[26] A year after her ordination as an elder, Harkness was offered a job at a Methodist theological school, Garrett Biblical Institute.

Harkness absorbed and was shaped by all of this: by her Wesleyan roots; her social gospel training at the Boston School of Religious Education and Social Service with its focus on work with immigrants; her education at Boston as a personalist philosopher; her experience as a teacher of ethics and the philosophy of religion; her travels across post–World War I Europe; her sabbatical studies with Whitehead, Hocking, Macintosh, Niebuhr, and Tillich; her membership and active participation in the Theological Discussion Group and the American Theological Society; her participation in ecumenical discussions; and her engagement in the social and political problems of the time. Drawing on all of these experiences and working with an eye on all of the major camps of the mid-twentieth century, Harkness crafted what she referred to as an "evangelical liberal" theology that incorporated and synthesized some claims of classical Christian teachings with central themes from various branches of liberalism.

Harkness, who had been a philosopher and philosophical theologian for most of her career, became professor of applied theology at Garrett in 1940 and stayed there until 1949. The early 1940s were trying years for Harkness. Beginning in the fall of 1939, she began to have health problems that worsened for several years and were one of the factors that (along with tensions at Garrett) may have precipitated the depression that she suffered during this period. In response to this difficult time in her life, she wrote the book *Dark Night of the Soul.*

In these same years, Harkness was passed over for a position that she thought was rightfully hers.[27] When she came to Garrett as professor of applied theology, Henry Franklin Rall, professor of systematic theology, was near retirement. Harkness was left with the impression, after her contract negotiations with Garrett's president Horace Greeley Smith, that she would likely be Rall's successor. At the time, systematic theology was much more prestigious and taken more seriously than applied theology, and it was, frankly, a man's field. It was also a field that was a closer match for Harkness's training and her previous teaching and writing than was applied theology.

Years later, historian Rosemary Keller interviewed Mary Durham, a close friend of Harkness who had lived in Evanston at the time but was not a part of the Garrett community. Durham reported that in the early 1940s, Harkness came to her very upset and "unburdened herself" about a difficult conversation she had had with President Smith. According to Durham's account, at a time when the salaries of the male faculty were being raised, President Smith called Harkness to his office and told her, "You will never get more salary. You will just stay at the same salary. . . . I didn't want to have a woman on my faculty, and I don't like having a woman on my faculty."[28]

When Smith began to look for Rall's successor in 1944, Harkness was not considered. The job and the new title, the Henry Pfeiffer Chair of Systematic Theology, were given in 1946 to a young pastor, Gerald O. McCulloh, who had very little experience as a teacher or scholar. He had left the doctoral program at Boston to complete his Ph.D. in Scotland because, according to Edgar Brightman's account, "he was not quite sure of making the grade with us." McCulloh would leave Garrett in 1953 and spend the rest of his career working as a staff person at the Methodist Board of Higher Education.[29]

Rosemary Keller maintains that this event was pivotal for Harkness and for the writings that she would do in the coming years. It was a bitter disappointment and likely had something to do with her departure from Garrett a few years later. After this crisis had passed, Harkness embraced the identity of an applied theologian and began to write almost exclusively books for laity. Keller sees this shift as "a positive, long-range consequence" of the difficulties at Garrett. Harkness "began to reconceive her professional identity of what it meant for her to be an applied theologian . . . [and] gained a new vocational vision of her work."[30] Although I do not disagree with Keller, I recognize that this shift also came with negative "long-range consequences." Harkness was not as engaged in internal academic conversations with other scholars in her disciplines after this point; if she had been offered the position in systematic theology at Garrett, she would likely have taken a different path and have had a different impact.

A bright note for Harkness during these difficult years was the beginning of her friendship with Verna Miller, who was her companion from 1943, when they were introduced by their pastor, until Harkness's death in 1974. On the dedication page of one of her books, Harkness described Miller in this way: "To Verna who shares my home and my life and to whom the book and its author owe much."[31]

Harkness spent the last quarter century of her life in California. In 1948 she was invited to give the 1949 Earl Lectures at the Pacific School of Religion in Berkeley. She later wrote, "I came to Berkeley; I saw; it conquered." After the Earl Lectures, she came back to the campus for the fall term of 1949 as a visiting professor to see how she liked it and then accepted a faculty position—again as professor of applied theology.[32]

She and Miller moved together to Berkeley in 1950 and stayed there until Harkness's retirement in 1961 when she was seventy years old. They spent their retirement years in Claremont, California, where they lived until Harkness's death.

This collection of readings stops in the early 1940s, but Harkness kept on working for another three decades—writing, teaching, and always pressing the case for a more just and peaceful world. When the Methodists voted in 1956 to give women full clergy rights, the General Conference, of which she was a delegate, acknowledged "the valiant fight she has waged for this cause for many years" and gave her a standing ovation. Harkness continued her work as a pacifist and was a strong opponent of the Vietnam War, writing a well-known article in 1966 that was entered into the congressional record by her former student George McGovern. Her associations with various Christian activist groups had earned her an FBI file as a communist sympathizer. She spoke out against racism and classism throughout her life, and toward the end opposed discrimination against gay and lesbian people.

The theology that Harkness had worked out through the 1920s and 1930s was the basis for her writings in the years that followed. In 1942 when she wrote the articles that close out this collection, the fifty-one-year-old Harkness had published eight books (including one book of poetry). In the three decades between 1943 and her death in 1974, she produced an additional thirty-one books, at a steady pace of about one a year. They range in topic from theological methodology to eschatology; from pacifism and sexism to racism and economic justice; from mysticism and Christian perfection to women's ordination and inclusive language; from capitalism, nationalism, and democracy to marriage, birth control, and abortion. Most of them were written in popular form for Christian laity and clergy.

These later, more popular books are the ones for which Harkness is most widely known. But it is the earlier writings from the late 1920 into the 1940s— the ones from which this collections draws—that are the more compelling. Here we see Harkness forming her theology in the middle of the whirlwind as the world suffered through economic crisis and political conflict. By setting out to study and work with thinkers from conflicting points of view, she sought to be shaped by and to shape the major American philosophical and theological camps of her day. And this theological engagement was extended as she traveled around the world to be in conversation with Christian theologians from Asia and Africa as well as the "continental theologians" from Europe. Reviewing Harkness's work as she drew on all these streams from the 1920s to the early 1940s, one sees the remaking of a liberal theologian.

II

"A Spiritual Pilgrimage"
How Harkness's Mind Changed

SECTION PREFACE

The Christian Century carried a series of articles in 1939 on the topic "How My Mind Has Changed in This Decade" and invited as contributors key theologians, ethicists, and church leaders including Karl Barth, Edgar Brightman, Reinhold Niebuhr, Henry Nelson Wieman, James Luther Adams, and John Bennett. Harkness wrote her contribution in the first days of 1939 as she sailed home from a major ecumenical conference in Madras, India.[1] Her reflections in the article "Spiritual Pilgrimage" (the first reading in this collection) reveal the impact the ecumenical movement and her encounters with world Christianity had had on her theology and her faith. She later wrote about Madras: "This conference with its disclosure of the virile quality of Christianity among the younger churches and its realistic, vivid demonstration of the reality of the world Christian community, was the most significant ecumenical gathering I have ever attended." As one of the drafters of a theological statement at Madras, Harkness had made it her "self-appointed task to keep the statement at least within speaking distance of liberalism by persistently objecting to the Barthian cast that [other delegates] wished to give it."[2]

The theological tensions that were evident at Madras were also a recurring theme in many of the contributions to this 1939 series of articles from *The Christian Century*. Harkness, like many of the other contributors, reflected on the debate that had raged through the 1930s between neo-orthodox and older liberal theologies as well as on the massive social, economic, and political changes that had occurred from the late 1920s to the late 1930s. By early 1939 when this piece was written, Germany had been arming itself and in October of 1938 had annexed the western side of Czechoslovakia. On *Kristallnacht*, November 9, 1938, many Jewish homes, stores, and synagogues across Germany were pillaged and burned. In "Spiritual Pilgrimage," Harkness describes the chastening of her liberalism in light of these world events and theological changes of the 1930s.

The rest of this collection is arranged roughly in chronological order by year from 1929 to 1942. We begin, however, with this 1939 article because it serves as an introduction to the changes that Harkness would undergo during this period and that are evident throughout this collection.

READING 1

The editor says that I am to be autobiographical. I shall take him at his word, for if I am at all faithfully to record what the past ten years have done to my religious thought I cannot refrain from saying what they have done to me. The collapse of economic and international security, of brotherhood and mutual trust, which the world has witnessed in this decade has affected my thinking, as it must that of anyone with a shred of ethical or religious sensitivity. The rise of continental theology has led me in part to accept it and in greater measure to reject it. Yet more determinative for me than what has happened in the political or theological world have been the events of my private world. If the reader is bored to hear about them or is unwilling to be patient with self-reference, perhaps it would be well for him to stop reading at this point.

I

At ten o'clock on the evening of February 8, 1929, I put the last words to the writing of *Conflicts in Religious Thought*. At the awareness that at last the long job was done I felt a wild exhilaration such as makes one want to "paint the town red." Being thoroughly conditioned to sobriety, I went to bed. The content of this book affords a measuring-point from which I can reckon the changes of the past decade.

These changes have been many. As I try to look at myself objectively I see quite a different person from the self of ten years ago. I think I have found something akin to what was called in the simple terminology of my childhood a "second blessing." Yet I am aware of no radical transformation of either attitude

From "A Spiritual Pilgrimage: Ninth Article in the Series 'How My Mind Has Changed in This Decade,'" *Christian Century* 56 (March 15, 1939): 348–51.

or belief. There is nothing in *Conflicts in Religious Thought* that I wish to retract. Were I writing it now there is much that I should wish to add.

What has happened in these years? I have become more of a theologian, probably less of a philosopher. My religion is more Christ-centered. I have rediscovered the Bible. Mysticism and worship have taken on added richness. I seem in a small way to have become a peripatetic evangelist, speaking often on personal religious living. I was a pacifist and a socialist ten years ago and still am, but my Christian conviction in both spheres has taken on greater clarity and firmness. I am more church-minded. Finally, I have seen a new vision of the world mission of the church. These words are being written on shipboard as I return from the Madras Conference, and what I say is likely to be colored by it.

How have these changes come about? Partly through the turn in external events and the turn in theology which has accompanied them. But not wholly. Within this decade I have changed colleges and have moved from a department of philosophy to one of religion; have spent a year and a half at Union Seminary; have published six books; have attended two world conferences (Oxford and Madras); have been influenced by an enlarging circle of Christian friends, particularly those in a hard-hitting group sometimes referred to as "the younger theologians"; have had my ego inflated by being elected to the American Theological Society as the first woman member; have discovered the spiritual release of writing poetry; have lost both my parents and have witnessed in my family the miracle of young growing life. If these experiences had not affected my religion, nothing would.

Let me try to state briefly what new light has come to me in four fields: theology, worship, social action, and the church.

II

Ten years ago I was a liberal in theology. I am still a liberal, unrepentant and unashamed. This does not mean that I have seen nothing in liberalism that needed correction. We were in danger of selling out to science as the only approach to truth, of trusting too hopefully in man's power to remake his world, of forgetting the profound fact of sin and the redeeming power of divine grace, of finding our chief evidence of God in cosmology, art or human personality, to the clouding of the clearer light of the incarnation. Liberalism needed to see in the Bible something more than a collection of moral adages and a compendium of great literature. It needed to see in Christ something more than a great figure living sacrificially and dying for his convictions. It needed to be recalled to the meaning of the cross and the power of the resurrection.

These correctives have come to us. I do not think liberalism ever had as many utopian illusions as it is now customary in retrospect to attribute to it, but its self-confidence has been challenged both by events and by theological trends. With many others in America I have profited from the currents coming out of continental Europe and too superficially called Barthian. These have come to me through books, but more through the forceful personalities of Reinhold Niebuhr and Paul Tillich—men with whom I do not agree very far but by whom I am stirred to rethink my faith. They have come at Oxford and Madras through wrestling with continental theology for the liberalism which I believe to have the truth.

My liberalism is, I trust, a chastened and deepened liberalism. But I am more convinced than ever I was before that God reveals himself in many ways and that only through the spirit of free inquiry can Christian faith go forward. I believe in the essential greatness of man, in a social gospel which calls us to action as co-workers with God in the redemptive process, in a Kingdom which will come in this world by growth as Christians accept responsibility in the spirit of the cross. My Christian faith has its central focus, not in Paul's theology or Luther's or Calvin's, but in the incarnation of God in the Jesus of the Gospels.

I said above that my religion was both more theological and more Christ-centered than formerly. These two movements are part of one process—a movement away from an ideal of philosophical objectivity to one of more overt Christian commitment. For many years the philosopher and the theologian in me have been, not exactly at war, but in friendly rivalry. My graduate training was taken mainly in philosophy, though in the personalistic school congenial to religion. For fifteen years I taught philosophy. My academic conscience has the conviction that philosophy should be taught philosophically, and with greater or less success I held to this conviction. But while I was teaching philosophy I was writing religion. When the opportunity came to transfer to a department of religion I welcomed it, and the change has done much to terminate the rivalry.

When I wrote *Conflicts in Religious Thought* it did not seem to me appropriate to include a chapter on Christ. I was trying to write a simple philosophy of religion which would rest the case for religious faith upon experience without theological presuppositions, and I do not think the omission wholly unjustified. But were I writing the book now, I should put in the chapter. Whatever other grounds of faith may be adduced, it is "through Jesus Christ our Lord" that the Christian finds God with life-transforming power. The manifestations of God in the order and beauty of nature, in human fellowship and progress, in the spiritual strivings of men of all faiths, are important and real. It is essential to recognize them, for nowhere has God left himself without a witness. Yet all such evidences are incomplete. Only in Christ is revelation ultimate and unequivocal.

I am not sure how long this conviction has been growing. It probably roots in the Christ-centered religion of my childhood. In recent years an awareness of the centrality of Christ has been deepened by attempts to interpret the Christian faith to students at their conferences. A fresh exploration of the Bible made in order to teach it has left the personality of Jesus high and lifted up. At Oxford the truth of the familiar words,

> The Church's one foundation
> Is Jesus Christ her Lord,

came to me with power, and this experience was renewed at Madras.

III

Worship has become more meaningful. This is due to no change in thought, for I have long believed in a God worthy to receive adoration and glory and praise. Apart from worship, faith lacks resonance and power. But I am by nature more of an activist than a mystic. In these years God has revealed his presence to me with greater vividness and warmth. In the midst of increasing activities I have been led to find a richer communion in living silence and in the great liturgies of the church.

In the turmoil and strain of this decade great numbers of people have been driven to look to God for the resources they did not find in themselves or in social relations. Students are more interested in personal religion now than they have been since my own student days. In part this betokens a recovery of the inner life of religion; in part it is, I fear, an escape from the difficulty of making decisions about social action in a world which seems almost at an impasse. This has deepened my realization that what I would try to impart I must first seek to possess.

Certain other experiences have contributed. The morning worship services in the Union Seminary chapel left with me much—more, perhaps, than the refreshing winds of doctrine which are ever blowing there. I share the general judgment that the services of worship in St. Mary's Church were the greatest and most potent factor of the Oxford Conference. Within this decade I have come to a fresh awareness of God in nature by the shore of an Adirondack lake and among the hills of my native northern New York. Recently, sitting silent before the exquisite beauty of the Taj Mahal, I felt a sense of the numinous such as has never been stirred in me by any Christian art. . . .

IV

My social philosophy has undergone less alteration than any other aspect of my religion. The changes of these years have deepened the conviction that only through a more just distribution of economic goods, and through the substitution of constructive good will for military force, can the world find peace. I am not unaware of the difficulty of translating the social message of Christianity into political terms. But unless we do so translate it, by more courageous and sacrificial action than the church has yet been willing to support, I see nothing ahead but continuing chaos. The world is meant to be the dwelling-place of the family of God, not a battleground. When we treat it as a scrimmage in which the strong or the sly may grab what he can, everybody loses—and through the lamentations the God of judgment speaks.

There is no space in which to state in full my social convictions. But perhaps I should explain why I have become a more convinced pacifist in a day when many better Christians than I have felt impelled to surrender their pacifism. The reasons are both pragmatic and theological. War destroys every value for which Christianity stands, and to oppose war by more war is only to deepen the morass into which humanity has fallen. I have talked with lovable, high-minded Japanese Christians who see nothing of aggression in what their country is doing. "Japan is fighting for two reasons only—to establish friendly relations with China and to preserve the peace of the Orient!" When a military system does this to the minds of sane people it is time to repudiate forever the illusion that by fighting we shall have peace.

But deeper than this is the realism which has come with the shattering of whatever illusions our liberalism had. I believe that life is inevitably a sphere of conflict and that our choices are not often to be made between good and evil, but between alternative evils. I believe that in all of life's dark areas the triumph which shines through tragedy comes not with the sword which our Lord rejected, but with the cross toward which he walked. I believe that only in the union of justice with suffering love is any human force redemptive and permanently curative, for only in such union is force more than human.

V

Finally, I believe the church to be the custodian of Christian gospel and its matrix for growth. I have never stood outside the church, for my parents took me to its services long before I can remember and with few exceptions since, I have entered into the house of God on the Sabbath day. Twelve years ago the Methodist Episcopal Church ordained me, and I have preached from the pulpits of most of the major Protestant denominations. Yet within the past two years the church has taken on new meaning.

Pacifist though I am, I find great vigor in the phrase "the church militant," and I see growing evidence of its reality. As a child I was stirred by the rhythm of "Onward Christian Soldiers," but came later to dislike not only the military metaphors of this hymn but still more its bombastic assertion of what seemed flat falsehood.

> We are not divided,
> All one body we,
> One in hope and doctrine,
> One in charity.

Was there anything the church more obviously was not than "all one body"? Until recently I should have said that these words, like many others we sing on Sunday, are to be endured but not believed. Now I find in them world-transforming truth.

The Oxford Conference is mainly responsible. There were enough divisions in hope and doctrine, if not charity, at Oxford to tear any group in the world asunder. Yet this group was knit together in unity. The conviction was borne in upon me, as upon many others, that the foundations on which the church rests are not of this world, and that the Body of Christ is more than a time-honored phrase.

Within the church as it is, with all its division, its compromises and its pettiness, Christ's true church is working. It encompasses some of the most strategic social action of our day, as it has in every day. Because it is a supra-national fellowship, it is the only truly international organism. When almost everything else trembles it is least shaken of all our major institutions. Into a world of strife and gloom it brings brotherhood and light. Both because of its foundations and its mission, the gates of hell cannot prevail against it. The Christian can be confident that whatever the outcome of the present turmoil, the church will survive and will go forward "with the cross of Jesus going on before."

This vision of the church came to me at Oxford. But it remained for Madras to show me what the church has actually accomplished in the world community. If one had had any doubt as to whether the missionary enterprise is worthwhile, it would have been dispelled at Madras by the fellowship which resulted from the presence of the able leaders of the younger churches. They gave their witness with power, both of word and personality, to what the church has brought to pass. When these achievements are set against the background of poverty, ignorance, superstition and fear which still prevail in large areas, one is overwhelmed at the magnitude both of what the church has done and of what it has yet to do.

At Madras we beheld in action the great democracy of God. I have never seen elsewhere so complete a transcendence of distinctions of race, color, age, sex, denomination, and (most difficult of all) ecclesiastical prerogative. One felt one's self in the midst of great Christians grappling profoundly with great realities. I do not mean that there were not radical differences of opinion! To work together with persons of equally strong but differing conviction for the expression of Christian truth in unanimity without compromise is an experience as difficult as it is creative. Yet again, as at Oxford, there was one faith and one Lord. Christ when lifted up draws all men unto himself.

This is my spiritual pilgrimage. Had my life for the past decade been more exposed to the storms which have shaken the world, the tale might be different. I can feel sympathy for the mood of temporal despair and apocalyptic hope which grips the minds of many Christians. But I do not think we ought to adopt it. I believe that God is in his world, that he works in and with his children, and that out of the distresses of this day his Kingdom is being the more surely wrought.

III

Conflicts in Religious Thought (1929)

SECTION PREFACE

Readings 2, 3, and 4 come from Harkness's book *Conflicts in Religious Thought*, which was finished in early 1929, eight months before the October 1929 stock market crash, and which bears the mark of the 1920s.[1] The book was addressed primarily to young people of what some called the "lost generation" who were indifferent to religion and suspicious of religious authority. Religion had been crowded out, Harkness charged, by loyalty to the scientific method and what she called "pseudo-science" (which denied the place for faith) and by the material prosperity that was proving to be America's "spiritual undoing." For many Americans, this material prosperity was at its height in the late 1920s, with record lows in tax rates for the wealthy and record highs in the stock market.[2] Many Americans—particularly those who were prosperous—were confident about the future and about American technology and science and did not see the need for religion. Harkness wrote in the early pages of the book, "The primary battle which religion must fight today is the battle to justify its own existence."[3] And in *Conflicts in Religious Thought*, Harkness sets out to make the best case for a credible religion. As we saw in reading 1, Harkness later described the intent of this book: "I was trying to write a simple philosophy of religion which would rest the case for religious faith upon experience without theological presuppositions."[4]

Harkness was still fresh from her doctoral training in personalist philosophy at Boston University and from her postdoctoral work at Harvard under W. E. Hocking and Alfred North Whitehead when she wrote *Conflicts*. She notes in the introduction that this book was shaped by three scholars: the personalist Edgar Brightman, who was her major professor and mentor during her doctoral work at Boston University; William Ernest Hocking, with whom she had studied while on sabbatical at Harvard in 1926; and D. C. MacIntosh, with whom she was studying as she wrote up this book while on a Sterling Fellowship at Yale during the academic year 1928–29. The influence of Alfred North Whitehead is also evident especially in the section, excerpted here, on "evidences for belief in God." She draws on these philosophers and philosophical traditions—particularly personalism—as she makes her case for religion.

The first reading of this section, "Shall We Walk by Faith?" is taken from a discussion of religious authorities. The rise of confidence in the scientific method, Harkness noted, had led many people away from belief in a God who could not be scientifically verified. Harkness begins to set out in this excerpt (as well as in the following one) her case for God. She begins here with a discussion of the grounds for knowledge about God and other things religious. A hallmark of liberal theology has been its refusal to rely solely on external authorities such as the Bible and the teachings of the church and its affirmation of internal authorities such as experience. In "Shall We Walk by Faith?" Harkness is at her most suspicious of external authority, which "lays the dead hand of the past upon its pronouncements and throttles progress." She sets up a choice between either the "dead hand" of external authority or the "way of inner experience" that "offers the thrill of adventure." She betrays here some unfair prejudices against Christians who place a high value on external authority. A decade later, Harkness had moved to a greater appreciation both for external authority used in tandem with internal authorities as well as for other Christian denominations and ways of understanding authority.[5]

In *Conflicts* Harkness shies away from more distinctively Christian claims and language in other areas as well. For example, she is at her most dismissive of the doctrine of original sin: "The doctrine of original sin is fast disappearing—and the sooner it disappears, the better for theology and human sympathy." She writes often in this book about God but rarely about Christ and hardly ever about the Holy Spirit. As she noted in reading 1, if she were writing *Conflicts* in 1939 instead of 1929, she would have included a chapter on Christology (as she did in the book she actually *was* writing in 1939). In *Conflicts* Harkness is also at her most confident about progress, "in the onward march of things—to be discerned in both biological and social evolution." Her positive view of human nature and the orderliness of the world as it moves toward purposeful ends are also typical of her liberal position (and, to a degree, of her Wesleyan heritage, which had a high view of human nature not in and of itself but as transformed by grace).

Over the course of the 1930s, Harkness gained appreciation for some traditional teachings and language of the church. Her faith and theology could not get through the 1930s unscathed. She was engaged in discussions about economic and political crises around the world. She met Christians from India, Africa, and around the world who did not do theology in the same way as many Protestant North American liberals. She spent a semester each at Yale and Harvard and three semesters at Union Theological Seminary. All of these things shaped her theology and faith.

She also moved from a philosophy department to a religion department in the 1930s (and to a theological school in 1940). *Conflicts in Religious Thought* is more philosophical and less theological than Harkness's later writings; this is no surprise given her doctoral training and then six years of teaching in philosophy. In particular, her indebtedness to Boston personalism is evident throughout *Conflicts*. She wrote in the preface that of "contemporary philosophers" Brightman is the one "to whom I owe a debt above all others." This influence is unmistakable in the next excerpt, "Is There a God?—Evidences for Belief." Her analysis is very similar to Brightman's (as well as to Bowne's before him) and also bears the stamp of Whitehead. Her personalist and larger liberal commitments are evident in her arguments for God's existence based on the evidence of, for example, human personality, a mind-like world, human religious experience, and the objectivity of values.[6]

Personalist themes are also evident in reading 3, "Personality, Human and Divine." For personalists the distinctive aspect of human life is personality. It undergirds the whole network of conscious human feelings and thoughts; likewise, God is understood through the lens of "personality." Harkness wrote in the excerpt included here, "We must think of God, if at all, in terms of the highest that we know. Life gives us nothing higher than personality."

These theological and philosophical reflections on God, method, and human nature are all offered toward a practical end. Observing a generation of young adults who, she thought, had lost their moorings and were not bearing their responsibilities in the world, Harkness was convinced that they would only find stability and direction in religion. Religion helped to "make men better and to make men stronger."[7] Yet they would turn to religion only if it could be made credible. Throughout this text, as she seeks to make religion credible, she is unmistakably liberal in her theological orientation.

READING 2

The legitimacy of any kind of faith is under fire these days, and particularly of religious faith. The advance of scientific method has led many to the conviction that nothing can be known, and therefore that nothing ought to be believed,

From "Shall We Walk by Faith?" *Conflicts in Religious Thought*, 32–36.

save what can be definitely verified and proved. This is obviously one of the primary reasons for the giving up of belief in God. Deferring for the present the question of God's existence, we must ask whether faith has a rightful place in the building of our structure of beliefs. First, let us see how the matter stands historically with regard to religious faith.

1. Roads of faith.

There are two main roads which religious faith may travel. One is the way of an infallible external authority; the other the way of inner experience and investigation. The first is precise and definite, and suits the temper of him who wants a conducted journey. The second has alluring by-roads and offers the thrill of adventure and the joy of new discovery. One leads along a highway trod through many centuries and is traveled often by primitive conveyance; the other pushes out into new territory and uses every available modern resource for charting areas hitherto unexplored. Sometimes the roads converge, but they proceed from different angles.

The Catholic faith follows the former of these routes. It rests its religious beliefs on the authority of the Holy and Apostolic Church, affirms the infallibility of its past pronouncements, and tries to preserve inviolate the truth delivered to the fathers. Its official doctrine is that which was formulated by St. Thomas Aquinas in the thirteenth century. The Church interprets the Scriptures for its adherents and prescribes what they shall believe. Deviations from the established path are not encouraged, and an incipient attempt at "modernism" in the Catholic Church was effectively crushed by the encyclical of Pope Pius X in 1907. The result is a type of thought which exerts a powerful conservative influence tending to maintain the *status quo*, but which leaves little opportunity for progress toward a more rational faith.

Protestantism owes its origin to a "protest" against the authority of the church, and an insistence upon the right of the individual to think his own thoughts, read his own Bible, and find his own way to God without the mediation of priest or mass. But Protestantism has by no means been free from the power of external authority. An infallible Book took the place of an infallible Church, and early in its history the authority-defying individualism of its founders gave way to a docile yet intolerant acceptance of a new set of dogmas. Present-day Fundamentalism, though externally at the opposite pole from Catholicism, is one with Catholicism in its reliance upon authority, dogma and creed. We have here, as so often in history, an example of the meeting of extremes.

Liberal Protestantism has been truer to its inherent genius. It has maintained that truth must be the final touch-stone of all belief, and that every avenue of mind and conscience must be followed in the quest for truth. It has found its authority, not in Church or Book, but in human experience. It has found in Church and Book great reservoirs of truth, but has maintained that Church and Book must themselves be scrutinized with the keenest intellectual and spiritual instruments available. It has tried to put a religion of the spirit in place of the religion of authority. It has attempted to conserve the contributions of the past and at the same time to go forward.

The temper of our times clearly reflects these dominant influences. While social changes have made inroads even upon Catholicism, there is no marked diminution of its power. It probably gains each year as many communicants as it loses, and the Anglo-Catholic movement is an evidence of a desire on the part of many to return to a safe haven of authority.[8] Fundamentalism is waning, but exerts much influence in America in all save the more distinctly intellectual centers. Representing the conservative element within Protestantism it dominates the majority of Protestant churches; and the church is still rare where a pastor trained in a liberal seminary can say frankly all that he believes, or does not believe, without fear of alienating the "pillars" and upsetting his church.

Religious liberalism is growing in power and is firmly entrenched—particularly in urban centers. To people of intellectual training and Protestant background, it is usually the only type of religious thought that has any appeal. But it still lacks solid ground. The wide-spread religious indifference of the day is due at least in part to the fact that we are crossing a stream: Fundamentalism has lost its hold on thousands and Modernism has not yet gained it.

There are complex reasons for Modernism's failure to have the hold on religious loyalties that Fundamentalism used to have. Some of these are found in the general social and economic turmoil of the times, and a remarkable material expansion with which our moral and religious ideas have not yet caught up. Others more pertinent to our study lie in the fact that the natural conservatism of the human mind makes many afraid to venture along new paths, even though convinced that the old are wrong. Liberal leaders, even without conscious timidity, are constantly aware that their message is under fire and are under temptation to compromise in the interests of diplomacy. And with the old foundations of external authority shaken, there are many—both of leaders and laity—who have not yet been able to find solid footing in an authority that is from within.

So we find ourselves in somewhat of a plight. External authority lends stability, and by it one may be comfortably guided—until he looks around and begins to suspect the guide. But external authority does not lead forward. It lays the dead hand of the past upon its pronouncements and throttles progress. The only "way out" that one may travel with assurance of going forward is the way of inner religious experience and a frank facing of the truth wherever the way may lead.

There must be a way out. We cannot go back; to stand still is to be engulfed in the stream. We must go forward, and the way out can be found only in a more solid intellectual basis for religious faith. We do not need a new "Protestant Scholasticism"; we do need a religious philosophy which common folks and college professors alike can grasp and live by. If religion is to survive, we must be able to walk by faith without walking in the dark.

READING 3

1. What is a person?

. . . My personality consists then in the totality of my mental processes—my thoughts, feelings, purposes, desires, etc.—not isolated or disconnected but *bound together by an awareness of their belonging together as mine.* I know that I am myself and not another; I know that I am the same person today that I was yesterday. I am aware of being the same person now that I was ten years ago, though every particle of bone and tissue in my body has been changed and a different set of thoughts goes coursing through my mind. . . .

This view regards the self as active—as thinking, feeling, willing, uniting past and future in the experience of the present. Such a self is able to perform all the functions which, as we have seen, set man apart from the subhuman world. The self is able consciously to profit by the past and to project its purposes into the future; it has the power of abstract thought and self-expression; it is able to form ideals of moral rectitude and experience communion with a Higher Self. Watching carefully our terminology, we are justified in saying, not that a person *has* a soul, but he *is* a soul.

A person is a conscious being. . . . Personality, or selfhood, consists in the total complex of experience which we call our conscious life. Self-psychology refuses to regard these experiences as merely the functioning of a physical organism, or as a mysterious something lying outside of consciousness, or as a disconnected agglomerate. It regards the self, or soul, as an abiding unity, changing yet permanent, reasserting its continuity over lapses caused by sleep and perhaps by death. The self is real, not as a material or spiritual substance, but as the whole of our organized, unified conscious experience. My soul is my self. *I am a* soul, and I *have* a body.

2. Is God a person?

Throughout this . . . consideration of what a human person is, little has been said of God. It is evident that until we know what we mean by human personality, it is impossible to decide whether to ascribe personality to God.

If a person is an animal or a physical organism only, God cannot be such a person. If a person is the embodied (or disembodied) soul of animism or the traditional psychology, the belief in God is a more consistent hypothesis— though it would be difficult to conceive how such a God could be immanent in the world as love and goodness and creative power. But if a human person is an active conscious self, God too may be such a self. As the human soul expresses itself through the body but is not identical with the body, so God may manifest himself through the world without being identical with the world. As the

From "Personality, Human and Divine," *Conflicts in Religious Thought*, 150–67.

highest reaches of human personality are found in love and goodness, wisdom and creativity, so also the personality of God may manifest these qualities in infinite degree.

There is a wide-spread tendency to damn the belief in a personal God by calling it "anthropomorphic." But just what do we mean by anthropomorphism? If "man form" means bodily form, the objection is justified. . . .

But is the anthropomorphism of bodily form or human passions the only kind of "man-form"? Obviously not. If human personality is conscious experience manifesting itself at its best in love, goodness, wisdom and creative power, then the assertion that the belief in God is anthropomorphic loses its stigma. In Chapter V we saw that *all* knowledge is in a sense anthropomorphic, for we can know only in the terms that human experience gives us. We must take our choice among anthropomorphisms, choosing what appears most consistent with the evidence.

We must think of God, if at all, in terms of the highest that we know. Life gives us nothing higher than personality. If therefore we ascribe to God the highest personal qualities that experience reveals, and if (as we found in Chapter VI) there are reasons for believing that such a God exists, the anthropomorphic character of the belief affords no argument against its truth.

If we are to believe in a personal God we must think of him in terms of the highest human personality we know. To Christians, God is most readily conceived as revealing his true nature in the personality of Jesus. The Christian revelation is not the only avenue to God, but it is the highest the world has seen. It is as "the God and Father of our Lord Jesus Christ" that we know God most perfectly. The essence of the doctrine of Jesus' divinity lies in the fact that in his life and teachings we learn what God is like. Fortunately one does not need to be versed in metaphysics to know the Father God to whom Jesus prayed, the Father God whose works he came to do, the Father God whose sustaining care he promised to the burdened hearts of men.

READING 4

. . . Religious faith is seldom intellectually generated. Yet it is often intellectually destroyed. The theist who *thinks* must be able to give a reason for the faith that is in him if he would preserve that faith; and he must be able to defend it with reasons if he would convince others that it is worth preserving. . . .

The considerations which in the author's judgment afford the most valid grounds for belief in God are as follows: (1) the unity and interacting harmony of the physical universe; (2) the existence of human personality; (3) the rationality and "mind-like" nature of the world; (4) the evidences of a guiding purpose; (5) the religious experience of humanity; (6) the nature of values.

From "Is There a God?—Evidences for Belief," *Conflicts in Religious Thought*, 106–48.

1. The cause of the cosmos.

"The heavens declare the glory of God."

Of the factors which support belief, the one which presents itself most readily is the need of a cause, or creator of the world. . . .

Speculative wisdom has added little to that ringing declaration of faith in the supremacy of the spiritual which is found in Genesis 1:1. But it is not enough to talk about God as a First Cause in the temporal order of events. To push the creative work of God back into the fringes of time and leave it there gets us into many difficulties. Deism, a theory widely held two centuries ago and still the uncritical view of many, assumes that the world was created by God in the beginning—set running, like a watch or mechanical toy—and then left to run by itself. Such a view gives us a First Cause but also gives us an "absentee" God, a God unconcerned with human values or with the present processes of nature. Religion needs an ever-present, ever-working, ever-creative God. Philosophy likewise asks what power it is that keeps the solar system and the electron each whirling in its orbit, and finds an answer in an ever-active God. We shall be wiser if, instead of talking of first causes, we regard God as the ultimate, under-lying, ever-present cause of the world, its eternal source and ground. God is forever *immanent* in his world.

The argument we have just been stating is a revised form of that which has been known historically as the cosmological—the argument from the need of a deity as creator of the cosmos. It would be presumptuous to claim that it *proves* there is a God. But science, far from destroying the grounds of religious faith, gives constantly new evidence that this is a marvelously intricate world, a vast harmoniously interacting cosmos. The more we learn about the world we live in, the more incredible its existence appears unless there is an Infinite Mind as the source and ruling guardian of it all. The cosmological argument is thus rein-forced by the argument from interaction. "How is a unitary system of interact-ing members possible? This is the problem. Only through a unitary being which posits and maintains them in their mutual relations. This is the solution."[9]

Let us take a little excursion into the land of starlight. Reviewing our ele-mentary physics, we remember that light travels at the rate of 186,000 miles a second. Our sun, only 93,000,000 miles away, gets *its* light to us in a little over eight minutes. Scattered through the heavens are other suns—stars, we call them—so many billions upon quadrillions of miles away that ciphers fail us and we measure their distance in terms of the years that have elapsed since their light rays started their long journey to our earth. The star nearest to us, other than our sun, is four and a half "light-years" away. Others are four thousand light-years distant . . . [and] stars have been discovered that astronomers believe to be a million light-years away.

Each of these heavenly bodies is whirling in its orbit, never deviating from its wonted path. Our earth (and we along with it) revolves about the sun at the rate of eighteen miles per second—a million and a half miles per day! Our sun is also hurrying along its own way. . . . Yet so smoothly are we carried that we feel not the slightest apprehension in our dizzy rush through space.

Turning our gaze in the opposite direction, we find in the vast littleness of things a staggering set of figures. Every bit of so-called "matter" is made up of molecules, and these of atoms, and the atoms in turn of protons and electrons which are simply positive and negative charges of electricity in certain numerical combinations.

What does all this mean for religion? It means that our earth is a comparatively insignificant planetary fragment, and this awareness ought to make us humble. It means too that we are living in a world of amazing intricacy and complexity, a world of ordered harmony, a world not only of space and speed but of infinite accuracy. The possibility that such a world "fell together" by chance is so remote that the suggestion is unthinkable. Science gives us new evidence daily that the world is a cosmos, a *universe*, an ordered oneness. And whence came this physical universe, with its unity and interacting harmony, save from a Unitary Creative Power? The heavens declare the glory of God, the firmament showeth his handiwork.

2. Human Personality.

"And God created man in own image."

It is an indisputable fact that man is here: of this we can be certain in a world of many uncertainties. The next question is, "How did he get here?"

Biologically, man's ancestry can be traced back to sub-human stages, back indeed to the one-celled amoeba. . . .

Through millions of years, so science tells us, man has been a-making. And what guided the process through all those aeons? Is man the result of undirected natural forces, stumbling hither and yon and falling by fortuitous circumstances into the product we call *homo sapiens?* The "survival of the fittest" is explanatory of many of man's traits; but, as has been aptly remarked, what accounts for the "arrival of the fit"? A distinguished biologist, Professor Lawrence Henderson, has shown persuasively that before the emergence of life upon the planet the inorganic world was ready for it, with exactly the right combination of chemical elements to support life.[10] This does not look like chance. Then onward through the ages favorable variations emerged, and were preserved, and an organism of increasing complexity developed. And at last, the organism was no longer an organism only; it was a living soul. To say that man is merely a "fortuitous concourse of atoms" is to offer an affront to common sense and to biological science.

It was once the fashion for theology to belittle man, thinking to glorify God by making of man a "worm of the dust." This concept has well-nigh vanished from theology, and the dignity and greatness of man gets its attacks from other quarters—from the astronomer who points to man's littleness in the vast immensities of space, from the psychologist who makes of man an animal and nothing but an animal, from the materialist who finds in man only a combination of physico-chemical elements. Anatole France calls man "a speck of dust on a ball of mud." Bertrand Russell speaks of "this petty planet on which our bodies impotently crawl." H. L. Mencken remarks that man is a sick fly taking a dizzy ride on a gigantic fly-wheel, and life a combat between jackals and jackasses.

From such estimates, it is refreshing to turn to words of another sort:

> "Thou hast made him but little lower than God,
> And crownest him with glory and honor.
> Thou makest him to have dominion over the works of thy hands;
> Thou hast put all things under his feet."

So sings the Psalmist in a paean of praise to the Creator, and to man, the climax of creative acts. This rapturous outburst is good poetry, good religion, and good philosophy.

Man, to be sure, does not always appear to reflect the character of God. Instead of being but little lower than God, he seems in some respects to be but little above the beast. In all of us there are traits which point to a survival from our animal ancestry. Man shares the instincts of animal life—"we cannot disown our poor relations."

Yet in spite of manifold resemblances, the fact remains that in that *ensemble* which we call man's personality, that combination of characteristics which makes each individual what he is, human kind is a long way removed from the animal world. Two capacities in particular set man so far apart from the animal that it is folly to attempt to describe human personality wholly, or even largely, in terms of biological categories drawn from the sub-human realm. These capacities are man's creative intelligence and his power of pursuing moral ideals. No animal has the power to think logically in terms of abstract concepts or to exercise creative genius. No animal has the power to subordinate an instinctive urge to an ideal of moral rectitude, or to strive consciously for the attainment of moral values.[11]

It is, moreover, a significant fact that rationality and goodness, these most distinctive attributes of human personality, are the very qualities which above all others God must possess if there be a God. A God who was not intelligent and rational would be useless as an explanation of the unity and interacting orderliness of the universe. A God who was not good—a God unconcerned with the moral welfare of mankind, would neither satisfy the demands of religious worship nor explain the existence of a purposeful and moral universe. If it be true that man's highest traits are those of God, it looks as if man had been made in the image—the rational and moral image—of the Creator. Human personality is the product either of blind material forces or of a higher mind. It may be the product of a Mind working through material forces. But its ultimate explanation is either personal or impersonal—we must take our choice. It seems more credible—more consistent with the nature of human personality in its most characteristic traits—to believe with the Hebrew seers that man is the supreme creative act of a Supreme Person.

3. A mind-like world.

"He that teacheth man knowledge, shall not he know?"

A third line of evidence comes from that department of philosophy called epistemology, or rather from epistemology in conjunction with its physical and metaphysical foundations. Epistemology is the theory of knowledge—the study which examines the possibility of our knowing the world in which we live. . . .

We are much in the habit of assuming that the ideas in our minds are correct copies of the objects they refer to. For example, we feel sure that when we look at an apple and think we see a red, round, external object we really see one. To raise any question on this point usually strikes the philosophically uninitiated as sheer nonsense. But the problem is not so simple as it looks. If one is color-blind, the apple is no longer red—which raises the question of what would become of the redness of apples if we were all color-blind. Seen in twilight, or through colored glasses, its redness is of a different hue. . . .

Physics deals roughly with our "common sense" assumptions. In fact, it tells us that the redness is not in the apple at all; that a color is simply a set of mathematically calculable vibrations of a certain wave length, impinging upon the sense organs of an observer. The solidity of the apple, which looks more substantial, vanishes too in an analysis of its minute electrons into charges of electrical energy. And the apple turns out upon investigation to be not the solid, external, independent thing it looks to be—but a system of activity, infinitely complex, deriving the qualities we attribute to it from a certain set of vibrations in conjunction with a certain set of sense organs.

One theory of epistemology holds that idea and object are one and inseparable (i.e., that the apple *is* the experience of it in the mind of an observer); another view maintains that every idea *refers to* an object which is other than itself. We shall not attempt to settle here this abstruse question, which has given Bishop Berkeley, John Locke, Immanuel Kant and innumerable others much cause for speculation. All we are concerned with here is the religious significance of the problem. It is enough to note that there is a problem, and a puzzling one. The question of how our minds can know the world around us *looks* simple—so does the rising of the sun in the east each morning. But when one probes behind either event it is far from simple, and the solution far from being what appears on the surface. We know the outer world, but *how?* . . . [T]he very ease with which we do it blinds us to the mystery and miracle of the process.

Not all philosophies have thought it necessary to introduce God as an aid in the solution of the epistemological puzzle, but many have. Most famous of these is Berkeley's doctrine that physical objects owe all the externality they have to their being ideas in the mind of God. The various types of absolute idealism that have emanated from Hegel agree in regarding the universe as a unitary system of thought, and accept the Hegelian dictum, "What is real is rational." All of these have an Absolute as the ground of things; some have an Absolute Self, or an all-knowing Mind, spanning the chasm between the finite knower and the object of his knowledge. . . . It was a major tenet of Professor Bowne's philosophy that the "parallelism of thought and thing" sets a gap between idea and object which can be bridged only by a metaphysical monism based on the activity of an Infinite Mind.[12]

Epistemology drives us back to metaphysics, for our minds can know the world around us only because the world itself responds to our knowing. Suppose we assume for a moment that no mind ever had anything to do with its making, and that it just fell together by accident. A comparable analogy would be a page of type that fell together as printer's pi. Would we expect to read any meaning from the page? Scarcely. The chance that the type would fall together to make one intelligible word is slight; the chance that the words would arrange themselves in an intelligible sentence infinitely less; the chance that sentences would arrange themselves in a meaningful paragraph or page so remote as to be negligible. Whenever we open a book and find meaning on a page, we assume that a mind has put it there. Likewise when we look at the world and find meaning in it—a world infinitely more intricate and full of meaning than any page of type—we can only assume that a Mind has placed it there.[13]

Not only can man read off the secrets of nature; man can control nature. Neither would be possible, were not the universe an orderly, intelligible, dependable world. The magnificent achievements of modern science are a double tribute to the greatness of man's mind and to the mind-like nature of the world that man is mastering.

To say that the intelligibility of the universe arose through mere chance or the undirected interplay of material forces is simply to confess our inability or unwillingness to grapple with the problem. There appears to be, to use the phrase of Leibniz, a sort of "preestablished harmony" between the universe and human minds.[14] The possibility of our knowing the world around us, of discovering meaning in it and bending it to human purposes, points to a Supreme Mind as the author both of human minds and the world of things.

4. Teleology versus mechanism.

"Yet I doubt not thro' the ages
One increasing purpose runs."

A fourth argument, usually called the teleological, affirms the belief in God from the evidences of purpose in the universe. It has as its correlate the atheistic argument from the presence of evil and the apparent indifference of the world of nature. The evidence is by no means all on one side, and the question as to whether the world is really guided by a world purpose or is merely a great purposeless machine is one of the deepest that confronts human thinking. Philosophers are divided on this issue into teleologists and mechanists.

Teleology is the view that the universe is purposeful—that it realizes ends and is concerned with the attainment of values. It says that the universe is not a mere aggregation of parts each having its own little function, but that the universe is a *whole,* or an organism, made of parts which work together in a unity and work toward some end. It boldly denies the mathematical dictum that the whole is equal to the sum of all its parts; for it says that the whole is *greater* than the sum of its parts.

Mechanism, on the other hand, maintains that the world is governed by unchanging natural laws which act automatically and with such precision that every event—whether of man or nature—could be predicted with unvarying accuracy if all the circumstances were known. It thus links itself with determinism in the field of human conduct—an aspect of the problem which will receive fuller consideration in a later chapter. It holds that every event is inevitably determined by the chain of previous circumstance, and bids us study these sequences instead of looking for purposes if we would understand the why of things. Mechanism rests its case on the push of the past: teleology on the pull of the future.

Mechanism is often misunderstood. As a scientific method, it is simply an application of the accepted principle that every effect must have a cause. The study of antecedent circumstances and the establishment of causal sequences is imperative to any scientific view of things, and has done much to banish superstition. But when a legitimate scientific method exalts itself into a metaphysics and tries to banish the spiritual aspects of man's nature by denying their existence—to say nothing of its banishment of a divine purpose—it exceeds its rightful bounds.

Mechanism used to be accepted as an indisputable principle in the realm of the purely physical. But no longer. The solid foundations of the older physics are breaking up with recent discoveries, such as the quantum theory and the principle of relativity; and Professor A. N. Whitehead, probably the most authoritative philosopher-physicist of the present day, has shown in his *Science and the Modern World* that a mechanistic philosophy is inadequate to account for all phenomena even in the world of physical nature. "The old foundations of scientific thought are becoming unintelligible. Time, space, matter, material, ether, electricity, mechanism, organism, configuration, structure, pattern, function, all require reinterpretation. What is the sense of talking about a mechanical interpretation when you do not know what you mean by mechanics?"[15]

Biological evolution, in the first flush of its popularity, was generally interpreted in mechanistic terms. "Natural selection" and "survival of the fittest" were thought to cover the whole territory. But not for long. Biologists have for many years been divided on the question as to whether all biological phenomena can be interpreted mechanistically. There are many "vitalists" who hold to the existence of a non-mechanical life force.[16] Vitalism is not necessarily teleological in the sense of asserting a divine purpose, and an impersonal Life Force *is* a long way from the God of religion; yet it joins hands with religion in denying staunchly that "creation walks with aimless feet."

Let us look at a few of the teleological factors discernible in evolution. One of these is found in the very meaning of evolution. Evolution implies progress. And progress is not mere change; it is movement *toward* something. To quote Professor Whitehead again, "The aboriginal stuff, or material, from which a materialistic philosophy starts, is incapable of evolution. . . . Evolution, on the materialistic theory, is reduced to the role of being merely another word for the description of the changes of the external relations between portions of matter. There is nothing to evolve, because one set of external relations is as good as any other set of external relations. There can merely be change, purposeless and unprogressive."[17] Yet progress is a fact. To talk of progress without guide or goal is to destroy its meaning.

We have noted the problem that mechanism faces (if it faces it) about the "arrival of the fit." Biologists confess that the origin, both of the primordial germ cell and the myriad variations from which new species have emerged, is shrouded in mystery. To attribute these emergents to chance is disloyalty to mechanistic method, for mechanism has no place for deviations from the established order. To attribute them to a directing cosmic purpose is to surrender the case to teleology. Mechanism is thus driven to deny all novelty, maintaining that everything apparently new has been potentially present from all eternity. But this simply multiplies mysteries, and does not tell us at all how it came to be present, or how it came to "unroll" as it has. The more tenable doctrine of "emergent evolution," which holds that at each new level something new emerges, easily correlates with theistic faith in a guiding purpose. . . .

The struggle for existence itself implies a purposive factor in the organism. Machines do not struggle. There is much in the struggle of a living organism that is mechanical; yet even in the subhuman realm, in such elemental urges as hunger, sex, and self-protection, there is a selective element in which consciousness plays a part. The horse, within limits, can choose its food; the automobile is yet to be invented that can choose its oil and gasoline! The presence of consciousness in the higher animals has had no little influence in the preservation of the organisms possessing superior intelligence and adaptability.

When man emerged, consciousness came to function in a vastly more important way; for in *homo sapiens* the course of "natural" selection was definitely interrupted by his power to act in accordance with rationally chosen ends. No longer does Nature take its course, for we are *human*, humane, humanitarian—preserving weaklings biologically "unfit" to survive. We do this because social evolution has superseded biological, and man is attempting—however feebly—to guide his destiny and that of his fellows on the basis of the supremacy of the good rather than the survival of the strong. In human evolution "fitness" takes on a new and finer meaning.

If mechanistic categories are inadequate to explain all the data of the physical and biological sciences, they prove still more inadequate in the social sciences.

There are undoubtedly many mechanistic elements in human thought and conduct, the discovery of which will furnish valuable tools for the direction of human action along better channels. But the ideal of the better, and the power to choose it, still stand as evidences of the purposeful. Many of man's acts are thrust on him from behind, and every act has a cause. But in his most significant acts he is lured from before, led on by ideals and consciously chosen ends. "The gleaming ideal is the everlasting real." To deny that man is capable of purposeful activity is to blind one's eyes to the facts for the sake of defending a theory.

What has the presence of non-mechanical factors in the realm of physical nature, and biological organisms, and human choice, to do with God? It has at least this to do with God: that the rejection of mechanism in these realms, for reasons scientific rather than religious, gives evidence that any theory of universal mechanism oversteps its bounds. It thus clears the ground for faith in a purposive, guiding God—a God of long purposes who works out his will through these mechanisms that we call natural laws, a God who *uses* law but is not the victim of it.

We can go further, and say that there are value elements—evidences of increasing worth in the onward march of things—to be discerned in both biological and social evolution. It is a long journey from amoeba to *homo sapiens,* but it is a journey that has been going somewhere. The emergence of an organism with the complexity and skill of the human body, to say nothing of the vastly greater complexity and skill of the human mind, is a sheer mystery in a mechanistic world.

It is of course impossible to see value or meaning in every step of the biological march. There are unfavorable as well as favorable variations; there is destruction as well as growth. One can gather data, if he will, to prove that Nature is "red in tooth and claw." But the surprising fact is that so many of the variations are favorable, so much of the destruction a stairway for progress. In a world of fang and claw, of bacillus and parasite, the natural conclusion would be—not progress—but universal death. But instead, there is life, and growth, and increasing complexity of structure and function. There is ugliness in the world, but much more of beauty also than is necessary for biological survival. There is pain, but life in most (perhaps all) of its stages shows a predominance of comfort over pain. Were it otherwise, the will to live would long since have atrophied. There is much that appears purposeless, but lacking the vista of eternity it is presumptuous to brand any phenomenon as purposeless. Looking broadly over the present, and looking backward with a long look, the life-current seems not ill-adapted for the pursuit of the higher values. It looks as if a value-loving Mind were immanent in the process.

Surveying the course of social evolution, we find further evidence of a "destiny that shapes our ends." Little by little, man has moved forward in the direction of the supremacy of the spiritual over the carnal. In spite of temporary eddies in human progress, such as the World War and its after-effects, a long look over the past reveals a tremendous advance from the ideals and standards of former days. We are far removed from cannibalism, and gladiatorial combats. Human slavery, even within a century, has been well-nigh banished from the earth. Within a decade, we have moved an amazing distance toward a warless world. In spite of the tendency of human nature to sigh for "the good old days," not many of us would be willing, if we could, to go back to the customs and conditions of the past.

Viewed from the perspective of the centuries it looks as if the world were not only moving forward, but moving in the direction of the attainment of higher moral values. How much of the upward progress of mankind is to be attributed to human agencies and how much to divine guidance is a question not to be empirically answered; for God works through human circumstance and human wills. But when human purposing and the force of circumstance have been fully taken into account, we have not accounted adequately for the correlation of the whole—for the direction of destiny toward the "far-off divine event." Human purposes are discordant, yet little by little unity has emerged from the chaos of conflicting ends. Men more than once have builded better than they knew. More than once men have laid down their lives for causes apparently defeated; yet the cause has outlived defeat and right in the end has triumphed. Shakespeare to the contrary, it is not true that the evil that men do lives after them while the good is oft interred with their bones! The evil is soon forgotten, or remembered to be avoided, while the good lives on as a component element in the structure of human progress.

In spite of the problem of evil, serious as it is, it looks as if the world were being guided by a power that makes for righteousness. Law, pain, struggle, even sin, have meaning in a God-directed universe. In an aimless world, neither cosmic nor human purpose has a meaning.

5. Religious experience.

"The Lord is my shepherd;
I shall not want."

A further line of argument rests on the evidence afforded by the fact of religious experience. With this we shall consider also the pragmatic argument from the effects of religious faith, for it is because the worshiping individual has believed that he found God, and through finding him has achieved self-mastery and peace of soul, that worship has maintained its perennial power over the human spirit.

The term "religious experience" is not easy to define. We shall use it in the sense of worship—a reverent reaching out of the human individual to a more-than-human power, a seeking that in the very act of *seeking* is in some sense also a *finding*. It is an inner commitment of life to the guidance of that which is recognized as Highest and Holiest. To one who has experienced it, it is an indubitable fact—grasped rather through first-hand acquaintance than through accuracy of definition. To one who has never experienced it, it is likely to appear as mere self-deception or self-hypnosis. . . .

To one who has . . . felt the personal presence of the divine, there can be little doubt concerning the reality of God.

The argument from religious experience must be scrutinized with care. As we saw in examining the criteria of truth, neither the universality of any belief nor the feeling of certainty with which it is held can establish its truth. The coherence test must be our court of last resort. We must proceed therefore to examine the argument from religious experience in the light of its coherence with what we find in the rest of our experience.

Looking into the historical aspect of the question, we find that while the belief in God cannot be said to be universal in the sense that every individual who ever lived has held it, religious experience appears nevertheless to be a characteristic human trait. It is not an instinct, but it is an instinctive tendency, the outgrowth of man's whole instinctive life. . . .

Furthermore, there appears to be a large-scale harmony between man's search for God and the rest of the universe. Religion emerges and is sustained by man's sense of need—a significant truth embodied in Schleiermacher's famous definition of religion as a "feeling of absolute dependence." Everywhere else in the universe, a deep-rooted sense of need has been met by an external reality corresponding to it. The whole process of evolution gives evidence of the adaptation of the organism, impelled by a need, to an environment which objectively exists. To gratify hunger there is food; to gratify the sex instinct there are mates. Man is not created with a sense of need for human companionship, and then forced to live alone. "To suppose that during countless ages, from the seaweed up to man, the progress of life was achieved through adjustments to external realities, but that then the method was all at once changed and that throughout a vast province of evolution the end was secured through adjustments to external non-realities, is to do sheer violence to logic and to common sense."[18] Unless the universe for once has deviated from its pattern, it looks as if man's age-long search for God must have a God to satisfy it.

The argument from the religious experience of the individual, as of the race, must be considered in conjunction with the rest of life. A personal experience of God—an intense conviction of his indwelling presence—is probably to most believers the strongest practical reason for belief. Taken by itself it proves only that a great many people sincerely believe that a real God is really present in their lives. It is conceivable that all may be deluded.

Yet, there are reasons for believing that the consciousness of God's presence which the devout believer feels is more than a great illusion. Chief among these is the fact that such an experience *makes a difference in living,* and makes a difference that harmonizes with the universe instead of running counter to it. Applying the coherence test to pragmatic effects, we find that the belief that a real God can really come into human life is consistent with the moral welfare of the world. If it were all a vast illusion, it is difficult to conceive how it could harmonize so successfully with the development of finer ideals and nobler living. Yet it does *so* harmonize, and history reveals an ever-increasing harmony. To be sure, superstitious notions and unethical practices have more than once been fostered in the name of religion. But witchcraft and the Inquisition have had their day and ceased to be—and they have ceased to be because they were antagonistic to the major currents of the universe as manifest in human affairs. Little by little, the elements inconsistent with the demands of moral progress perish. The belief that God can enter into human life and lift it to higher planes has persistently survived.

The belief in God has had tremendous consequences. In spite of ghastly perversions, it is the most potent idea that the world has known. The idea of a good God demanding goodness in men, when linked with a personal experience of the divine, has afforded an unparalleled dynamic to moral living. It has turned men again and again from sin to righteousness, and has enabled them to triumph gloriously over the ills of life. It has brought a richer, fuller life to thousands, and has lifted men from despair to hope through a conquering faith in the Eternal. The belief that there is a good God who wants men to be good and who is aiding them in their moral struggles is a simple doctrine—but it is a doctrine without which the world would be a very different place.

History bears witness to the potency of the idea of God. Not all the great figures of history have been impelled by religious motives. But if the influence of all whose work was motivated primarily by the ideal of obedience to the will of God were to be stricken from the world's history, the story would lose its richest elements. Moses, Isaiah, Socrates, Jesus, Paul, Augustine, Aquinas, Luther, Lincoln, Gandhi, and hundreds of lesser figures, have learned of God and molded destiny. If we turn to the literature of the ages, the verdict is the same. The world's greatest epics have been religious epics—Homer, Dante and Milton bear witness to the potency of the idea of God. Goethe, Browning, Tennyson and a host of other poets and seers have found in religious faith an inspiration to creativity. The world's greatest literary masterpiece is the Bible, and the influence of the Bible has permeated all other literature. In the field of art, the greatest themes are religious themes. Phidias and Praxiteles, Raphael and Michael Angelo [sic]—each in his own way has portrayed his conception of the reality of the divine. . . .

Religious experience is built upon belief in a real God. The consequences of the belief do not prove its truth beyond all question. But they indicate that the belief in God makes a difference, and makes the kind of difference that it ought to make in an orderly, purposeful, moral universe. The God-idea seems to coincide with the ways of the universe—not to thwart them. If the world is built on rational principles, it would be strange indeed if the most powerful and the most inspiring idea that humanity has known should turn out to be merely men's imaginings.

6. The objectivity of values.

> "On the earth the broken arcs,
> In the heaven a perfect round."

We come now to an argument for God which is of very uneven standing among philosophers. Some regard it as the most cogent of all—so forceful as virtually to constitute a proof. Others deny it any standing whatever. . . .

By the *value* of anything—whether a dinner, or a sunset, or an experience of worship—we mean its worthfulness or desirability. That is, the amount of satisfaction it brings to the person who values it. The most important values, such as the love of friends and family, a clear conscience and a contented mind, cannot be bought or sold. . . . The values which any person loves and lives for—his dominant desires—are the truest index of his character. . . .

By the objectivity of values is meant the belief that there are certain types of value which every rational mind *ought* to prize; and that these values depend, not on our subjective preferences and shifting social standards, but on something solid and dependable in the nature of the universe. The objectivity of values implies that there is a real goodness, a real truth, a real beauty which is good or true or beautiful quite regardless of whether you or I may think so. . . . And since neither individual opinion nor social codes yield any true objectivity, these values, if they are genuinely objective, must be grounded in something *more than human*. In a word, grounded in God.

Are values really objective? Could we answer with a decisive yes or no, we should have gone a long way toward solving the problems of both religion and philosophy. Upon this question hinges the issue as to whether we strive merely for ephemeral goods, or for goods that are eternal because grounded in an eternal determiner of destiny. The question cuts across metaphysical systems and divides them into optimistic and pessimistic, into idealistic and naturalistic. The dominant trait of metaphysical naturalism is not its stand on the inner nature of so-called "matter"; it is its negative reply to that deepest of all human queries, "Is the universe friendly?" Naturalistic ethics, says Professor Hocking, is man's gesture of heroism on the scaffold of a universe that will eventually write a cipher as the sum of all his works. "It lacks the vista of eternity, and the resonance of a divine concern in its inward vitality." It is this note which faith in a personal God as the ground and goal of values supplies to men.

The religious spirit has not always been able to formulate the logical foundations of its faith that values are objective, but it has clung tenaciously to the conviction that somehow its highest ideals must be real. It has refused to believe that its aspirations toward the higher reaches of the soul are but fleeting fancies. Idealistic poetry, the devotional literature of the Bible, the liturgies of the Church—every medium through which religious experience has translated itself into words, gives evidence of a deep conviction that ideals have cosmic meaning because grounded in an All-Perfect. And that, in a word, is what the objectivity of values means. . . .

The sum of the argument is this. Only persons can be wise or good: values cannot float about the universe as etherial entities residing in no mind. Only a Supreme Person can be all-wise or all-good—the ground and goal of all the values worth striving for. If values are cosmic yet personal, they must be grounded in a personal God.

Nearly a thousand years ago Anselm, philosopher-theologian of the Middle Ages, tried to prove that there must be a real God because the idea of God is the most perfect men can form, and where there is perfection there must likewise be existence. This argument, called the ontological, was easily enough demolished by Anselm's successors; for, as Gaunilo showed, the idea of a perfect island is something very different from the existence of such an island. Yet the argument in one form or another has persisted through the ages. Men have refused to relinquish the faith that the highest and best they can imagine must be true. Men have staked their all, and have died for the conviction, that their ideals are not mere transient fancies but are grounded on an eternal Rock of Ages. Today the ontological argument, transformed to faith in the objective reality of men's highest ideals, is perhaps the strongest of reasons for belief in God. Not as a hard and fast logical proof does it afford indisputable evidence. But as a way of life and a practical attitude toward the deeper problems of existence, it leads men boldly and triumphantly to stake their lives on the belief that there is a God—a good God who wants men to be good. Faith is reason grown courageous:[19] faith is vision plus valor.[20]

We have followed a long trail in our quest for the foundations of theistic belief: let us look back over the path. The universe which our experience gives us points to the belief in a Creative Mind as the source of the cosmos with its ordered harmony. Man's personality points to a Supreme Personality for its explanation. Man's knowing mind discovers a mind-like world responding. Man's religious experience impels him to believe that a real God comes into human life, and acceptance of God's reality affords richer practical consequences both for happiness and moral living than does denial. Finally we have seen that the world as it is, with all its limitations, points to the reality of a world as it ought to be—a world of ideals and values existing in the acts and purposes of a more-than-human Person.

We cannot presume to assert that the belief in God has been proved beyond all cavil. The quest is not finished—the road stretches ahead. But unless the universe is a chaotic complex of inexplicable mysteries, it looks as if there must be a God.

IV

The Resources of Religion (1936)

SECTION PREFACE

Readings 5 and 6 come from Harkness's 1936 book, *The Resources of Religion*, which Harkness described as a "companion and supplement" to *Conflicts in Religious Thought*.[1] Harkness sought in *Resources* "to set forth the basic elements of a Christian philosophy of life and a Christian strategy for meeting the neo-paganism of our day."[2] In *Resources*, as in *Conflicts*, she is addressing a culture that is experiencing a "lostness" linked to secularism and remedied only by religion and its moral demands.

The world had changed dramatically between February of 1929 when Harkness finished *Conflicts* and the fall of 1935 when she wrote *Resources of Religion*. The material prosperity that she described in *Conflicts* as America's "spiritual undoing" had itself been undone by the stock market crash in late 1929 and the Great Depression that followed. The book was written as massive social programs were being initiated to help the poor. In May of 1935, the Works Progress Administration, a federal program to create jobs for the unemployed, had been formed. August saw the creation of the Social Security program to provide for the elderly and the passage of the "Federal Revenue Act" increasing taxes on the wealthy. Over these same months, the U.S. government passed laws to protect the rights of workers and to regulate businesses, limit monopolies, and restructure the banking system.[3]

The European context had also changed. In the 1920s, Harkness had been very sympathetic to the cause of post–World War I Germany, whose people were going hungry and whose government was very weak in part because of reparations that had been required in the Treaty of Versailles. In two articles published in January 1925 ("Germany and the War-Peace" and "Germany's Place in the Shadow"), Harkness criticized the treaty for its harsh measures against the German people and maintained that the treaty contained the "seeds of future wars." "Instead of placing all the blame on Germany," Harkness wrote, "we [had] better blame economic imperialism, secret diplomacy, and the whole war system. Until we, who call ourselves Christian, can bury our grudges and learn to love our enemies, there is not much hope of peace on earth and good will towards all."[4]

By the mid-1930s, these "seeds of future war" had taken root. Hitler was in power and, by late 1935 when this book was written, had reinstated a military draft and begun rearming Germany in violation of Versailles. In 1935—as in the several years previous—a string of restrictions were placed on German Jews. Just the year before, in 1934, Karl Barth, Dietrich Bonhoeffer, and others had written the Barmen Declaration, which objected to Hitler's largely successful attempts to control the church and insisted, in opposition, on the church's integrity and independence. These world political and economic crises were pivotal for Harkness and this book. In this very different context, she is writing not, as she had in 1929, simply about why religion was credible, but also about what religion demanded in a time of crisis.

Harkness wrote *Resources* not only in the shadow of the Depression and world crises, but also literally in the shadow of "the spires of Union Theological Seminary and Riverside Church." The book, Harkness reported in the preface, "owes as much to this environment as to any individual." Even so, she does highlight the particular influence of one person, Reinhold Niebuhr, noting that *Resources* was "written during a period when I was accepting and rejecting a torrent of ideas expressed by him in five lectures weekly, and only omniscience could determine how much of the book is the product of the fertilization of his thought."[5] Both of the readings from *Resources* show the imprint of Niebuhr and of the social and political crises of the time.

In the first reading from *Resources,* "A Christian Society—Ends and Means," some of the language is very similar to Niebuhr's, but overall Niebuhr serves as a foil for Harkness's reflections on the kingdom of God and the Christian society. The chapter is a counterargument to Niebuhr's pessimism about the possibility of good societies formed around love. Harkness, seeking to find a way between "unrealistic idealism and an unidealistic realism," offers here an alternate vision. A Christian society should model itself on the life of a healthy family where the members respect each other and exhibit "respect for personality," humility, and "friendliness," and where justice is sought and won by peaceful means using nonviolent coercion. Means and ends, Harkness insists here, must be in harmony; only peaceful means will bring peaceful ends. In this liberal rejoinder to Niebuhr, Harkness tries to wed a greater realism with a liberal confidence about the possibilities of forming a good society that seeks peace through friendliness and that helps to build the kingdom of God.

In "Our Enlightened Paganism," Niebuhr serves less as a foil than a friend. Harkness examines the things that she believes stand in the way of full loyalty to God and God's kingdom—capitalism, nationalism, scientific determinism, and other aspects of culture in the mid-1930s. Harkness is keen to shift the focus of her readers away from a sole preoccupation with the sins of Marxism or German and Italian nationalism toward a greater recognition of the sins of U.S. capitalism, nationalism, and racism.

READING 5

1. Some Preliminary Observations

It is not the purpose of this chapter to compete with Sir Thomas More or Edward Bellamy in setting up a Utopia. Paper utopias in plenty have already been established, not only by my socialist friends but by the idealists of every age from Plato's to the present.

Such patterns of ideal states are not to be disparaged because they have not been wholly brought to fulfillment. Ideals rooted deep in a sense of social justice are not mere pipe-dreams; they are the most powerful realities in the universe. Ideals alone are strong enough to stand against man's most powerful physical impulses—sex and hunger—and bring out of them a reasonably ordered civilization. It was ideals that abolished gladiatorial combats, infanticide, the burning of heretics at the stake, the hanging of old women as witches, the owning of persons of darker skin as chattels, and numerous other things of which—with all our present lack of civilization—we are happily rid. In our own day an ideal of a classless society has brought into being in Russia the most far-reaching social experiment of our times—if not, indeed, of all times; while in India an ideal of non-violence has enabled a little man of unprepossessing appearance to give anxious moments to one of the mightiest nations of the earth. Let no one despise the power of ideals, for ideals are the stuff that great movements are made of.

This chapter will be concerned mainly with ideals. It will have something to say of what society would be if it were built along the lines of a Kingdom of God. The approach, however, will not be the setting up of an ideal state but the attempt to see what a Christian strategy might be in bringing into being such a "realm of God" as every Christian desires. Though the chapter will not be

From "A Christian Society—Ends and Means," *Resources of Religion*, 43–71.

devoted specifically to the question of war and peace, citations will be largely in this field both because it is intrinsically so vital and because it illustrates all the major issues of a Christian strategy. We shall perhaps say more of means than of ends, regarding means and ends as inseparable though not identical factors in the building of a better world.

Ends are important. Without them we are lost in a welter of confused gropings, following the trial and error method of rats in a maze which the psychologists have made so familiar to us. . . . [The rats want] to get to freedom. Their major problem is how to get there.

Somewhat comparably there are very few Christians who, so far as they think at all, do not want a society built on love. State this ideal in sufficiently general terms, and every congregation will assent. Dress it up with sufficient oratory, quote poetry or Abraham Lincoln at the proper moment, and people may call it a great sermon! But what we do not agree on is, first, what *principles* and second, what *techniques* to follow in getting to this goal.

This study will deal mainly with principles; for in principles means and ends converge. To suggest a principle of Christian strategy is to try to say both what we want to achieve and along what main routes we should try to achieve it.

It is significant that one naturally talks about what a Christian society *would be*. It would be presumptuous and a bit shocking to anyone acquainted with the present world situation to try to say what a Christian society *is*, while there is no corresponding sense of shock at speaking of what a Christian person is. This simply bears out Reinhold Niebuhr's thesis, so obviously true that it is strange we did not recognize it more clearly until his *Moral Man and Immoral Society* forced it on Christian thinking, that we can have a high degree of achievement of the Christian ethic in individual life without its greatly affecting group relations. There is danger of falling into either of two extremes; the one a pessimistic cynicism that says Christian ideals have never done anything of importance to remake society, the other an over-optimistic liberalism or evangelism that says we need only to educate or convert the individual to make society what it ought to be. The truth lies not in either extreme, not even in a mid-point between, but in a synthesis of what is true in both views.

2. Of Respect for Personality

When in the last chapter we made a brief analysis of the ethical demands of Jesus, we found respect for personality standing at the center, the most concrete embodiment of the ideal of love. An individual's ethical sensitivity or dullness can be measured by the degree to which the happiness and well-being of other persons seem important to him. However zealous in religious activity, if a person is cruel to his competitors or flames out in harsh words toward members of his family there is something wrong with his religion. . . . The impulse to vengeance is the outcropping of a primitive sadistic tendency not yet civilized. There is no need to labor the point that there is a good deal of this left in human nature even after religion has effected something of a "conversion." . . .

However, in limited social groups this sadism is successfully suppressed, and in rare individuals completely overcome. Perhaps every reader of these pages has been privileged at one time or another—though I suspect not often—to participate in the type of family atmosphere where there are differences of opinion, but never scolding, direction and even coercion of the immature but never anger or violence. In such families individual wills are not crushed, but are subordinated to the general good in a common enterprise. Each member, including the three-year-old, has work to do appropriate to his powers. Each has his time for relaxation as well as work, with much of this relaxation family fun—merry table talk, picnics, good-natured pranks. Each has opportunities for growth according to his tastes and each respects the hobbies of the others. Each has a place in the house he can call his own, with his own things in it, while the house is not the property of one or two (though the father may pay the taxes) but is the joint possession of all. In such a household there is not only biological love; there is the rarer quality of *friendliness*. In such a household there is achieved the ideal of respect for personality.

Such a family is the best symbol of the Kingdom of God. It is the kind of society we might have if Christians took seriously enough the fatherhood of God and the brotherhood of man. Yet it is pathetically patent that we do not have it. Let us carry a little further this central figure of the Christian faith.

The family relation demands that when the budget is in straitened circumstances, all must sacrifice—perhaps not equally but equitably, and that when there is abundance all may share in the luxuries available. A family in which some children were pampered by being given ermine play-suits, rich rugs and tapestries for their rooms and all the spending money they wanted, while the others wore rags and cast-offs and did not have enough to eat, would not stay a family very long. At least, only till the underprivileged were strong enough to break loose, and it would be hardly reasonable to expect these underprivileged members to be complacent if they saw that food enough for all was being deliberately destroyed.

The family relation demands that when quarrels over possessions or powers break out, as is likely to happen in the best regulated of families, they be settled by talking things over—by mutual concessions if both contestants are wrong, by arbitration if necessary. Fistfights settle only the question of which has more muscle or more finesse in using it, with the advantage usually on the side of the older child. When an issue is settled by the ancient method of bare knuckles, what usually happens is that the bystanders get drawn into the fray, and one fight merely brings on another.

It is unnecessary to carry the figure further. It is evident that if we really had upon earth the family relation in which the Christian ethic centers, we should not have the starvation in the midst of plenty, breadlines side by side with skyscrapers, Japan gobbling up China and Italy Ethiopia, Hitler hounding Jews,

Russia stifling freedom in pursuit of justice, colossal expenditures for armaments while our whole economic structure totters. We should not have such stains on our civilization as the Sacco-Vanzetti case, or the Tom Mooney case, or the Scottsboro case, or the case of Angelo Herndon.[6] Yet we have all these.

The reasons are deep-seated. They root in tendencies of human nature so permanent and permeating that modern psychology has given grounds for a revival of the ancient doctrine of original sin.[7] The myth of the fall of man rests on the truth of the unending conflict between nature and spirit. This conflict does not occur because nature is all bad and spirit all good, but because there is in each an inchoate mixture of good and evil. Sin arises when man's spirit eats of the fruit of the tree of knowledge, and with intelligence quickened to discern good from evil, obeys the call of evil.

The primary human impulses are sex, security and the will to power. What happens to each of these depends on the degree to which one respects personality. Sex may be hallowed into the most sacred of human relations, as in the family described above as typical of the Kingdom of God, or it can degrade persons to the level of the beast until we come to think characteristically of "animal passion" as synonymous with lust. Desire for security for one's self and one's family is the mainspring of economic effort, and it is also the main source of economic cleavage and international strife. The will to power when joined with respect for personality gives moral impetus to make the most of one's capacities. Divorced from it, it is perhaps the primary root of sin, for through it one is impelled to think of himself more highly than he ought to think and to claim for his exclusive possession or prerogative what ought to be universal.[8]

Respect for personality, cultivated in even a large number of high-spirited individual Christians, will not automatically make a Christian society. The four absolutes of the Oxford Group movement—absolute honesty, absolute purity, absolute unselfishness, absolute love—are all forms of the virtue of respect for personality. It is unlikely, in fact inherently impossible because of human finitude, that any of these absolutes will be "absolutely" embodied in any human life. As regulative ideals, they have immense power to modify conduct for the better and create a type of personality compatible with self-respect. Because of this power as determining ideals, they ought not to be esteemed lightly. Yet there is no record in history clearer than the evidence that honest, pure, unselfish, loving personality in large numbers of individual Christians has not abolished war, capitalism or race prejudice from the earth. As long as society has colossal systems antagonistic to respect for personality, individual character will be like a flower rooted in a muckheap—it will shed beauty and peace, but it will not obliterate stench and filth.

On the other hand, there is no hope of redeeming society except as there are redeemed individuals[9] to make the fight, with intelligence and vigor, for a better world. This is the truth which lies at the heart of the Buchmanist movement and every other great evangelistic effort, and lies also at the root of the liberalism so much under fire at the present. While neither evangelism nor education will abolish war without international machinery for settling disputes, neither will such machinery abolish war until moral ideals are vivified and intelligence quickened in enough of the masses of the people to make a peace machinery workable. This is why not only peace education but an aggressive pacifism is vitally important. Individual murder, like cannibalism, would be relatively rare in most civilized communities even without laws against it because the principle of respect for personality in regard to it is sufficiently established to make it the most revolting of crimes. Only as this revulsion is extended to include mass murder can war be permanently abolished.

The principle of respect for personality as applied to a Christian society is an ideal having immense power to hold in check man's baser impulses. Only as it is established in small groups can foundations be laid for its establishment in the larger world society. Attainments of it even on a limited scale are sublimely significant—but are not to be trusted too far.

3. Of Humility

We must examine the place in a Christian society of another basic virtue—the virtue of humility. It was not without reason that the medieval churchmen held *superbia* (pride) to be the worst of all the seven deadly sins. They saw human pride overcoming man's sense of "creatureliness," to use Von Hügel's favorite expression, and would tolerate nothing that detracted from the greatness of God. Almost any belief held widely for a long time has some truth in it, and this is no exception. In a revised setting we can now see that man's quest for power and possessions has created a machine age in which we are spiritually proud but morally unwise; in short, it has been responsible for the "cultural lag" the sociologists are so fond of talking about. If there is anything in what was suggested above—that a misplaced will to power is the primary root of sin, perhaps the medieval fathers were not so far wrong.

We shall not delay long to discuss humility as an individual virtue. It may be taken for granted that a "becoming" modesty is an attribute of good manners as well as good morals and good religion. Nothing so quickly betrays a personality maladjusted as display of an overweening sense of one's own importance. Nothing more surely cuts one off from friendship. On the basis of a plain utilitarian desire to make a social success, a proper humility is a greater asset than books on how to converse, or remedies for halitosis.[10]

The Christian religion has gone far toward instilling a type of humility which is not only superficially but profoundly attractive. There are many "great persons" who in gentle simplicity vaunt not themselves and are not puffed up. As in respect to the sacredness of personality, we should thank God and take courage that this is so. But the presence of a large sprinkling of such sweet-spirited, beautiful characters in a group is no guarantee that the group will not "behave itself unseemly." Anyone who has ever witnessed the *superbia* let loose in a faculty meeting when a matter of departmental prerogative or prestige is at stake will not need argument to convince him that the actions of groups fall far below those of individuals! Family pride may be a wholesome incentive to its members to live up to a great heritage; it may also be a demonic source of division which sunders Capulets from Montagues until the only resolution of tragic conflict is in death.

Multiply a family feud of the Scottish Highlands or the mountains of Kentucky a thousand times, and one gets the situation on either side of the Rhine. For national honor, which means group *superbia* on a grand scale, Christian men will fight to the death other Christians against whom personally they have not the slightest animosity. National honor is a more insidious cause of war than economic imperialism, for it is easier to deck it out in fine apparel which will make people think they are making the supreme sacrifice for a God-given cause. People could never be induced to fight by the slogan, "Come, now, let's grab some territory!" Mussolini has come nearer to this than any other war-maker of recent times, and for this perhaps deserves the tribute due to honest assertion of purpose; yet as I write, the morning paper states that he announces himself the benefactor of Ethiopia whom wise Ethiopians will welcome for bringing order out of chaos! Proclaim an ideal of national honor, or extend the call of national pride to include making the world safe for our kind of government, and states can enlist millions.

What has been said of war can be said with equal pertinence regarding the economic situation, where the "class struggle" is not merely a Marxian doctrine but a stern and terrible reality. The class struggle is not just a mood of rebellion on the part of the underprivileged. Any attempt to treat it as such is both to blind one's eyes to facts and to defeat in advance any attempt to heal the breach. It is a case of large-scale conflict of interest in which an owning class, able to impose its will by economic advantage, hereditary power, social prestige, usually superior education, and a mass of other interwoven factors, exercises political control in behalf of its group, while a growing class consciousness on the part of the workers generates organized resistance. The way to meet it is not for employers to discharge men for joining labor unions, or drive out of the city radical ministers who attempt to organize workers or arbitrate strikes.[11] The first need is to recognize that any great class cleavage implies that there is right *and also wrong* on both sides of the gulf.

I am not suggesting that to repent of collective sin is a simple short-cut to the solution of colossal social problems. But it is the first step, and one without which any "implementation" is bound to be ineffective. It is a step to which Christian ministers with great profit to all can lead their people, provided it be done with sincerity and not with sham. The great danger is that in the confession of any collective sin, we shall confess the sins of others and forget our own. No sin is really confessed until the confession is made in a mood of repentance and the will to reform.

Approaching the world situation of the present day in this mood, we see clearly that there are four great nations which predominately want peace. These are Russia, Great Britain, France and the United States. There are three great nations which, though they do not want war, want territory and are willing to engage in war to get it. These are Japan, Italy and Germany. The substratum of this fact is that the nations which want peace already have what territory they need; the nations willing to have war want to do what these other nations have already done. It is not hard for a nation to be peace-loving when it has enough; it is hard to be when its territory is too small to feed its millions. Similarly it is easy to be complacent about capitalism, even with shrinking dividends and salary cuts, when one is reasonably secure and comfortable; it is when fear or hunger grips men that revolutions are imminent. We shall not have a Christian society until large numbers of individuals are willing to look these unflattering facts in the face and say in deep humility *mea culpa, mea maxima culpa.*

4. Of Peace through Friendliness

The principles of respect for personality and Christian humility find concrete embodiment in friendliness. Fellowship is an equally good word when divested of organizational or institutional connotations, but friendliness is a richer term to designate that combination of good will and sympathetic understanding whereby each desires the well-being of the other and is willing to recognize the right of the other to maintain his individuality—even to his pet peculiarities. It is a better term than love to describe this relation, for love is always in danger of being sentimentalized. Limitations of time and space make it impossible to love in a deeply personal sense more than a few of the world's millions, but there are no limits to the possibilities of friendship. When Jesus called upon his disciples to love one another and show their love by the keeping of his commandments, he summed up his relation to them in the words, "Ye are my friends."

It may be taken as axiomatic that a truly Christian society would be a friendly, and therefore a peaceful, society. This does not mean a situation in which there would be no differences of opinion. In any relationship which can be conceived as existing among men, some measure of working at cross purposes must be expected. Persons could not be *persons* without individuality of thought and act, and unless persons are mechanized and regimented out of the possibility of expressing any individuality there is bound to be a measure of tension. This tension may be the healthy growing point of action, like the clash of minds in a friendly argument or the physical re-creation of a friendly game of tennis; or it may be the divisive, destructive force that corrupts personal relations when bad sportsmanship creeps in. When one says of any group (and church groups are no exception) "there is a bad spirit here," what one really means is that the redeeming power of friendliness to make tension profitable has fled, leaving in its place a demonic force which our fathers readily conceived in terms of the devil. Magnify this demon to colossal proportions, and one gets international war.

The depth of the Christian message may be measured by the breadth of its reply to the lawyer's question, "And who is my neighbor?" A world society dominated by true neighborliness would be a peaceful and safe society—one in which many individuals would make contributions, according to their diverse gifts, to the good of the whole; one in which differences would be a wholesome stimulus to a mutual search for knowledge, beauty, and cultural progress. Such a state of peace through friendliness prevails in the well-ordered school or church or community, and in some international relations. It is this which makes the (as yet)[12] unguarded border between the United States and Canada the safest international boundary in the world. It is the lack of it that keeps the dogs of war baying at most of the border-lines of Europe and yapping frequently across the misnamed Pacific.

Granting the desirability of a world in which peace and progress toward higher values would prevail through friendliness, the question is how to get it. This will take us again into the matter of means and ends.

5. Of Non-Violent Coercion

As was suggested earlier in the chapter, it is impossible to make a clear separation between means and ends. This is because any means adopted and held before the mind with great energy becomes an end. Neatness in a home should be a means to comfortable and happy living; when the over-meticulous housekeeper exalts neatness into a dominant passion, she sweeps the family out of doors.

To discuss means and ends together is not to obscure a distinction, but to unite two elements often tragically sundered. The doctrine that "the end justifies the means" has been one of the most insidious in human history. It has justified war and mutual slaughter in the interest of protection of humanity; economic exploitation and mutual bondage under guise of freedom. We are likely to go on defeating good ends by using bad means until we learn that any end worth attaining has a worthy means to its attainment. Thus Henry P. Van Dusen aptly says in *God in These Times*, comparing the Christian with the Communist strategy for achieving social change:

> It is implicit in Christianity's certainty of the ethical unity of reality that it places confidence in no methods for the accomplishment of social change—however worthy the goal—which are not themselves consonant with the goal desired. To employ injustice, violence, ruthless coercion for the achievement of socially desirable ends, is to let loose in the world forces of evil which—the universe being a moral organism—are certain to take their toll from those who employ them and to qualify, and in some measure nullify, the good ends achieved.[13]

This I believe to be true, and thoroughly Christian. The path which Jesus followed when confronted by colossal evil was the way of the cross, not the way of the sword. Had he attempted to combat evil with ruthlessness and violence he would have been a long-since-forgotten revolutionist. It is because he chose the way which led to temporary defeat and ultimate victory that he was able to release forces which for twenty centuries have been shaping the world's destiny. Because he staked his life on the power of love to conquer sin, men worship him as God.

Yet the problem is not as simple as religious idealists have often made it. If one is to adhere to a love ethic in the midst of the diabolical forces contending for mastery today in the international and inter-class struggle, his conviction must not be too cheaply won. Only as one vivifies and undergirds his idealism with a vast deal of realism has one a right to put his trust in the power of love— to rest his strategy in "the victory of persuasion over force."[14] The plain prose fact that one needs with open eyes to see how bad the world is, and how weak human beings are, has perhaps been nowhere better stated than in the words of a great idealistic poet:

> The common problem, yours, mine, everyone's
> Is—not to fancy what were fair in life
> Provided it could be,—but, finding first
> What may be, then find how to make it fair
> Up to our means: a very different thing!
> No abstract intellectual plan of life
> Quite irrespective of life's plainest laws,
> But one, a man, who is man and nothing more,
> May lead within a world which (by your leave)
> Is Rome or London, not Fool's paradise.[15]

When Rome imperils London's interests, shall those in London who believe that this is not "Fool's paradise" proceed to do as the Romans do? The question of the application of sanctions to restrain Italy has brought the whole problem sharply into focus, and even for the most high-minded the answer is not simple. Members of the Fellowship of Reconciliation[16] whose members are committed to absolute pacifism are by no means of one mind as to the legitimacy of using either military sanctions, or economic sanctions which may lead to war. The fact that George Lansbury, a Christian saint in politics, was forced either to surrender his pacifism or his leadership of the British Labor Party gives evidence of the difficulty of bringing Christian ideals and political realities into cohesion.

Still more complex is the question with reference to class war. It may be taken as axiomatic that no one in his right mind really *wants* war, either international or inter-class. Yet when a state of war actually exists—when the clubs of the police fall upon the bodies of those engaged in peaceful assemblage or machine guns are trained upon strikers petitioning for redress of grievances, it is a bit unrealistic to say, from the vantage point of comfortable security, that one will have nothing to do with such a situation.

Three things are imperative, if we are to steer a proper course between an unrealistic idealism and an unidealistic realism. The first of these is to surrender frankly the hope of a *safe* course, for nothing is safe in the kind of world we live in. To seek one's own safety rather than the service of the common good is both to lose one's security and one's soul, as the experience of terror-stricken individuals and nations amply testifies, while a large measure both of inner and outer security may be found through mutual good will. But there is no guarantee against disaster. Both the way of the sword and the way of the cross are ways of hazard and pain.

A second need is to distinguish clearly between forcible coercion and violence. No society—not even so small a group as the family—could exist without some kind of coercion. Immature members must be taught and in some cases forcibly directed by coercion from the more mature, lest they destroy themselves and others. In the larger society a police force is imperative to restrain the results both of ignorance and sin. Within both areas, physical coercion under some circumstances is born curative and necessary. There are times when children need to be spanked; there are occasions when intoxicated persons need to be thrust forcibly into a police car. It is better to disperse a lynching mob with tear gas than to let them lynch their victim.

Coercion ceases to be legitimate force and becomes violence when either physical brutality or mass destruction replaces the spirit of redemptive restraint. To imprison an offender is coercion; to flog him is violence. To disperse a mob with a gas causing physical discomfort but no permanent injury is coercion; to ride ruthlessly through it and let human beings be trampled under horses' hoofs is violence. There is probably a legitimate coercive use of night-sticks and guns by the police, but there is certainly an illegitimate use of these when an arbitrary and brutal demonstration of power replaces the maintenance of order.

Violence corrupts much family discipline; it impregnates the police and penal systems with arrogance; it is the very nature of war. And whenever coercion gives way to violence it destroys its end; for it sets in operation forces of anger, cruelty and retaliation which in their essential nature are destructive rather than curative.

A third essential is to trust the power of love beyond the evidence of surface appearances. Until those who believe in "the power of non-violence" of which Richard Gregg has so ably written are willing to put it into the political milieu at personal cost, we are not likely to have more than the first stepping-stones toward a peaceful world. To call non-violence impractical is to speak with great presumption. Non-violence has great political power, as manifest in Gandhi's use of it; and even a few people, seriously committed to the use of it, could have far-reaching political influence. It generates the energy of endurance, which in the long run is the most important kind, and wearies out the opposition. It increases both intellectual and spiritual power through decrease of fear. Of St. Francis of Assisi it is written, "His dress was mean, his person insignificant, his face without beauty. But with so much power did God inspire his words that many noble families, sundered by ancient blood feuds, were reconciled forever." Through such strategy does non-violence work.

Let us see now what these principles mean in terms of the problem of the abolition of war. Great numbers of "peace talks" heard in churches and women's clubs are futile, if not worse. They are futile when they merely intensify the horror of war which every sane person has already. They are dangerous when people are led to substitute an emotional loathing for war for an intelligent consideration of its causes and of ways to get rid of it. No great amount of exhortation is needed to make most people agree they would rather not have their sons killed! It requires no great testing of spirit to put one's name to a petition for general disarmament, though there is in it enough political strategy and personal commitment to make it probably worth doing. The real issues are not touched until one faces something deeper. These ultimate testing-points are two: (1) whether one is willing to use a peace strategy to obtain peace, and (2) whether one can stick to this determination in the face of titanic forces driving toward war.

I do not mean to disparage the importance of educational propaganda for peace. Few things are needed more, provided it includes promotion of international acquaintance, sympathy and understanding. But unless it links peace *means* with peace *ends*, it may drive the world into war the sooner by generating the fear which lies at the root of the race of armaments. An illustration of this is the way war pictures showing "the horror of it" have been turned into propaganda to support greater appropriations for the War Department.

In theory, the principle scarcely needs to be labored that lasting peace can be obtained only by peaceful means. The idea of fighting "a war to end war"—however high-minded the thought of the great Christian statesman who gave the world these words—has been discredited by the logic of events. The mere mention of the words in most groups now is to call forth cynical laughter. As I write these words, a World War seems at least as imminent as in early July of 1914, and more consciously feared by millions of people. However little understood the causes of the depression may be, it has been beaten in upon the thought of great numbers of people that somehow the war helped to cause it. It is not possible for four and a half years to have billions of dollars' worth of goods literally get "shot to pieces" and "go up in smoke" without so upsetting world trade that there has to be a day of reckoning—a day which has stretched to years and caught us all. In theory, any intelligent person would admit that fighting a war is a foolish way to get peace!

In practice, of course, the situation is vastly more complicated. This is why every nation is racing to increase its armaments, thereby bringing catastrophe nearer by rolling up to ever larger proportions the vicious circle of fear, armaments, and war; then more fear, more armaments, and again more war.

If one is to take seriously the conviction that the way to get peace is to use a peace strategy, three things are necessary. The first is to demilitarize the popular mind and substitute internationalism for the dominant nationalistic psychology. This requires both the spreading of knowledge of the historical and economic roots of international relations and the cultivation of friendly emotional attitudes toward other nations. This is the most basic step, and there is ground for rejoicing that it is being done extensively in churches, schools and civic organizations. But great danger lies in the assumption that this, which is relatively easy to do, is all that needs doing. Note that I do not say it is easy; only that it is much easier than the next two steps.

The next thing—not next chronologically but logically—is to bring about legislation calculated to preserve peace by peace means. This means a concerted, never flagging effort to defeat political action for increase of armaments, the militarization of the schools, the display of armed force as a threat to Japan or any other country. It means a corresponding positive, aggressive action for disarmament, the World Court, and every other measure calculated realistically to substitute arbitration for combat. Good will is the most powerful force in the world, but good will can operate only in terms of political coercion. Such legislative strategy must be directed as much toward the removal of the economic causes of war as toward war itself, for it is unlikely that war can be permanently abolished while capitalism, with economic imperialism as its eldest son, is the ruling system.

Concrete, dynamic effort for legislation is difficult and dangerous. But the third step in a peace strategy is still more so. This is the position of absolute pacifism.[17] Held to in war times as in peace, there are few things that try men's souls more searchingly. It is infinitely easier to preach and teach internationalism and to work for disarmament than to risk one's position as a conscientious objector. Furthermore, it is easier to lose one's job and perhaps go to prison for one's convictions than it is *inwardly* to stand firm in these convictions when the whole impact of human relations is against them. I do not say that every person who reads these words should become an absolute pacifist. One should adopt this position only when it is a compelling conviction, rooted in the deeps of his nature.

The clear verdict of history is that the way of reconciliation and persuasion, where it has been tried, has contributed vastly more to the world's progress than the way of the sword. Reconciliation works *with* the cultural arts, the sword against them. Violence begets violence; kindliness evokes a recognition of the fundamental kinship of men and promotes cooperative endeavor. But the way of non-violence is not an easy path to follow. If we are to be "able to withstand in the evil day, and having done all, to stand," we must find our resources in more than human strength.

6. Of the Resources of Religion

We have now suggested in outline what a Christian society would be. It would be a society in which respect for personality and far-reaching friendliness would be achieved in humility of spirit through non-violent coercion. In such a society all the higher values of life—science, art, literature, creative work, recreation, physical well-being and spiritual culture—could have their place, growing up on the foundation of economic security and competence. It would be such a society as the Utopias have described and Christian idealism has always dreamed of.

But can these things be "on earth"? When we pray for the will of God to be done *on earth* as it is *in heaven*, are we not asking the impossible—that the transcendent and unconditioned break through into the welter of earthly relativities and harmonize the clashing strains of earthly discord? We are asking just that, but we are not asking the impossible. This is where the resources of religion come into the situation.

Man lives on three levels[18]—not, indeed, levels in the sense that they are disparate and sharply differentiated steps, but levels in the sense that human nature grows from one to the next above, and through the higher finds power to overcome what could not otherwise be vanquished in the lower. They are the levels of physical and social coercion, of human ideals, and divine grace.

Every human being does many things that he does not want to do. Some of these coercions are placed upon us by the fact that we have physical bodies to be fed and clothed and imperious impulses that will not be long denied; some by the fact that in the long history of culture society has worked out largely by trial and error certain techniques of control by which we manage to live together. One may live a reasonably decent, but not very idealistic, life on the basis of these coercions.

The person who accepts voluntarily such of these controls as his intelligence approves and courageously challenges others has risen to the second level. This is the field of human brotherhood and ethical idealism. Here one mainly lives "above the law," though his ideals may so far outrun his group that he finds himself on the wrong side of man-made law, imprisoned or crucified for a cause. This is high morality.

But if one's struggle and crucifixion are to have in them anything more significant than the death of one more human being who must die anyway, there is a third level on which one must ground his life. Here that which is *in heaven* enters into that which is *on earth*, transfigures it, and knits it into the pattern of absolute and eternal values. Out of man's weakness emerges strength, and a sense of cosmic resources makes the battle for right seem worth fighting even in the darkest hour. Gethsemane leads on to Calvary, and Calvary to the resurrection. This is divine grace; and through it "the trampling march of unconscious power"[19] which is one aspect of life's realities gives way before the sure advance of the power to love. On this level lies high religion.

A Christian society would be a society built on respect for personality. If we would help to bring it into being, faith and hope must be conjoined with love. Faith in the strategy of peace through friendliness, hope born of the conviction that divine grace *can* break through to man, love that leads to a cross—these three will build on earth the Realm of God. But they will not build it in a day.

READING 6

The Church has always had as its special function the guardianship of religion against the onslaughts of the world. Many valiant efforts have been put forth to save the soul of man, not only from the flesh and the devil, but from the world in which both are incarnate. With what feebleness the Church of the present is making this struggle has been suggested [earlier in this book]. The reason may

From "Our Enlightened Paganism," *Resources of Religion*, 103–36.

lie in a loss of its prophetic message, or it may lie in the overwhelming strength of the forces of opposition—forces more titanic than the Church ever had to struggle with in simpler times. To see the part played by the second element we must look at the paganism of our day.

1. The Meaning of Paganism

The term pagan is not used in a disparaging, but in its classical, sense. A pagan is not a cannibal or one who believes in temple prostitution—not necessarily one who believes in any killing or any prostitution! My dictionary defines the word, first, as "an idolater, or worshiper of idols or false gods"; second, as "a person having no religious beliefs." Modern society is largely pagan in both these senses.

These two definitions of pagan are not identical, but they converge with reference to modern civilization. There is more than an accidental conjunction between the worship of the false gods of money, luxury, prestige, power, race and state, and the loss of religious belief. A religion which puts personality at the apex of its scale of values and bids its followers "seek first the Kingdom of God and his righteousness" is by its very nature in eternal tension with an attitude of life which glorifies the possession of things and exalts a human group—whether one's class, race or nation—into the place of highest loyalty.

That the term is not inappropriate is evidenced by the fact that Christianity finds itself now in a state of peril such as it has not faced since the end of the Roman empire. There is, of course, always danger of overstatement due to lack of perspective in analysis of one's own times. A sentimental pining for "the good old days" is sound procedure neither historically nor ethically. However much the doctrine of automatic progress was overstated by Herbert Spencer and the nineteenth century idealists, there has been progress—not only in science, industry and general education but in ethical sensitivity; and the author has no desire to dispute this fact. Yet it is also true that in reference to Christian standards of thought, and action, the world is more pagan now than it has been since Constantine established Christianity as the official religion of the Roman state.

What is meant by this statement is not that the world is living up to Christian standards less than formerly, but that the standards themselves are being *repudiated* as they have not been in the past. There has always been acquisitiveness in the world; there has always been cruelty, self-seeking, strife, sexual debauchery. Society, with greater or less success, has fought these tendencies in the Western world with a power born of the conviction that they are antithetical to the Christian way of life. Medieval warfare killed many people but there was a Truce of God; puritanism suppressed many wholesome impulses but sought to make cleaner living prevail. The now discredited "mid-Victorian" era was an era of prison reform, of woman's suffrage and temperance movements, of eradication of slavery, of increase in educational facilities, of the spread of democratic privilege, because these changes were thought to be in keeping with the Christian valuation of personality. Not all who fought for these ends were professed

Christians, not all the means used were Christian; yet a Christian scale of values lay always at the base of social effort.

What is now happening is not merely that Christian ideals are not being lived up to but that they are being rejected *as ideals.* Humility, democracy, non-violence, sexual restraint, *caritas* in all the rich meaning of that term—these are being widely challenged; and at the same time the roots are being cut from under the religious undergirding by which efforts to put these ideals into actuality have in the past been sustained. It is this double repudiation which makes the modern world largely pagan.

2. Economic Paganism

It is impossible to discuss our current economic paganism without discussing capitalism and saying some uncomplimentary things about it. And in any fair-minded estimate of our present chaos, it is necessary to hold in mind two paradoxical factors which are often sundered.

In the first place, it is not capitalism which has created chaos; it is *sin.* With the evil tendencies of human nature uncurbed, no system—however much grounded in a philosophy of love and justice—can bring love and justice into active functioning in human society.

But lest this pessimistic affirmation bring too much comfort to the exponents of a purely individual gospel, I hasten to say that it is not simply human depravity which has created our present chaos; it is the capitalistic system. A mechanized, competitive, profit-seeking order is the surest road to ruin, for it runs athwart the moral order of the universe. When a system persistently treats the world as a battlefield rather than a family, it is not surprising that from it ensue battle and carnage.

The clearest line of demarcation between Christian and Marxist socialism lies in the fact that the Christian takes sin seriously. He does not expect a classless society to be brought into being solely by a rearrangement of economic forces.[20] He finds his ideal society in a Kingdom of God in which justice shall be rooted in love, and looks to divine resources for the undergirding of human effort toward its establishment. This is quite different from Marxian utopianism. Yet they meet in the deep-lying conviction that a system rooted in injustice must be rebuilt from its foundations if even an approximation of justice is to be brought to pass upon earth. From the Christian viewpoint we must now see why the prevailing order is one of paganism.

In a remarkable book, *The Religious Situation,* Professor Paul Tillich traces the sources of the "self-sufficient finitude" which was produced by the movements of the nineteenth century and has come to fruition in our time. Natural science, technology and capitalism have served as an unholy trinity to generate in man an overweening sense of his own importance, centering his attention on the temporal rather than the eternal. Professor Tillich writes:[21]

What now is the meaning of such a spiritual situation? . . . Evidently it is an extreme example of a self-assertive, self-sufficient type of existence. This applies to mathematical natural science which pursues the goal of demon-strating that reality is governed wholly by its own laws. . . . It applies to world-ruling technique with its will to conquer space, time and nature and to make the earth a well-furnished dwelling of man. It applies, finally, to capitalist economy which seeks to provide the greatest possible number of men with the greatest possible amount of economic goods, which seeks to arouse and to satisfy ever-increasing demands without raising the question as to the meaning of the process which claims the service of all the spir-itual and physical human abilities. In all of this there is no trace of self-transcendence, of the hallowing of existence. The forms of the life-process have become completely independent of the source of life and its meaning.

Yet this is not the last word in the matter, he thinks, for all three came into being originally, and are rooted in, eternal elements. Mathematical natural sci-ence was born out of the desire to know the laws of God's creation; technology was a revelation of the power of spirit over matter; liberal economy and capitalist society were based on the idea of the freedom of the individual. But emancipated personality, seized with an unlimited desire for economic power, profaned what should have been holy, and the capitalistic spirit has become a symbol of the self-sufficient secularism which is "closed against invasions of the eternal."

There is much to ponder here. It points to the deep-lying truth of the words, "Ye cannot serve God and Mammon." In much the same tenor Max Weber thirty years ago predicted that unless there should arise either new prophets or a great rebirth of old ideas and ideals, the spirit of capitalism would even-tuate in "mechanized petrifaction, embellished with a sort of convulsive self-importance."[22] It would be hard to find a more apt description of what has actually come to pass as capitalism with steady aggressiveness has pushed God out of current thought and life. It has done this through two different but inter-related media, the one ethical and the other psychological.

An unholy glorification of profit, dulling the sense of human brotherhood, undercuts the religious life. In the paganism generated by the injustices and inhumanities of our economic system both victor and victim are caught. The high-minded employer who wants to treat his employees as human beings is forced by the system, under penalty of going to the wall himself, to forget human suffering; while in turn the underprivileged in his struggle for indepen-dence and livelihood forgets that the capitalist is human—with the virtues as well as the vices of humanity. The person on the under side of the economic struggle is, furthermore, unable to get much spiritual bread while his body is undernourished, and he is likely to resent the robes of sanctity with which he sees comfortable middle-class clerics and their vestrymen adorning themselves while his children go underclad.

Such a straining of the bonds of brotherhood does more than generate uneth-ical action on both sides of the chasm. It does that, but it also causes the sense of the reality of God to slip out of one's life. "If a man love not his brother whom he hath seen, how can he love God whom he hath not seen?" Multiply this situation to one of dominant control in the lives of millions of people on either side of the class struggle, and one gets the economic paganism of our day.

The second channel through which capitalism drains off the living vitality of religious experience is the plain fact of things and material processes. Capitalism is "faith in wealth as the primary source of all life's blessings and as the savior of man from his deepest misery. It is the doctrine that man's most important activity is the production of economic goods and that all other things are dependent upon this."[23] Here again its paganism makes inroads into both sides of the capital-and-labor cleavage. On the capitalist side there is more of ostensible belief in and worship of God—even the sincerely motivated endowment of churches for the glory of God—but in practice a very general assumption that "business is business" and not to be too much cluttered up with religion. God thus passes out of the picture, not usually by outright rejection, but by preoccupation with what seems more important.

On the labor side of the gulf, there is much more of plain-spoken rejection both of God and the Church. This is due in part to Marxist influence, for many who do not know much about Marx know that he called religion the opiate of the people. But it is due more to the daily, necessary preoccupation of life with *things* in order to live. A contemporary analyst of the place of God in the common life describes vividly the effect of our mechanized industrialism.[24] "Snipping endlessly the pieces of cheap cloth for shoddy garments; punching endlessly the paper and split leather soles for bargain shoes; feeding endlessly the rods, wire, and sheet metal that become ten-cent hardware; selling endlessly cheap merchandise in a cheap market; finding romance in cheap movies and woodpulp magazines. Who is fool enough to look for God, even if one were sure there is a God, in this dreary modern warehouse?"

With the fulcrum of thought and action in modern life the possession of material things, God can be served but feebly. This is not to say that we can dispense with material things, and any theory either economic or religious is foredoomed to futility which assumes that if we were idealistic enough, we might become discarnate spirits without bodies to be fed and clothed. But to recognize the needful place of the material is not to exalt the material into primacy. This is what capitalism has done, and any thing-centered civilization is idolatrous.

It is, perhaps, unnecessary to say that not all capitalists are idolatrous; not all the fruits of the system are pagan. Yet a structure which is off-center at its foundations cannot satisfactorily be pulled into place by guy-wires at the top.

3. Nationalistic Paganism

Economic paganism has been gradually accumulating virulence since the birth of capitalism at the end of the Middle Ages. Its most rapid advances, striding forward with the introduction of machines at a geometric progression of increase in speed, have been made in the last century and a half. The past six years have witnessed the collapse of the structure which supported it, but not much headway toward the building of a new one.

The type of paganism now to be discussed has followed a somewhat different course. It was in full force at the beginning of the Christian era; then for many years was semi-dormant, and has emerged in our day with many of the characteristics of its early history.

We are back now in a pre-Constantine setting. Until the acceptance of Christianity as the official religion of the Roman state the Christians were obliged through the coercion of their faith to fight against a hostile state which demanded primary allegiance. In turn they were persecuted. Nero and other emperors who threw Christians to the lions acted with entire consistency when they tried to stamp out by force a sect which challenged the deity of the state.

The relations of Church and State since they were married by Constantine have not, of course, run along with complete domestic felicity. A great deal of secular history deals with quarrels within this union. In Europe the relation has been quite generally maintained in the form of an Established Church; in the United States something like a Platonic friendship has existed instead of the marriage relation. There have been at times illicit adventures—such as, for instance, the rejection of candidates for office because of religion, and legislative attempts to throttle biology instruction because of certain religious views. But in this country Church and State have not ostensibly had a closer connection than that implied by the custom of beginning each session of Congress with prayer. A great deal of domestic trouble has thus been avoided.

The situation, however, is now changed both in Europe and America. There is in progress what may prove to be a death struggle between two forms of worship. As in the days of Nero, the issue is joined between worship of God and worship of the State. This is more than an attempt to patch up a disagreement between Church and State as to property or prerogative. What is at stake is the fundamental question of *primacy of loyalty*.

This struggle finds its most conspicuous form in the totalitarian state. The meaning of this term has been thus defined by Dr. J. H. Oldham:

> The totalitarian state is a state which lays claim to man in the totality of his being; which declares its own authority to be the source of all authority; which refuses to recognize the independence in their own sphere of religion, culture, education and the family; which seeks to impose on all its citizens a particular philosophy of life and which sets out to create by means of all the agencies of public information and education a particular type of man in accordance with its own understanding of the meaning and end of man's existence. A state which advances such claims declares itself to be not only a state but also a Church.[25]

In Nazi Germany it is evident enough that the totalitarian state has exalted itself into a Church. Great professions of religion are made in the name of National Socialism, while a pagan cult of blood and soil and *Volk* are being substituted for the world brotherhood of Christianity. Non-Nazi Christians who cannot reconcile anti-Semitism with the religion of the Galilean Jew who was Christianity's founder, and who dare to say so in defiance of the State, are in the position of the early Christian martyrs. That this martyrdom does not take the form of outright bloodshed is a score on the side of progress, but deprivation of privilege, loss of position, imprisonment and exile are no less real forms of martyrdom for conviction.[26]

The foregoing citation from Dr. Oldham continues:

> Even where the state sets itself to destroy all forms of religion and to impose a view of life which is wholly secular, it makes on men the same total claim as religion makes and demands from them the same complete surrender. If its view of life may not properly be called a religion, it is offered as a substitute for religion and becomes its powerful rival.[27]

This is the state of affairs in Soviet Russia. Here the claims of the totalitarian state are pushed to the limit, and the crushing of religion is pursued with religious passion. Here the Church is in the final stages of a life-and-death struggle—a struggle which now looks like almost certain death, but from which the unquenchable power of the religious spirit may yet wrest some form of victory.

Other types of totalitarianism are found in Italy, in Turkey, in Mexico, in Japan. Whether the State makes religion its tool, denies it the right to propagate itself, or forbids it to exist, there is a common element in the result, namely that he who would put God and conscience first in his life is brought into inevitable conflict with the State.

We shall not linger to discuss the issues in these countries, partly because the issues themselves are too complex to be adequately discussed without giving them more space than is here possible, more because there is grave danger lest, in damning Germany, Russia, Italy or Japan, we forget that nationalistic paganism lies all about us. Indeed, so insidious is its force, we may be a party to it without suspecting our guilt.

It was a conspicuous mark of nationalistic paganism when, during the last war, churches became recruiting stations taking orders from the State; and in shuddering at the horrors of concentration camps in Germany today, it is a sobering thought that hundreds of high-minded citizens like Evan Thomas and Harold Gray[28] were confined for many months in Fort Leavenworth prison for the crime of obedience to a Christian conscience. Since 1918 there has been a movement away from the opprobrium then heaped upon the pacifist, but there is no assurance that in the event of war it would not return with all its former virulence. The Macintosh case, and all other less famous cases in which conscientious objectors have been denied United States citizenship, are signposts of paganism. The ironic character of such denial is evidenced by the fact that a naturalization system which refused citizenship to the Hungarian reformer Madame Rosika Schwimmer gave it freely to Zangara who in the spring of 1933 almost changed the destinies of America by his attempted assassination of its President-elect.[29]

Other signposts of paganism are found in the wave of sedition bills and red-baiting hysteria which seems to be rapidly rising. Loyalty oaths can never be a real test of loyalty, since only the person conscientious enough about his patriotism to have a scruple would hesitate to affix his signature; but they can be an insidious and annoying challenge to academic freedom. Sporadic attempts to keep high-minded prophets of peace and social justice from talking by official black-lists, or by pressure leading to the cancellation of engagements, usually are more disturbing to the organizations implicated than to the individuals attacked; but they indicate that freedom of speech exists in this country more in the written word of the Constitution than in the social order supposedly regulated by it. So also do the many frantic flourishes which under guise of preserving the Constitution, are really trying to preserve the *status quo* "with perhaps a loving reminiscence of old war times," or at least with a reminiscence of the halcyon days of Coolidge prosperity which followed the last great war.

By a strange quirk not to be justified by logic but understood from long association of ideas, a great proportion—probably the majority—of the American public regard an attack on the capitalistic system as tantamount to an attack on the State. Everywhere in press, radio, political addresses, service club speeches, women's clubs, and even sometimes in schools and churches, socialism is a sign of lack of patriotism. We have not yet graduated from the attitude which links together socialism, atheism, free love and treason in one embracing category and damns them all.

As nationalism and capitalism are mixed up in one pot together, so are nationalism and race prejudice—with religious prejudice thrown in to make the brew still more unsavory. There is difference in the cleavages which separate Negroes from whites; Jews from Gentiles; Orientals from occidental Nordics. But there is more likeness than difference, with a common meeting ground in the *superbia* which is antithetical to a Christian society. Class pride marries itself to a bogus patriotism. It is a natural but unholy union; and when trouble ensues, as is inevitable, violence follows. This takes the form of anything from fisticuffs through race riots to lynching and war.

The Ku Klux Klan has somewhat gone into desuetude in this country, but what it stood for in racial intolerance and the lawlessness of vigilantes is with us still. While we are condemning Hitler for treating the Jews in Germany obscenely, it is sobering to remember that a few years ago the high priest of American efficiency was launching diatribes against "the international Jew" in his *Dearborn Independent*. In almost every American community there is an accumulated body of racial and religious prejudice which parades in saintly robes under guise of preserving "the sacred traditions of our American democracy."

These circumstances which lie all about us are signposts of paganism; first because they hallow the relative and give it absolute sanction, for an earthly allegiance, exalted into the position of deity, trammels up the Christian conscience; second, because the true Christian patriot who is keen-sighted and resolute enough to resist, as most of us are not, faces persecution as surely as did any early Christian martyr. The ghosts of the Caesars walk again.

That the persecution faced in the twentieth century is less drastic in form than that of the first or second is ground for optimism—but not too much. To lose one's job is to be preferred in most cases to losing one's life. But in a society where there is no guarantee of economic security, and he who loses his job must either lose his body in physical deprivation or his soul in the enervating influences of unearned public relief, it is not far from the truth to say that one's job *is* one's life.

But did not Jesus say, "Render to Caesar the things that are Caesar's and to God the things that are God's"? In some areas of life it is possible to do this without conflict. In the increasing complexity of our social organism, these areas grow smaller. We all must compromise. To pay taxes if one has taxable income or property is a public duty; to pay taxes is also to implicate oneself in an unholy use of public funds for implements of destruction. No person can live in a social organism, as we must, and extricate himself wholly from corporate guilt. But by ethical sensitivity and courage it is possible to reduce the areas of implication, and contribute somewhat to the changing of the system. This cannot happen if one recites glibly this great saying of Jesus and makes it an excuse for that which Jesus himself repudiated when he chose the way of the cross rather than the surrender to the engulfing nationalism of the times.[30]

There cannot be two masters and one supreme loyalty. It is as impossible to serve two deities in God and the State as to serve God and Mammon. Yet our pagan world is full of attempts to do this.

V

The Recovery of Ideals (1937)

SECTION PREFACE

Harkness wrote *The Recovery of Ideals,* as she had *The Resources of Religion,* at Union Theological Seminary while on an extended leave from her undergraduate teaching, this time in the fall of 1936.[1] Again, the Union environment helped to shape her thought as she was listening to Fosdick preach at Riverside Church on Sundays and attending lectures with Niebuhr and Tillich during the week. In the preface, she noted her indebtedness to both Tillich and Brightman for reading the full manuscript.

Harkness is responding again to the problems of the "lost generation," young people who, "bewildered" and "shell-shocked,"[2] lacked not only good jobs and a secure future, but also ideals that would give purpose to life in the midst of difficulty. In light of these problems, Harkness set about describing the "dissolution of ideals" and laying out a plan for their recovery. Even more serious than the economic depression of the time was this "depression of morale."[3] Given both the economic and political crises facing the world community in the mid-1930s, the need for ideals was all the more pressing. A person "cannot live with hope and courage," Harkness wrote, "unless he has worthy ideals by which to regulate his life with an inner authority."[4]

"The Place of Ideals in Human Nature," reading 7, reflects the influence of Reinhold Niebuhr both positively in the language she uses and the way she frames some of the problems, and negatively as she makes the case for a more liberal view of human nature and the role of ideals. Harkness believed that people of her time were beset by a sense of loneliness and fear that could be overcome only through "the recovery of ideals." Only then could humans find "direction and power to resist temptation and to overcome limitations. . . . [One] finds through them not only personal mastery but the impetus toward the creation of a society where none need be inhibited by artificial barriers. . . . In the power to live by ideals . . . lies salvation."[5]

These ideals are rooted in the religious and moral realms, the very areas about which humans have the least certainty. In order to move toward the recovery of ideals, then, one must try to understand—and then move into relationship with—the God who is the source of ideals. To this end Harkness offers, in the next reading included here, "Synoptic Supernaturalism," a method by which to "find such certainty as is possible to find in the field of religious knowledge."[6] Her synoptic method uses all available resources and draws from them a "coherently unified view" that provides not complete certainty but "certainty enough to undergird our living as we go. This is all any man knows, and all he needs to know."[7] When Harkness writes here of "ethical, aesthetic, or mystical" intuition, she is making a similar argument to that of John Wesley, who, out of his empiricist framework, drew on the idea of spiritual senses of talk about how humans could know about the spiritual realm.

In readings 9 and 10, Harkness, using the synoptic method, turns to the questions of who God is and how God is limited. In both readings, Harkness's reflections reveal not only her personalist formation but also the influence of Whitehead and Tillich. In reading 10, "How God Is Limited," Harkness makes a break with several claims of personalist theology. Harkness had insisted previously, with Brightman and other personalists, that only personality—divine and human—was real. Other things in the world besides human persons that seem real are actually part of the divine personality. If only human and divine personality are real, then how could personalists account for the existence of evil and suffering without finding its cause in human or divine persons? Brightman's solution was to insist that the evil and suffering of the natural world come about because of a recalcitrant factor within God's nature—a "given"—with which God must struggle. Brightman wrote that this given, recalcitrant factor "constitutes a real problem to divine power and explains the 'evil' features of the natural world."[8] In laying out an alternative solution that affirms the existence of realities beyond divine and human personality, Harkness breaks with a key tenet of personalism and embraces what she calls "theistic realism."[9] Throughout these readings from *The Recovery of Ideals*, one can see that Harkness is taking on more of the traditional language and even teachings of the Christian tradition; she does this with a chastening but not a disavowal of key liberal claims.

READING 7

In the preceding chapter we examined some of the processes which have contributed to the shattering of ideals in our time. We shall now look at some of the deeper and more permanent elements in the situation, and shall hope thus to find clues pointing toward a way of reconstruction.

We shall begin by examining the nature of man. This procedure is based on the simple pedagogical principle of going from the known to the unknown. Man's existence is indubitable; about his nature we do not know everything, but we know by experience a great deal. If we say we have certainty of God or of the cosmic status of ideals we speak with insufficient caution, and whatever degree of certainty we do possess comes through our knowledge of man, the workings of the human spirit, and our convictions as to man's place in the cosmos.[10]

The most dominant characteristic of man is that he is a citizen of two worlds. Original sin and original goodness contend within him; so likewise do finitude and infinity.

1. Original Sin and Original Goodness

By original sin I do not mean just what St. Augustine and the orthodox Christian tradition have meant by it. The Babylonian epic of the fall of man, adopted by Semitic tradition and narrated with moral beauty in the third chapter of Genesis, mixed by Augustine with the Platonic myth of man's pre-existence in a supramundane world of perfect archetypes, and transmitted into the tradition of the church to be literalized into plain, prose doctrine—this myth has been the source of much bad psychology and bad theology. But there is both psychological and theological truth in it which we ought not lightly to disregard.

Psychological study gives plenty of evidence of man's inherent tendency to sin, if we are not afraid to let a much shunned word into our terminology. Any realistic view of childhood will see there traces of "original sin" in the ever-present tendency of the child to *demand, demand,* then *demand more* of a sick, tired mother, or of any one who is accessible for the satisfaction of desires. Children by nature are egocentric little animals, with a dominant concern to obtain for themselves a maximum of satisfaction. . . .

Social conditioning and the emergence of altruistic tendencies tone down somewhat this fundamental selfishness. But what adult can say with honesty that he is free from it? Its roots run through the entire emotional life, mixing with pride, anger, envy, and the rest of the seven deadly sins, and many more, to

From "The Place of Ideals in Human Nature," *Recovery of Ideals,* 32–57.

corrupt our natures and distort our living. Probably its most insidious form is that tendency to rationalize the will to power which cloaks even our higher moral impulses in self-righteousness to the point of making us oblivious of its existence.

Egocentricity pursues us where we least suspect its presence, easily substantiating the belief in a personal devil. I do not, on metaphysical grounds, accept belief in such a devil, but there is everything in our psychological natures to make us feel as if we were in the grip of a power not ourselves which makes for evil. This inherent tendency to selfishness, projected from the individual into a social order made up of selfish individuals, is the root of exploitation, war, and chaos.

Selfishness is not merely self-reference. There is a good deal of popular and academic cynicism which claims that even our noblest acts of service are subtly motivated by a desire to please ourselves, and therefore reduce to selfishness. This is a half-truth which as usually stated becomes an untruth. It is true that all motivation has self-reference in it. What a motive is, is simply an urge toward the satisfaction of a desire sufficiently compelling to induce one to act. Whenever I act voluntarily, I act because I want to satisfy something in me; and I can no more be satisfied by another person's urge to the fulfillment of desire than my body can be nourished by the food another person eats. This holds of the most altruistic as well as the most selfish acts. Kagawa, like Mussolini, is driven by an urge toward the satisfaction of an impulse within his nature. But this self-reference, native to us all and inevitable, is not what I meant by sin.

Sin enters at the point where this urge toward the satisfaction of desire becomes a *narrow* and *exclusive* interest.[11] Exclusiveness, whether an exclusion of values essential to the wholeness of our own personalities or an exclusion of other persons from the range of interest, is the basic form of sin. When I will to be less of a person than I might be, I sin. When I will to secure values for myself which I am not willing to help others to secure for themselves, I sin. When I will to secure values for myself which I am not willing as far as circumstances permit to share with others, I sin. The phrase "as far as circumstances permit" is both a necessary safeguard against fanaticism and an easy door through which to escape responsibility. Presumably it is not my duty literally to sell all my goods and give the proceeds to the poor; yet I am selfish and therefore sinful when, recognizing this fact, I make it an excuse for living in comfortable indifference to the fact that thousands of human beings die annually of under-nourishment because of an unjust social order.

To illustrate again, it is not sinful to seek knowledge in order that one may be a wiser person and therefore have more to share. But to seek knowledge to the exclusion from life of health, friendship, beauty, or holiness is sinful; to seek it for private gain is to make it the tool of a subtle will to power which corrupts personalities and undermines societies.

Sin enters most often in connection with economic goods because these are by nature exclusive values while wisdom, worship, friendship, and beauty are more readily shareable. But "love of money" is not "the root of *all* evil." The most insidious forms of evil are those wherein a value which by its nature is meant to be shared is hugged as a private possession. Snobbishness, whether intellectual, ecclesiastical or social, is not simply one of the most unlovely of human attitudes; it is one of the most demonic.

This tendency to the exclusive enjoyment of our own ego and its appurtenances is the permanent meaning of "original sin."[12] There is a perpetual "fall" when man, seeing the good, narrows the range of his self-satisfactions to do evil. Such a stranglehold does it have upon us all that it is not surprising that Christian theology has held redemption to be possible through divine grace alone.

With the marks of original sin, we bear in us also traces of original goodness. This does not mean, as Rousseau held, that human nature left to itself will turn out all right. Romanticism like the doctrine of human depravity is a half-truth which is also at least half error.

Yet the shrewdest judge of human nature who ever lived would not have set a child in the midst and said, "Of such is the kingdom of heaven," unless he had seen there elements of an inborn divinity—or, since we are not yet ready to talk about God, elements of a native moral perfection.

Wordsworth probably went beyond the bounds of psychological realism in his famous ode:

> Heaven lies about us in our infancy!
> Shades of the prison-house begin to close
>   Upon the growing Boy,
> But he beholds the light, and whence it flows,
>   He sees it in his joy;
> The Youth, who daily farther from the East
>   Must travel, still is Nature's Priest,
>   And by the vision splendid
>   Is on his way attended;
> At length the Man perceives it die away,
> And fade into the light of common day.

Taking this for what it is meant to be, not a psychologist's analysis of statistical data but an artist's vision, there is the sound of truth in these words. One must be quite lacking in discernment who does not find in the same three-year-old referred to above not only egocentricity, but intimations of a realm of spiritual reality beyond the crude attainment of either child or adult life. Children are neither little devils nor little angels, but there is in child nature something both demonic and divine.

So much of our goodness has to be "coaxed along" as we grow to maturity that it is less easy on empirical grounds to make out a case for original goodness than for original sin. Yet none of us could achieve goodness at all, either through divine or human effort, unless goodness were in some sense native to us.

As the roots of sin are in selfishness and exclusiveness, so goodness roots in a common human tendency to project interest outward toward other human beings. It appears in the child's capacity to love and attempt to please, first those on whom he is dependent, and then a wider circle. Such other-regarding interest is less spontaneous than our egocentricity and requires much fostering: but there is in all normal human nature the capacity to be motivated by concern for the well-being of others. The degree to which it manifests itself, as well as the form of action it takes and the persons upon whom it is directed, is determined in large part by the social inheritance and in particular by early training. But the significant fact is that neither the social inheritance as a whole nor any training in particular could make us act altruistically, in opposition to powerful egoistic impulses, unless the capacity for altruism were an original endowment of human nature.

Man, whether in the relatively unmodified state of childhood, or in maturity after society and some measure of self-direction have done their work, is a mixture of original sin and original goodness. There is in him no such clearly drawn warfare between flesh and spirit as Paul and Augustine envisaged. But rooted in both flesh and spirit and manifest in both flesh and spirit, an eternal conflict between good and evil is being waged. Evil is mixed with good, and good with evil, and this very fact of mixture serves to complicate and accentuate the fact that the personality is being pulled by opposing impulses. It is a conflict so disrupting to man's nature that he must somehow find a way out of it. And because he is a human being and not simply a biological organism, he does find a way which frees him—never wholly, but in part—from the clashing currents in his members.

2. Human and Animal Nature

In this conflict between evil and good impulses, the personality has both assaults and reinforcements from without. But the issue is primarily settled by impulsions and inhibitions *from within.* As the growing personality achieves maturity and force of character, there is less and less dependence on external coercions. The fully mature person does not have to be kept in check by physical or legal sanctions, or even by public opinion, for he has learned to regulate his life from within with relative indifference to outer enticement or assault; and in acts of heroic fidelity to his own ideals he defies society to the point of accepting ostracism or death rather than compromise. That there are few such "fully mature persons"—probably no living person is completely so—does not nullify the fact that the more ethically mature a person is, the more he relies on inner rather than outer restraints.

This capacity to live by an *inner non-coercive authority* to which one yields his life is man's most distinctive trait. It is here that man differs most from the subhuman animals, whose behavior may be either attractive or perverse according to human standards, but is neither good nor evil in a moral sense. An animal reacts to a stimulus; a man responds to a situation. Such response is complex, and conscience is obviously not the only element in it. Yet it is of supreme importance that man is motivated, at least in his most *human* acts, by an inner authority which acts upon him with the power of an objective force. Though we ordinarily call it conscience, or a sense of moral obligation, it could equally well be termed the power to live by ideals.

The fundamental distinction between human and animal intelligence is often stated in terms of reason and imagination. I do not wish to deny the importance of either. Both enter into this ideal-forming, self-directive capacity. Yet it is not identical with either, for one may reason or project goals in imagination without acting. John Macmurray in his *Creative Society*[13] links the fear of death with reason as the primary human capacity unpossessed by animals, and makes this the root of religion. I believe this distinction to be overdrawn, and in any case, subordinate to the more fundamental difference that a man can definitely envisage *what he ought to do* and set himself, against the weight of conflicting impulse, *to the doing of it.* It is intimately related to reason, for it involves the human capacity to bring together past, present and future in an act of conscious thought. But it is more than a cognitive matter. It roots in a fundamental difference in the emotional life whereby human emotions take on moral significance and impel the individual to self-directed action; while animal emotion is the bare, uncontaminated and unglorified, outcropping of instinctive impulse. To be ruled by emotion in the same "un-self-directed" way the animal is, is to throw away one's human birthright and sink toward the level of the beast.

3. Finiteness and Infinity

Man, then, is a mixture of good and evil, a natural endowment which is his to build upon or be crushed beneath. But we said also at the beginning of the chapter that man is a mixture of finiteness and infinity. This requires further examination.

Man in his inner life is fundamentally fearful, lonely and bewildered—a state of affairs accentuated by recent social phenomena but basically characteristic of human nature. His most fundamental impulses are sex, acquisitiveness, and the will to power.[14] With each of these impulses are mingled deep-seated, profoundly disturbing emotions.

Fear stalks its way through life introducing ghoulish specters into what might otherwise be joyous experiences. The lover fears that he—or she—may not win the object of devotion, and when the family is established fears still that loyalty may slip away. Fear besets sexual satisfaction. It engenders terror, even in a personally courageous man, at the thought of injury which may befall his family. Almost everybody, whether with family responsibilities or not, fears that he may not possess enough to make his economic status certain, and having won possessions, fears that he may lose them. With economic stability relatively assured, fear of losing caste or prestige is still a haunting terror, making one feel driven by the pressure of his group, however circumscribed, to conform to its demands.

Human fear is more intense and devastating than any animal fear could be, for the reason that to biological fear is added that which comes with the enlargement of outlook and the awareness of all that is at stake. For the same reason, there is probably more fear in an advanced than in a primitive society, where in spite of many superstitious terrors now banished it was true that "ignorance is bliss." A homely example of this is the fear of germs, amounting in some almost to a mania. . . .

Loneliness, like fear, besets man's life. The home is intended by nature to give intimate companionship, but if one may trust the testimony of many in family relations which seem on the outside to be satisfactory, it gives conjunction of clashing temperaments more often than genuine unity of spirit. Economic activities in all but the rarest of instances are divisive rather than soul-uniting agencies. The quest for power and prestige elicits social recognition but not true understanding.

Isolation, like fear, grows more devastating as man advances. It is doubtful whether animal loneliness can compare in intensity with the human awareness of lack of inner comradeship; and the more complex society becomes, the more the individual feels himself lost in the great shuffle. The child lost in a swirling crowd of unfamiliar faces and crying for those he loves is symbolic of the experience of many adults who feel an overwhelming sense of loneliness in the presence of human indifference and nature's "great unknowns."

To fear and loneliness are linked confusion of soul. To live is to face a future of which the platitudinous "You never can tell what's going to happen next" is an apt description; while to die, for those not rooted in religious faith, is a leap in the dark which a natural biological impulse to self-preservation invests with terror.

I have referred to the importance Macmurray attaches to the fear of death, making it the basic symbol of human fear. There is no reason to deny the place which death and its correlative, the hope of immortality, have occupied in all human experience. Religion might have existed without it, but would have taken quite a different trend. Yet I doubt whether, except in the presence of imminent danger, death is dreaded by most people as much as life. Death is dreaded when one thinks about it; life has to be thought about—that is, faced and somehow grappled with—all the time. Life is feared not only because it is dangerous, but more because it is chaotic, turbulent, beset with uncertainties which may turn out to be nothing but in anticipation loom large with awful possibilities. Confronted with them, it is easy to say to another a cheerful "Don't worry. Things will come out all right." But not many who give this advice blithely can follow it themselves.

So this is the state in which we live. A war or an economic crisis, a sudden and irreparable physical injury or a blasting of hopes may bring these turbulent emotions vividly into the foreground. But they are always in the background, lurking like the legendary three-headed Cerberus to leap upon the wayfarer. It is to these forces that even with the best of inner buttressing, we are largely subject.

I do not wish to paint an over-gloomy picture from which pleasurable satisfactions are omitted. There is plenty of joy in life: friendship, family, love, laughter, and sunsets have their place and only the dullard or misanthrope fails to find enjoyment in them. But yet however much we may desire to—and have a right to—look on the brighter side of things, it is to drug oneself with optimism if one fails to see that there is an element of original unhappiness and chaos in us all which relatively few people successfully surmount. This is the deep-lying truth in the commonplace, bitter ejaculation, "Life is hell!"

In so far as we surmount this condition, it is through ideals. This does not necessarily mean religious ideals, though it is through religious ideals that the most effective conquest comes. In so far as our idealism is thin, we are a prey to impulse and circumstance, living conventionally acceptable or socially stigmatized lives, as the accident of environment may dictate, but never living with true self-mastery. Such an existence may be a negatively tranquil but is never a genuinely happy life; it is the victim of too many evil forces pressing from within and without. Of such are the peevish, the complaining, and the bored.

It is through ideals that the element of infinity becomes operative in us, redeeming in a measure the finitude which otherwise possesses us. By infinity I do not mean any mysterious supernatural power. That there may be something of mystery in it and something above the natural I do not deny, nor is it necessary at this point to affirm it. What I mean is simply the empirical fact that human nature is so constituted that it can rise above the forces which would otherwise condemn us to live in darkness and dread—the victims of confusion and chaos. I call this capacity to surmount limitation *infinity* because, just as fear, loneliness, and bewilderment hedge us in and set barriers to our living, this capacity releases us to live victoriously in a manner to which there is no setting of upper limits.

4. The Function of Ideals

Ideals, though acquired, are our natural birthright by virtue of our human heritage. Apparently no animal possesses them, and no normal human being is wholly without them. They vary both in quality and force, and in the degree to which they are higher or lower, more or less regulative, lies our escape from "hell."

There is an important difference, and at the same time no clear line of demarcation, between our escape from sin and our release from limitation. Between a bad will and a weak will—an evil deed and a foolish one—there is a real difference which needs to be preserved lest moral responsibility be lost. A person *sins* when he might do better and "misses the mark"; a person *fails* when nature or society has laid upon him burdens too grievous to be borne and he sinks beneath them. Yet though it is imperative to preserve this distinction, it is equally essential to avoid any pharisaic drawing of rigid lines between the sin and the weakness of other men.

Some sin, some limitation we all must have as long as we remain human. But there is vastly more of both than is necessary. To say of any evil or weakness, "That's only human nature," is to miss the greater fact that there lies within human nature a channel of release.

It is through ideals that we discover direction and power both to resist temptation and to overcome limitation. If our ideals are as inclusive as they ought to be, we find through them not only personal mastery but the impetus toward the creation of a society where none need be inhibited by artificial barriers from living at his best. The function of ideals is both individual and social. In the power to live by ideals, whether directed against sin or chaos, lies salvation.

We are not ready yet to say whether this power is of God. It may be, yet some of the channels it takes—as we shall see presently—are quite ungodlike. The prior fact is that *ideals cure*. Because they are, men live differently. Because some ideals are both pure and potent, some men find salvation from inner catastrophe. There is no man living who can say without self-deception that his escape is absolute. Yet a road which leads even to partial salvation is of supreme worth, so long as it leads forward.

READING 8

1. Some Definitions of Terms

. . . The type of epistemological approach by which I believe we can best arrive at dependable religious knowledge I shall call a *synoptic supernaturalism*. The term is chosen with the awareness that both parts of it are easily subject to misunderstanding. I must begin, therefore, by trying to make clear what I mean.

Synoptic means "seeing together" . . . [and] implies the principle of inclusiveness. The synoptic vision is that which sees things from all angles in a related whole. Whether the description of what is thus seen is stated in a paragraph or in a five-foot shelf of volumes is irrelevant, though the chances are against any true synopsis in a view so cluttered with detail that it takes a vast deal of verbiage to describe it. The synoptic view, when one really achieves it, is simple—but not with the simplicity of the simple-minded who fail to see complexity. The simplicity which is won through taking pains to see everything discernible is a long way removed from the pseudo-simplicity of failing to discover that there is anything to see.

Supernatural means "above the natural." In adopting this dangerous word—the storm-center of much theological discussion in these days—I do not mean to affirm any abrupt cleavage of the natural from the supernatural. The supernatural does not rest on top of the natural like the upper story of a house with a ceiling between. Still less is it somewhere up in the sky where "visibility unlimited" makes what lies within and beyond it invisible. . . . All these connotations supernaturalism has had, and because it has had them it has gone out of favor with realistically-minded people. But it is a good word badly misused, and because it expresses more exactly than any other a great idea which I believe to be a true one, I should like to try to help restore it to favor.

The supernatural, as the "more than natural," does not connote a separate realm of being, but an aspect of the world of existence which permeates and gives meaning to all existence. To assert belief in the supernatural is not to assert dis-

From "Synoptic Supernaturalism," *Recovery of Ideals*, 89–102.

continuity but the most intimate kind of continuity with the world in which we all must live. The supernatural is not identical with the natural, for super-nature is the ultimate source of existence and the goal of values which gives meaning to nature. Though it is not identical with the natural, neither is it severed from it.

This can perhaps be illustrated by an analogy. The knack of walking depends on the ability to keep one foot on the ground while the other is off. No child could learn to walk who did not discover this trick. To keep both feet on the ground is either to stand still or be dragged; to try to keep both feet off the ground is to be successful only in a leap or a hop which cannot last long. There is a situation here by which to understand the relation of the natural to the supernatural, if we do not push the analogy too far. The supernatural is not a separate world to leap off to; it is that in integrated union with the natural which allows us to go forward toward ends achievable only by such union. Anybody who would find its meaning, either practically or in speculation, must "keep one foot on the ground." But not both. To keep both feet on the ground is to be a naturalist; to take both off is to be a transcendentalist, an extreme mystic, or an authoritarian dogmatist. What we are looking for is a method by which to have progressive certainty and progressive moral achievement.

To use less figurative terms, our knowledge of the natural order of things is essential but not complete. If one sets out to try to explain either man or the cosmos in purely naturalistic terms, he leaves out the most important aspects. Origins, purpose, destiny—all require something "above the natural" for an understanding of what is natural. What this means more concretely we shall attempt to discover in the remainder of the book.

2. Elements of the Synoptic Approach

By the synoptic approach I mean that authority, intuition—whether ethical, aesthetic or mystical, the pragmatic test in individual and social living, the evidence of the natural sciences, and the demands of logical consistency, not only *do have* but *ought to have* their place in enabling us to formulate our idea of God and related concepts. This does not mean that any idea we get from any of these channels may be held along with any other. I am not advocating a philosophy of higgledy-piggledy. Were one to rely on the method of authority, unpurged, he would certainly not be able to rely with equal assurance on the method of the physical sciences. For example, one cannot at the same time believe that God created the earth in six days and rested on the seventh, and that creation is a process which it has taken geological aeons to bring to its present state. But fortunately, one does not have to find himself in this predicament if his use both of authority and of scientific method is truly synoptic.

What I am suggesting is not merely an eclectic but a coherently unified view, an approach in which the defects of each method find a corrective in a due consideration of data available through other channels. Only so can philosophy fulfill its function of thinking consistently about the meaning of life *as a whole.*

The synoptic approach is empirical, but not in any narrowly limited sense. Starting from authority, which is second-hand truth mediated to us through first-hand experience, it regards the pronouncements of authority as something to be tested by further experience. Such experience may be intuitional or sensory; it usually is neither one alone but is bound up with life in all its complexity. If intuitional evidence is sought—or not being sought presses in upon us—it may come in the form of the moral imperative, or the artist's insights, or the mystic's vision. None of these evidences is to be thrust aside as irrelevant; each is to be subjected to further testing. One way of testing it—but not the only way—is the objective verifiability of sense experience and the drawing from it of scientific inference. Another—the pragmatic way—is to submit our fragmentary experience to the test of consequences in the more complete experience of life in the large and in the long. Not as a separate method to be used in isolation from the rest, but in conjunction with them all, is the test of logical consistency. The White Queen could believe six impossible things before breakfast, but not the philosopher with a conscience.

As an illustration of the synoptic approach I shall take a familiar problem probably settled for most of the readers of this book, but still debatable enough in many minds to be illustrative of clashing claims. This is the problem of man's biological ancestry.

For centuries before Darwin, at least since the days of Anaxagoras, there have been people who believed in evolution. The authority accepted by the masses, however, was on the side of special creation until Darwin appeared. After 1859 the issue was clearly joined, for the authority of the Bible, as then interpreted, and the authority of the church was against man's animal ancestry and that of scientific thought was for it. One who tried to settle the problem on the basis of *authority only* found himself the prey of psychological rather than logical considerations, for he either continued from long association to hold the view accepted in his childhood or, if he changed it, he did so on the basis of hero-worship rather than cogency of argument.

In the midst of this clash of authorities, with a growing number of liberals in the church going over to the position affirmed by science, the method of one "say so" over against another was both corrupted and corrected by intuitional considerations. When the Darwinian theory was so interpreted as to exclude God, belittle man, and put man's most precious values into the discard, not only the religious but the ethical and aesthetic intuitions of spiritually-minded persons rose up against it. One finds in the poetry as in the theology of the past seventy-five years a fundamental intuitive unwillingness to let the highest human values be explained in subhuman terms. This resistance, on the one hand, retarded the advance of scientific truth, and on the other it purged nineteenth-century materialism of some of its cruder implications.

Meanwhile the frank acceptance of evolution by liberal religion in conjunction with spiritual values made for religious as well as intellectual progress. The death of William Jennings Bryan after the Dayton trial, victim of fidelity to a lost cause, is symbolic of the way intuition fights to the death; and whether its cross is a mark of shame or triumph depends on whether it has the truth-validating forces of the universe on its side. Often, as I believe to have been the case with Bryan, these "come mixed."

Neither authority nor intuition could settle the question, which was factually one of scientific evidence and spiritually one of interpretation of these facts. As the factual evidence piled up through knowledge of anatomy, embryology, paleontology, and many other fields, conflict waned. Pragmatically the theory of evolution worked as a unifying explanation of many otherwise disconnected phenomena, and the law of parsimony demanded its acceptance.

From the Darwinian *hypothesis,* as a guess or supposition to be tested, the evolutionary view passed into the stage of a *theory,* and now is generally accepted as *fact.* It is accepted by most people not on first-hand knowledge but on the testimony of those trusted to be credible authorities; and these in turn base their conclusions on the coherence of scientific evidence and the working value of this hypothesis as an explanation of empirical data. Intuition has nothing to do with the truth of the theory as scientific fact, but it has a great deal to do with the truth of the deductions for living which are drawn from it.

Any one of these approaches, taken alone, would yield either an incorrect or an inadequate conclusion. When brought into conjunction and allowed to correct each other, they make possible an important advance toward truth.

3. Truth and Value

What I am advocating as the synoptic method is a form of the criterion of coherence. To many minds coherence connotes a barren logical consistency—a viewing of things with "the round glass eye of the Absolute." But what is needed to enable us to arrive at any truth—particularly truth in a field which relates to the whole of life—is a synoptic vision full of rich and many-sided content from which values are not excluded. When we have got all the evidence available—material and spiritual, short range and long range—we are able to draw a conclusion which is as near correct as we can get. We shall not then have absolute truth. But we shall have knowledge enough to enable us to advance toward more, with certainty enough to undergird our living as we go. This is all any man knows, and all he needs to know.

The last statement is perhaps reminiscent of Keats' cryptic words,

> Beauty is truth, truth beauty,—that is all
> Ye know on earth, and all ye need to know.

Whether Keats intended to identify truth and value I do not know. I do not intend so to identify them, though neither can be understood apart from the other. To cite again the illustration of the preceding section, the truth of biological evolution and the spiritual meaning of creation are not identical. Bryan in my judgment was right in one sphere but not the other. Nor are the existence of God and the spiritual meaning of God identical. It is possible to have a high measure of confidence in one of these without the other. But *the truth about a value is as important as any other truth;* and in morals and religion, impregnated in their every nature with values, to disregard values is to cut off an important part of the approach to truth. The synoptic method requires, therefore, that mystical, aesthetic and moral experience have their place along with scientific evidence.

4. The Legitimacy of Supernaturalism

The term supernaturalism is full of pitfalls, not only for reasons earlier suggested, but because it may represent either an epistemological or a metaphysical position. It is with the former we are now mainly concerned, though the greater part of the remainder of the book will deal with the latter.

In a metaphysical sense, the term refers to the existence of a more-than-human and more-than-natural Controller of the universe and Determiner of destiny. In an epistemological sense, it implies approach to knowledge of this Being through other than the methods appropriate to a study of physical nature. For this "other than" there are many terms, but the best is the oldest and richest—namely, faith.

If faith were our *sole* approach to deity, the method followed could be neither empirical nor synoptic. Yet without some faith by which to appropriate revelation we could have knowledge neither of God *nor of anything else.*

Revelation, which is the correlate of faith on the objective side, permeates all knowing. Without revelation nothing would be given for our minds to act upon. I do not mean here revelation in a special religious sense, but "in the natural light of reason"—as natural a light as one may wish. The essential "givenness" of things is the starting-point of all knowledge, and knowledge of what is given is an appropriation of revelation. In the simplest act of sense experience, such as looking at a tree and seeing something there which from the standpoint of practical certainty one knows to exist, there is a response in our minds to what is objectively revealed.

The degree to which this appropriation of revelation falls short of absolute certainty, and therefore is in part inevitably a matter of faith, has been discussed in the preceding chapter. It would be easy to over-shoot the mark and affirm, as is often done, that the inevitability of faith in sense experience erases the problem with reference to religious experience. I believe that supernaturalism is valid in both fields, but that this does not justify hopping blithely from the conditions of one field to the other.

The philosopher of religion who has grappled most earnestly with this problem in our times is Professor Wieman. Supernaturalism, whether in its epistemological or metaphysical meaning, is not in my judgment antithetical to empiricism; but Professor Wieman thinks it is and rests his philosophy of religion upon this distinction. I accept his statement of the requirements of the empirical method, "that every belief be formed and tested by sensory observation, experimental behavior and rational inference."[15] I believe, however, that no sensory observation, and no experimental behavior, can be interpreted without the assumption of postulates which go beyond the bare occurrence of events in nature, and that rational inference requires at a minimum the faith that rational inference is trustworthy.

The extent to which it is possible to reach a supernaturalist conclusion by an empirical approach depends on the radicalness with which sensory observation, experimental behavior and rational inference are employed. Used part way, it leaves one with only such knowledge as can be gained through science. Employed all the way, or at least as far as we can take it, it makes a place for the data gleaned through all the avenues of a synoptic approach. If in this *thorough-going* use of empiricism we find data which can be satisfactorily accounted for only on the assumption of a more-than-human and more-than-natural deity, we need not hesitate to affirm that such a deity exists.[16]

A synoptic approach, starting from empirical foundations and employing both faith and rational inference to appropriate the "givenness" of revelation, points toward a supernaturalist metaphysics. There is a difference in our knowledge of a tree and our knowledge of human nature, another difference in our knowledge of human nature and of God. Yet the difference lies not in method of procedure, but in the kind of data which objective reality gives to us when we employ radically the synoptic method.

5. A Recapitulation

The discussion thus far has centered about ideals, and while I have tried to show that the current assumption which sets up an antithesis between ideals and reality is false I have avoided making metaphysical claims for the objective validity, or cosmic status, of ideals. The remainder of the book will deal mainly with God and the relations of God to the ideals by which men live. Before going forward to examine the metaphysical questions involved in the problem of God, it may be well to look back over the ground which has been covered.

An examination of the current scene reveals a trend towards the dissolution of ideals. For this there are many causes, and various projected cures. Only a multiple approach toward creative idealism is adequate. More significant than the contemporary situation is the fact that, as human beings, we are all doomed by our nature to be a prey to evil, egocentric impulses and to profoundly disturbing emotions. Yet at the same time we are blessed by our human nature with the capacity to generate ideals by which to escape, in part, from our sin and limitation. These ideals are concepts of what ought to be, accepted by us as mandatory upon conduct. They are principles of action which have an emotional foundation and a volitional effect. They are in part attainable, though possibilities of further attainment are inexhaustible. They are not illusions. Though the question of whether they reflect the existence or the will of God may be held in abeyance, they have at least an important psychological reality which is attested by their potency. They have moral validity, though in varying degrees, and exercise a moral imperative. They come to us; yet we make them. Being not merely animal organisms but human personalities, we choose in part what ideals we shall follow and how far we shall follow them. We can live on the level of prudential adjustment, or socially respected character, or triumphant religion, but only on the third level do we truly attain salvation.

In spite of the fact that the majority of people feel no compelling desire to live on the level of triumphant religion, an empirical consideration of the condition of man and society suggests that this level must become a normative ideal. It can be achieved only by a dual emphasis upon life and thought, for an ideal is an idea made dynamic through feeling. The road to the emotional inception and galvanizing of ideals is through incarnation in life—a process achieved through prayer, through the redemptive power of suffering, through many other channels among which personal example and personal participation in vital action are indispensable. The road to religious knowledge, which is difficult because of the paradoxical fact that the most important knowledge is the least certain, can best be found through a synoptic approach which starts from empirical foundations and leads into a supernaturalist metaphysics.

Such synoptic supernaturalism does not give complete knowledge of religious truth, but it gives practical certainty through a joint consideration of scientific fact and man's value experiences. This knowledge, though incomplete, is all that is available by any method, and all that is needed for living triumphantly.

Truth and value are not to be identified, but neither are they to be viewed in isolation. A synoptic approach necessitates consideration of all the ways of knowing—authority, intuition, scientific observation, practical consequences and logical consistency. This approach, though rooted in faith which is the correlate of revelation, uses rational inference radically and inclusively rather than partially. So used, it finds a supernaturalist epistemology legitimate and points toward a supernaturalist metaphysics. If upon following its lead we find validity in the idea of God, we shall have discovered firm ground to stand upon while moving toward the creative idealism of triumphant religion.

READING 9

By considering what God is not, I trust we have cleared the ground somewhat for considering what God is.

1. What God Is

No human mind can do more than touch the fringes of mystery at this point. "The purple mountain mystery of his majesty" looms above and beyond us. But

From "What God Is," *Recovery of Ideals*, 151–63.

we can find trails that lead upward. These trails I find in four convictions which I shall first state as propositions, and shall then attempt briefly to develop. These propositions are:

1. God is Organizing Mind.
2. God is the source and goal of ideals.
3. God is the Cosmic Companion.
4. God is the Poet of the universe.

a. God is Organizing Mind

By saying that God is Organizing Mind, I mean that the interacting orderliness of the universe, with its integrated structure of physical and chemical elements and its emergent levels of evolutionary development, points to the existence of a Mind with both a capacity and a concern for order as a dominant characteristic.

As was earlier suggested, this Divine Mind cannot be held to be just like ours. It has neither biological history nor physical limitation. It is completely active; our activity is but partial and diffuse. It is all-wise; our wisdom but "a torch of smoky pine." It is all-good; the goodness of even the best of us is full of inner corruption and external compromise. But this Mind can do, and on a scale of "grand strategy" does, what human minds do on a small scale. It creates; it initiates and directs meaningful activity; it has concern for goodness and moves toward ends; it brings what would otherwise be chaotic elements into system and order. The term mind is not a misnomer because *nothing else but a mind can do these things.* At least, nothing else we know of does them, and to assume that something else might, though it is within the bounds of theoretical possibility, is to leave certainty for supposition.

Although at some points to be noted later, I do not wholly assent to Plato's theory of creation, I see no reason to set aside the essential meaning of these classic words from the *Timæus:*

> Let me tell you then why the creator made this world of generation. He was good, and the good can never have any jealousy of anything. And being free from jealousy, he desired that all things should be as like himself as they could be. This is in the truest sense the origin of creation and of the world, as we shall do well in believing on the testimony of wise men: God desired that all things should be good and nothing bad, so far as this was attainable. Wherefore also finding the whole visible sphere not at rest, but moving in an irregular and disorderly fashion, out of disorder he brought order, considering that this was in every way better than the other.[17]

The words, "so far as this was attainable," are significant and suggest, I believe, a truth left out of the dominant Christian tradition which has assumed God's power to be wholly unlimited. God works with and through both man and nature to erect an ever-growing structure of meaning and value. This means that the world is still in part unfinished. Instead of throwing up one's hands—and one's religious faith—before this idea, one might better find a challenge in the thought of a dynamic God who is always doing things—a God who "worketh hitherto" and still works to bring order and richer meaning into his universe.

b. God is the source and goal of ideals

To say that God is the source and goal of ideals is to say that while all ideals have a socio-biological history, those which make for true goodness have also a cosmic foundation. While all ideals have an end to achieve in the temporal order—else they would not be ideals, our higher ideals point beyond it towards perfection. That in which such ideals are grounded, and the moral perfection to which they point, is God. God is both the source of the supremely worthful in human life and the object of supreme worth.

The question may—and must—be asked as to where the dividing-line lies between those ideals of which God is the source and those of which he is not—those which are pointers toward his perfection and those which are subtle rationalizations of our own arrogance and pride. If man attempts to *be* God he sins the worst of sins, giving himself over to the soul-destroying selfishness of the will to power. If man attempts to *live like God,* to the limits of his wisdom and moral capacity, he finds all of life transformed into richness and power. He does not then attain moral perfection, but he does attain triumphant living. It is more than an academic question to know what ideals are of God.

So important is this question that later a fuller section will be devoted to it. It may be said here, in anticipation, that God is the source of all biological and human life and therefore in one sense the source of all human ideals with their biological and physical matrix. As independent personalities, we form and act upon some ideals which are good, some which are evil, some which do not seem to make much difference. Yet in a moral sense, God can be thought to be the source and goal only of those ideals which, viewed most inclusively, are seen to enhance the values of life. We have noted how the evidence of history substantiates the judgment that there are eternal moral principles written into the structure of the universe to be thwarted at our peril.

As to which specific ideals do, and which do not enhance human values, inclusive judgment in the light of the supreme worth of personality must be the arbiter. Fortunately, no normal human being is wholly lacking in the intuitive and rational capacity by which to judge some things to be better than others. Where such judgment is mistaken, empirical study of factual circumstance and a union of reason with love is the corrective.

c. God is the Cosmic Companion

The climax of creativity, according to Professor Whitehead, is the love of God for the world whereby God becomes "the great companion—the fellow-sufferer who understands."[18] This is perhaps the profoundest insight of Christian faith, and one we could least afford to surrender if we had to give up any. It is also the one most open to self-deception, and to caricature. I have no great admiration, either theologically or aesthetically, for that gospel song, the chorus of which affirms ecstatically:

> And He walks with me, and He talks with me,
> And He tells me I am His own,
> And the joy we share as we tarry there,
> None other has ever known.

Yet while I should never select this hymn for a service of worship over which I had any control, it affirms a deep-lying truth which is at least as much responsible for its popularity as are its sentimental words and lilting melody. When a person says or sings that Jesus walks by his side, he is of course speaking symbolically, and if he did not *know* he were speaking in symbols he would be the victim of an hallucination, headed for a hospital for the insane. Fortunately, most of the people who sing this hymn are aware that Jesus does not literally walk and talk with them.

All deep emotion must speak in symbols. What is here symbolized is a sense of being not alone in the midst of a lonely world. One feels, and must describe somehow, the intimate Presence of a sustaining personality. This personality like the most satisfying human comradeship alleviates fear and confusion and gives moral support, yet unlike any human comradeship can be relied upon with implicit trust in the midst of any difficulty, however dark.

Whatever may be said of the psychological explanations of this assurance, metaphysically it does not rest upon illusion. God is that Power within the universe that enables us to feel within ourselves that we are not alone, that we have more than each other, that there is something objective and eternal to give us direction and leadership. There are many ways to say this, all falling short of the depth of meaning in which such confidence is grounded. One of the great historic ways of saying it is the Biblical figure of the pillar of cloud by day and the pillar of fire by night. If God's leadership today is by the clouds of the subconscious or the fires of imagination, this does not make such companionship less real.

d. God is the Poet of the universe

Of all the symbols by which we speak of God, the one most familiar is that of fatherhood. I have no desire to supplant it with a rival, fraught with meaning as it is through its familiar use by Jesus and many centuries of Christian testimony. Yet when the early creed-builders wrote "I believe in God the Father Almighty," they immediately had to add "Maker of heaven and earth." A Latin word for maker is *poeta*,[19] and it seems not inappropriate to speak of God as the Poet of the universe. God does what a poet must do.

What must a poet do? At least five things mark off the work of a poet from that of a rhymster. (1) A poet must create something, and the thing he creates must be both a mechanism and an organism. That is, it must conform to definite requirements of interrelated structure, a structure not only related part to part, but part to whole. (2) The created work must possess beauty, with a unity and symmetry of form in which the form is the inconspicuous but essential vehicle for the conveying of a meaning to which it is appropriate. (3) The poem must say something worth saying. The meaning must not be too obvious. The poem must not too plainly point a moral. But it must make its contribution to the richness of life. (4) What the poet creates must say something which comes from his own personality as a revelation of its nature, yet projects itself outward to meet a response in other minds. Only appreciative minds can make this response. (5) The poem must possess universality of meaning. It may delight the senses, or intrigue the fancy, or rend the heart, but a real poem must somehow touch the deeper emotions and leave the hearer or reader with a sense of having been lifted out of himself, and upward, by a miracle of beauty.

All these things God does in his universe. We can call him Poet only in terms of symbol and analogy. It is to commit the logical fallacy of undistributed middle to make a syllogism and say:

> A poet creates—
> God creates—
> Therefore, God is a poet.

Yet we may keep within the bounds of logic and affirm that God creates a world of interrelated structure, of beauty of form, of oft-hidden but majestically discernible meaning, of self-revelation to kindred minds, of eternal significance which lifts the religious spirit upward and outward to new heights of goodness, truth, and beauty. If God does this, we are entitled to speak of him not only in terms of fatherly care but of artistic creativity.

2. God and the Problem of Evil

Any one who has ever tried to write a poem knows that there are moments when the words, almost of themselves, shape themselves into symmetry and beauty; and there are other intervals, sometimes long arid stretches, when achievement is slight and *any* achievement is by pain and struggle. It is not inappropriate to suggest that something like this may be the experience of God in the making of his world.

The problem of evil divides into two interrelated parts, the problem of sin and the problem of suffering. Of these the former is the more important, for it is worse to sin than to suffer, harder to muster moral forces to get rid of sin than to exercise intelligent caution to prevent suffering. Yet most people are more troubled over the second than the first. In an intellectual analysis, it is harder to reconcile a suffering world with a good God than a sinning world. Leaving the problem of sin and salvation for later treatment, we must inquire how to fit the fact of suffering into the framework of belief which has been stated as describing something of the nature of God. . . .

The argument [of liberal theology] runs, in general, like this: God, though in a true sense all-powerful, has voluntarily limited his power to create a world of human freedom and natural law. Man, in using this freedom, misuses it and brings disaster on himself and others. God, in willing the existence of a world of law, commits himself to the possibility that in its operation disasters may ensue. Yet freedom, an interrelated society, and law are blessings worth the price. It is man's duty to try to prevent suffering, relying upon an Almighty God for cooperation in the task. I believe this to be, in the main, a true answer, but not wholly adequate for reasons to be stated presently.[20]

Some voices have been raised within the precincts of philosophy and liberal theology to challenge frankly the belief that God is infinite in power. John Stuart Mill believed in a Finite God, saying that if God is infinite in power he does every day things that man would be hanged for doing. William James developed this view further, and it is the main point of Professor Montague's "Promethean God" set forth in *Belief Unbound*.

Among these and others who have spoken for a Finite God, none has spoken with greater eloquence or clarity than my honored professor, Doctor Edgar S. Brightman. He maintains that the facts of existence negate the possibility that an all-good, all-powerful but voluntarily self-limited God is in control of the universe, and he defends the view that there is a recalcitrant Given within the nature of God which God himself must fight to overcome. The Given does not denote moral imperfection but limitation in the possibilities of action. God is a finite-infinite Being, finite in power but infinite in loyalty to reason and goodness, and in the capacity to make good come out of evil. This view has aroused much fruitful discussion. It has not gained very wide acceptance, for it seems to many to place a sort of stigma upon God and thus to prevent him from being the All-perfect object of devotion and trust.

The view which I shall present is not exactly like any of these. While a thoroughly satisfactory solution of the problem of evil is probably a hopeless quest, it seems to me possible to avoid some of the difficulties of these positions while preserving their contributions.

The usual liberal affirmation of the voluntary self-limitation of God in the creation of a world of human freedom and natural law may be accepted. But it is impossible without the glossing over of real evils permeating in scope and colossal in scale to explain all the pain, waste, and frustration of existence upon this basis. In addition to God's self-limitation through human freedom and the orderliness of nature, perhaps God is limited by elements of recalcitrance in nature itself and by chance in events. If so, God and man must work together to overcome such limitation, with the prospect of much frustration as well as victory in the process.

One who holds to a personalistic philosophy is obliged to place all recalcitrance either within human persons or the Divine Person. Hence to Doctor Brightman the Given is within the nature of God. But if persons are not the only metaphysical realities, the opposition may come from another source. It is then "given" both in the divine nature and in the structure of the universe that some things should happen which God does not will to have happen. To explain what this means it will be necessary to state wherein I dissent from personalism regarding the concept of physical nature. This will carry us into another chapter and will make clearer a theory of evil at which I have thus far only hinted.

It is, perhaps, sufficient to say here that if God is really organizing mind, source and goal of ideals, cosmic companion and poet of the universe, he is a God whose wisdom, goodness, sustaining care and creativity transcend our power to think. Before such a deity we may bow in reverence, or rise in action, but so great is he that we shall never encompass his meaning to confine it within our grasp.

READING 10

It is seldom that philosophers of religion take the trouble to explain what they mean by nature. Even philosophers whose interests do not lead them into religion are more often concerned with epistemological questions as to how to know nature than with what is to be known. It is imperative if we are not to fall into all sorts of loose thinking about the relation of the physical world to God to try to state what we are talking about when we mention it. This calls, in turn, for further statement of what is real.

1. What Is Real?

I was reared in the personalistic tradition which holds that God and human persons are the only metaphysical realities. Such a view does not, of course, make physical nature an illusion. It makes physical things the acts of God. That is, it regards nature as an eternal system of divine activity; not something God has created, or still creates, but something God *causes* with consistent regularity. Human persons, being relatively independent real units of existence, are created; physical things are caused.

To this view I still assent in part, but only partially. My present view comes closer to a form of theistic realism. I now see no valid sense in which it is possible to say that only persons are metaphysically real. Only persons initiate intelligent activity, have rational apprehension of the world, act freely, or are governed by ideals. But it is to beg the question to say that anything which does not possess such ultimate causal activity lacks metaphysical reality. There are at least three other types of interrelated reality: events, things (living or inanimate), and eternal forms.[21]

An event, as the word suggests, is anything which happens. . . . The point which is here significant is not the obvious fact that events do happen, or the

From "How God Is Limited," *Recovery of Ideals*, 164–82.

more disputable but very important question as to which ones ought to happen. Rather, it is that events have a reality which is in part independent of the agent causing them.

To illustrate, suppose one makes a speech. This is a "real event"—whether a good speech or not—which would not take place without the activity of an agent. In one sense, then, the speech is dependent on the speaker. It expresses some aspects of his personality, and therefore partakes of his nature. But anyone who has ever made his choicest address, only to find it garbled and distorted beyond recognition in next morning's paper, knows that speeches have a way of doing surprising things. This is because they have a reality which is not dependent on the speaker only but on the total set of circumstances, among which the previous thought patterns of the hearers and the physical environment are among the most important. All human activities, dependent on their agents though they are, have some measure of independence from the agent. Even such subjective but psychologically real events as fantasy and illusion owe their nature in part to combinations of circumstance in which past experience in a social milieu and present physical stimuli give rise to new associations of ideas.

The relevance of this fact to the problem of evil we shall presently state more fully. In anticipation it may be said that events which are "acts of God" are not uncaused; but neither are they necessarily occurrences in which everything happens as God would have it. It may be that God also is limited by circumstance.

But events in the sense of overt happenings are not the only events there are. Mathematical physics has demonstrated something which has to be taken on authority by most of us, but which there is no good reason to doubt: namely, that *physical objects also are events.* That is, they are systems of electronic activity. There is one kind of activity by which your eyes move to read what is written on this page; there is another kind which is the page itself. The page exists because a vastly complicated, invisible, but mathematically calculable, system of electrical energy is in operation. Professor Whitehead, in spite of introducing confusion into philosophical terminology, has rendered much service by showing that from the standpoint of modern physics any "actual entity" can just as well be called an "actual occasion."

What this does to physical things is not to dissolve their reality, but to reinterpret it. As much as one likes, one may describe an apple-tree in terms of moving electrons rather than matter, and still the tree *to our experience* remains a tree, and the apples which grow on it remain apples to eat and not merely to make computations about. The tree is a thing of beauty to look at—perhaps also a thing to climb into, to seek shelter under, or later to burn in the fireplace—certainly a thing from which in its prime to get apples which please our taste and nourish our bodies. In these experienced aspects, the tree is a real *thing,* not to be identified with, nor separated from, the system of real *events* comprising its inner structure. Likewise, as we shall note presently, if the tree is a manifestation of the activity of God, as the *experienced product* of that activity it has a meaning and function other than what it has in its correlative aspect as a *process* of activity.

But what of the reality of eternal forms? This is a problem which has teased the minds of philosophers from the time of Plato to the present, and this is not the place to review the history of controversy which has centered about their nature. Let us look again at the two illustrations cited above.

A speech, in so far as it makes any intelligible sense which another mind can grasp, embodies certain structures of meaning. The speaker composes his ideas; yet he *finds* them. The ingredients of his thought do not merely come to him out of the inheritance of social cultures. They have existed in these cultures and have survived to be passed on precisely because they were sharable ideas with a universal meaning to be appropriated by any mind rational enough to understand it.

The tree to which we referred also has certain structures which distinguish its nature, and make it something in particular instead of everything in general. Whether in its inner nature as electronic activity, or in its more observable qualities such as color, shape and texture, or in its value as a thing of beauty and usefulness, it is described in terms of certain recognizable characteristics. It might be other than it is, as it would be if it were a cherry instead of an apple tree; but we could not know it to be this tree *as it is*—like a cherry tree in bearing fruit but unlike it in bearing apples and not cherries—unless there were common forms and meanings by which to make the comparison.

Such forms—structures of meaning and value—must exist in minds or events or things. It is difficult to conceive how they could exist except in something which embodies them. Yet neither could minds, events or things exist in any sort of intelligible order unless they embodied the eternal forms,[22] which do not have to be made but *are*. Thus we are justified in asserting their reality, though it is reality integrated with the rest of existence and not in isolation from it.

2. God and Physical Nature

We are ready now to see what bearing this has upon the relation of God to physical nature.

It was earlier suggested that the physical universe is an integrated system, put together as only an organizing, unifying mind could make it. Viewed from the standpoint of its creation, the physical world is a complicated but marvelously interrelated system of processes. These processes in physical terms are pulsations of electrical energy; in metaphysical terms, the systematic activity of an organizing mind, the Poet of the universe, who labors to make his on-going world in conformity to eternal structures of meaning and value. The world *as created* is a process in which God has priority over the world in the sense that he makes the world and is not made by it. But this does not mean that God, at any point in time, created the world out of nothing. It seems more credible to think of the created universe as an eternal process—the never-beginning and never-ceasing activity of an immanent yet transcendent deity.

Yet the physical world *as apprehended* by us in our experience is not process primarily, but product. We see change everywhere, in the movement of waves, in the drifting of clouds, in "the gay motes that people the sunbeams." Some of these events seem to flicker and pass; from others we see relatively permanent results emerging, suddenly as in the falling of great rocks by which the contour of Niagara is changed, gradually as in the weathering away of this rock. But for the most part, physical nature looks like a relatively finished system of created things rather than an unfinished system of creative processes. It is important to recognize that it is *both,* and that one aspect of its being is as real as the other.

In the creation of any tangible object, whether a physical universe or an object of human art, all four types of reality described above are present. They are *distinct, yet interrelated,* aspects of creation. Each of these has a meaning and significance not to be subsumed under any other.

This last statement is essential to an understanding of the theory of evil which I shall state presently. First, however, it may be well to show their relations by reference to a case of human creativity in which it will not be necessary to think about God or the inner structure of an atom.

A person writes a book. Neither the process of the writing, nor the written product, is identical with the writer. They manifest his purpose, and reveal much about him. He is responsible for writing as good a book as he can under the circumstances. But when the tangible created product passes from under his surveillance and is read by unappreciative persons, he cannot be held entirely responsible for the outcome.

Thus far we have three "reals"—person, event and thing; creator, process and product—entering into an act of creativity. But without the fourth the creation could not take place at all. A book could not be *written* by one person and *read* by another unless there were structures of meaning common to the minds of both, and common to all persons sufficiently instructed to have some idea of what it is about. In so far as what is written has sense, these structures of meaning are embodied in it. In so far as either author or reader understands the sense of what is written, he participates in their nature.

In the creation of a book, there is both order and spontaneity. Nobody writes a book except through the operation of certain definite mechanisms which it is the business of physics, physiology and psychology—perhaps even histology and bio-chemistry—to understand and describe. Yet a book of which the writing was wholly mechanical would not be worth writing—and still less worth reading. It is the spontaneity of the author's insights and his nuances of thought and expression which give the book its meaning and charm. Another kind of spontaneity, the accident of circumstance such as a chance conversation or a periodical dipped into while the writing was on, may give it a turn for better or worse.

Spontaneity, then, may express itself either in intelligent purposeful creation or in chance variations. Both kinds are usually present, though it makes a big difference in outcome which is dominant. Both kinds of spontaneity exist within the book's orderly system; neither kind can be reduced to order and explained away.

Let us get back now to God and physical nature. The analogy fails in one aspect, that the human author has his physical materials given him to work on, while God creates his materials.[23] This is important enough so that it needs to be held in mind to avoid befuddling the argument. But at the points which bear on the four types of reality and their interrelations, the analogy holds. God (the creator) creates the physical world (the product) through his intelligent purposeful activity (the process), and it has meaning for our minds because he uses eternal, universal structures of meaning (forms) in its creation.[24] All are interrelated, but neither creator, product, process nor form is to be identified with any other.

The physical world, as created by God, is both something which happens and something which is. In human creativity, the process of creating a book is readily distinguishable from the book which is the created product. It is at this point that the distinction between the human author's making his book out of materials given him and God's making his own materials becomes relevant. Yet even in God's creating, there is not real identity of process and product; for as I have tried to show, the physical world as it is being eternally created (a system of events) is not identical in experienced meaning with the world as potentially or actually apprehended (a system of things).

This is not to say that one thing is two things—one of them a process and the other a product. Nor that a product is just a way men have of looking at a process. Rather, a physical thing as the product of God's creative activity means something and does something which it does not mean or do as a process of that activity. This is because it exists in an interrelated world—with relations which extend not only to God who creates it and men who perceive it, but to very many other things in a very intricate structure of events.

What all this means in terms of a specific physical object, like a cherry-tree,[25] is that it exists as the product of a process of electronic activity functioning according to the agency of Mind in an interrelated system. As perceived or thought about by human minds, it is distinguishable from other physical objects by the fact that it contains within itself certain combinations of form—that is, certain qualities and characteristics—which other objects unlike it do not possess. It comes to have these qualities through existing in an ordered system, within which there is both intelligent purpose and chance. Sometimes human order and spontaneity enter in to determine its nature, as in any manufactured thing or product of human art; sometimes not. But there is always *both order and spontaneity* present in its creation.

This means, in brief, that physical nature is the derivative product of Mind, event and form; but also that it has a character of its own which though derived from these cannot be submerged in them. If this is clear, we are ready to take up the question of what it is that limits God.

3. What Limits God

To ask, "What limits God?" is to imply that something limits him. To some minds it is sacrilege or presumption to raise the question. Is not God infinite in power, as in wisdom and goodness, the "absolute sovereign" of all our destinies?

To this the reply is that unless we are to refuse to open our eyes and look around us, we can scarcely say that everything in the world is the way a good God would want to have it. "From war's alarm and deadly pestilence" we may well ask God to save us, but there would be no point in asking God to save us from them if we thought God wanted them to happen. Though there is deep meaning in the Leibnizian phrase, "the best of all possible worlds," which is often missed by those who jeer at it, nobody without optimistic myopia could take seriously the idea that the world, just as it is, is just the way it ought to be.

What then prevents the world, with its destinies controlled by a good God, from being what it ought to be?

The first answer, and it is a valid answer as far as it goes, is the voluntary self-limitation of God in the creation of a world of human freedom and orderly natural law. This answer is valid *unless it is made to go too far.* It often has been.

There seems to me to be no adequate way of dealing with the problem of human sin, with its resultant sequence of outer calamity and inner dissolution, unless it is recognized that man has some measure of freedom of choice. What happens when freedom is denied is the wholesale elimination of a sense of sin. But while sin may thus be theoretically ejected, it stays by us nevertheless, even more potent in its hold from the fact that "if we say that we have no sin, we deceive ourselves." The problem is met, theoretically, a great deal more satisfactorily by admitting without blinking both the fact of sin and the heinousness of sin, and saying that God created us with the power to do evil in order that we might have the power to choose to do good. To have the power to *choose* our goodness instead of having it thrust upon us is God's greatest gift to man, and by it God limits himself.

I have suggested that God works in the physical world by a procedure in which there is both order and spontaneity—regularity of functioning and ideological creative advance. This is another way in which God limits himself. Though the orderliness of nature and the progressiveness of evolutionary development as a whole may be conceived to be God's will, some things that happen in them can be held to be so only in the general sense that God has willed that there be a world in which, for the greater good, regularity at some points may thwart value.

To say that God has voluntarily limited his power by the creation of a world of human freedom and natural law is only to say what liberal theism has long said. God is still in an important sense omnipotent if all that limits him is something which happens within his purpose. It is important here to distinguish between what he purposes in the kind of world he has made, and what he wills in specific instances. To cite a familiar analogy, as parents for the sake of letting initiative be developed in their children may permit them to act as they would prefer them not to act, so God to fulfill the conditions of a larger purpose may *permit* a frustration of value which he does not *will.*

However, there is within the world process more of the kind of spontaneity which crushes value than can credibly be set down to voluntary self-limitation on the part of God. God is limited by *inertia in things* and *chance in events.* What these terms mean I shall defer saying for a moment. It is best to get at their meaning through illustration.

Death is the most inevitable necessity of life. It may be a blessing, or a stark tragedy. For creative advance, death is a biological necessity in order that the earth may be cleared of organisms that have had their day. Without it, the on-going currents of new life would have no opportunity. In individual experience, quite apart from its racial value, death in senility is a blessing. When powers have failed and the spirit, "clogged with the pollutions of mortality," has no longer richness to give to the world or get from it, it is better that death cut off the struggle. In such instances, there is no blasphemy in saying that what happens is God's will.

However, the real problem of evil emerges in the fact that not all death is of this sort. In fact, the greater part of it is not. Death in infancy with life as yet unlived, or death in maturity with function unfilled and rich values yet to be achieved, is tragedy. Violent death may be fitted into a sequence of cause and effect relations, but hardly into a concept of the will of a good God. Gloss it over as we may by saying that something worse might have happened, the fact remains that by any canons of judgment we know such premature or violent death ought not to have come *then* or *in that way*. If any person faced by bereavement of this type finds comfort in believing that God wills it so, I should hesitate to rob him of this comfort. Yet it is an illogical comfort, and there are securer foundations on which to build a structure of life's meaning in the face of desolation.

For the occurrence of death as a biological necessity, the system of nature provides adequate mechanisms. These we may legitimately say are God-given. But in their operation, these mechanisms do not act with due concern for values. There is an element of "cosmic drag"—almost as if nature were telling us not to set too high a store by our cherished dreams, an element of fickleness that invades our best-laid plans and brings them to apparent nothingness, an element of spontaneity that by no means works invariably for intelligent advance but seems, like the rain, to fall on just and unjust, and like the lightning, to strike at random.

The operation of such forces, apparently illogical and unconcerned as to what they smash, is most visible in the human realm where values are most precious. But it is not limited to the human. In the premature, violent death of even the lower forms of animal life, the will of God is thwarted. We should take the problem of evil much more seriously than we ordinarily do if we faced with due concern the weight of unmitigated misery in the animal world. A clear-thinking philosopher who can scarcely be accused of sentimentalism has written:

> It is not, however, the pains of the conquering strong that call for our pity, but rather the pains of the utterly vanquished and crushed. Pains, for exam-ple, of small rabbits delivered as playthings to young eagles or fox pups by their mothers to be nibbled, gnawed, or pecked at slowly; toads beneath the harrow, cats beneath the wheels of our cars, or captured mice in the claws of those same cats. For such pains there is no compensating heroism, no high

religion or philosophy to snatch victory from defeat—nothing but writhing and screaming, trembling, terror, and despair.

There is an old, mean piety that would justify the ways of God at any price, even at the price of conscience, pity and sincerity. Contemptuously disregardful of all animal suffering, such piety concentrates on those few cases in which human pain can cancel human sin or hang a moral to a tale. There are such cases, but they make so small an islet in the seas of nature's agony that one needs must have the mind of a fool and a heart much worse to treat them as "solving the problem of evil" and freeing from blame a supposedly omnipotent creator. The puzzled, mounting wretchedness of a single dog lost on the streets of a city would be enough to damn with shame any God who ever lived in heaven if with omnipotence to draw upon he had ordained it so.[26]

It is this haphazard, undirected, often cruel spontaneity which constitutes inertia in things and chance in events. By inertia I do not mean merely the bare fact that things do not move until they are moved. I mean, rather, that things have no concern for values and therefore do not "bestir themselves" to advance them. Such inertia is as evident in the destruction which falls swift and sure as in lingering torture. It is as manifest when things move too much as when they do not move at all.

By chance I do not mean any deviation from the orderly system of nature. In what we call an accident, physical forces keep functioning in their regular way, sometimes in intersection with human freedom as in most automobile accidents, sometimes quite apart from any human will as in earthquakes and landslides. Some of these accidents could be prevented by taking thought; some could not. Chance is present, however, in the fact that by no criterion of judgment which we should think of applying elsewhere can these particular juxtapositions of circumstance be held to be the manifestation of a system of values.

Our freedom, the regularity of nature, and our social interconnectedness whereby we participate in others' good as well as evil, are our greatest blessings. But this does not tell the whole story. As a human author's book has effects which he does not will because there are combinations of circumstance which he cannot control, so does nature have effects which God does not will and cannot control. There is a sturdy recalcitrance here, not a recalcitrance of free human beings who sin, not a recalcitrance of purposed regularities imposed by God upon himself, but the recalcitrance of inertia and chance.

Such inertia and chance God does not ordain, but struggles to overcome. The opposition is not to be placed wholly within his nature, for real things and real events present this opposition. This they do, not freely or maliciously, but because they lack freedom and know naught of either malice or good will.

What limits God? In part, human sin, ignorance and carelessness. In part, a God-given system of ordered and calculable nature which requires, for a greater good, that things happen as they do even though many things happen as neither God nor man would have them. In part, sheer inertia and sheer chance, woven into this structure of human opportunity and nature's dependability so inextricably that it is futile to attempt to say where one begins and the other ends.

If the foregoing statement is accepted, one must say frankly, without any hedging about to preserve a theoretical omnipotence, that there are actual limitations upon God's power. This means, from the standpoint of values and their achievement, a dualistic universe with conflict as a necessary element of its nature. But if what was said earlier in the chapter about the interrelatedness of persons, events, things, and forms be accepted, the universe is still a *universe*. It is not necessary to impute to things and events any freedom of their own, or to personalize them as a demonic power. By being what they are, in part inert and in part fortuitous, they oppose the advance of values and thus the will of God.

4. What God Does in Tragedy

Can we stop here, and say simply that disaster happens through inertia and chance and God can do nothing about it? By no means. To do so is to affront the great conviction of the Hebrew-Christian faith that "God is a very present help in trouble."

God is a present help in trouble precisely because "when the whole creation groaneth and travaileth in pain," God agonizes with it. To some minds the idea of a suffering God is repellent. Yet if there is one sure insight of the Christian Gospel, it is that the cross means something deep and permanent in the experience of God—a union of suffering love with spiritual triumph. It is the place where love and sorrow meet to make meaningful a crown.

What God can do in tragedy, and experience amply testifies that he does do, is to be "the great companion, the fellow-sufferer who understands." God is the source and goal of ideals by which to live triumphantly in the face of starkest grief. The sufferer who finds God as the strength and mainstay of his life does not merely acquiesce before the inevitable with stoic fortitude. He looks the tragedy in the face, and looks up to new heights of spiritual beauty to which he may mount by using his grief as a stairway to God's glory. The cosmic companion supports him with energizing power; the poet of the universe reveals to him insights hitherto unglimpsed. So led and imbued with power, the sufferer transcends his grief to become the suffering servant of humanity and to reincarnate in his own life the eternal meaning of the cross.

If God does this, he does the greatest thing which any deity could do. How he does it, we must subsequently examine. But if we view clear-eyed the fact that all is not in this world as God would have it, we must with equal clarity survey his agony and his redeeming power. God delivers us from evil; and to him belongs the kingdom and the power and the glory forever.

VI

Theology and Theological Ethics in Conversation and Crisis (1938–41)

SECTION PREFACE

Readings 11–13, which range in date from 1938 to 1941, show Harkness in conversation with several different theologians and theological movements. In her 1938 article "The Abyss and the Given,"[1] Harkness continued to address the themes of the previous readings concerning who God is, how God is limited, and the nature of human knowledge about God. The focus is on the theology of Paul Tillich, with whom she had been in conversation during her sabbaticals at Union in 1935 and 1936. In this reading, written for the ecumenical journal *Christendom*, Harkness describes Tillich as well suited "to be a mediator between Continental and American thought," and she would later include Tillich in a short list of theologians and ethicists who "are concerned to preserve the truth in liberalism while correcting its shortcomings by a more biblical faith."[2] Harkness often drew on Tillich's theology in her own work, and he would later express his gratitude for her role in interpreting his theology to American liberals.[3] In this article, Harkness is interested in the problem of the relation of God to evil and the demonic. Tillich's work is set in contrast to the ideas of Brightman and Harkness herself. She continues here to work out her own mediating position.

Note that even in this very technical article, the international conflict of the time is not only in the background but is explicitly included in the analysis.

Reading 12 comes from an address entitled "Nature as the Vehicle of Grace" that Harkness gave in the spring of 1940 to the "Theological Discussion Group" (previously known as the "Younger Theologians"), of which she had been a member since 1933. The group met twice a year, normally at Yale, to hear and discuss papers by its members. In the fall of 1939 and the spring of 1940, the general topic was "Nature, Grace, and the Sacraments," with papers given by eight scholars including Walter Horton and Roland Bainton (in the fall) and Benjamin Mays, Henry Van Dusen, and Harkness (in the spring).

Harkness, drawing on the long Christian tradition of understanding nature as somehow a "vehicle of grace," examines in this reading "two approaches now widely current" that she finds deficient precisely because they have, in her judgment, ultimately "denied that nature is the vehicle of grace." The naturalists have so reduced everything to nature that there is no inbreaking of grace into nature. In this article, the primary foil among the naturalists is Henry Nelson Wieman, whose theology had been referenced frequently in Harkness's writings.[4] In contrast to the naturalists, the neo-orthodox have so focused on the fallenness of the world and the radical otherness of that God who saves that nature is devalued as a vehicle of saving grace; only God is such a vehicle. After presenting the deficiencies of both positions, Harkness lays out her own understanding of "nature as the vehicle of grace" and reflects on the difference this issue makes for how one understands salvation and how one conceives of the role of religious education.

Reading 13 comes from a series of articles by various scholars—James Luther Adams, Robert Calhoun, George Thomas, Georgia Harkness, and others—carried in the ecumenical journal *Christendom* in 1941 and responding to Reinhold Niebuhr's *The Nature and Destiny of Man.* Calhoun was caustic in his response, arguing that in *Nature and Destiny* the various thinkers "are swiftly divided into sheep and goats. The former are treated with enthusiasm and insight, the latter dismissed as not worth much bother. Swiftness is the word always."[5] Harkness responded more tactfully but still maintained that Niebuhr had dismissed liberal theology unfairly.[6] Her chief complaint was that Niebuhr had identified "Biblical" with the Old Testament and the Pauline Epistles while giving very little attention to the Jesus of the Gospels. Harkness contended that the fact that Niebuhr gave short shrift to the very part of Scripture that she emphasized (the Gospels) accounted for their different understandings of Christian "social action" and democracy.

This difference in understanding of Christian social action was no small matter at the time. By the fall of 1941 when this article was published, the debate in the United States about whether to enter World War II was at its most intense and would be resolved in December after the bombing of Pearl Harbor. Both Harkness and Niebuhr were key Christian voices in this public debate about the U.S. role in World War II—but they took opposite sides. (See reading 19.)

Their contrasting positions on the war were shaped in part by the differences that Harkness notes in this article.

READING 11

What A. N. Whitehead is to American philosophy, Paul Tillich is to American theology. Both are men of massive intellect, steeped in Old World culture and saturated with history. Both came to America after they had made significant and highly original contributions to thought in their own countries. . . .

The American theological world, for the most part, discovered Professor Tillich in 1932 when *The Religious Situation,* a translation of *Die religiöse Lage der Gegenwart* made by H. Richard Niebuhr, was recognized as an important contribution to religious sociology. . . .

On the Continent Tillich is very generally regarded as unorthodox while here we call him a Barthian (as we do everyone else who strays from the broad way of nineteenth century liberalism!). This charge of unorthodoxy roots not only in his religious socialism, but in his Christology and in his use of philosophy as handmaid to theology. He holds a left-wing position regarding the historical Jesus, believing that while Christ is the "center of history," what we have as the center of history is the Christ of first-century Christian experience rather than the Jesus of the Gospels. To talk of a religious *a priori,* as Tillich does, is heresy to one whose thought is set in the framework of a transcendent God condescending to man in divine grace. His approach through human experience seems to some to be indistinguishable from humanism. Tillich's God is transcendent but without the remoteness of the God of the Barthians, accessible through human experience but without the immanentism of the liberals. The resultant difficulty of classifying him indicates how admirably he is fitted to be a mediator between Continental and American thought.

II

Tillich's approach to God is anthropological and phenomenological. This means that in questioning human experience, finite and limited though it is, one finds an answer in that element of it which is unconditioned. Man's life is characterized universally by finiteness, by contingency and anxiety, by guilt and despair. From these man must find salvation. From these he does find salvation—not through social adjustment or through Stoic resignation—but through a Power which is within him while it is so much more than he that his very being depends upon it. God is not a Being among other beings, a Person among other persons. Rather, as the medieval scholars characteristically maintained, God is *the* Being. Also, as the mystics have always held, God in his ultimate nature is indefinable. We may call God the Unconditioned, but this is not to attach to God a predicate; it is to assert that the ground of all being lies beyond predication.

From "The Abyss and the Given," *Christendom* 3 (Winter 1938): 508–20.

Man's idea of God is an expression of the experienced fact that human finiteness is comprehended in a transcendent infinity; that human contingency with its bewilderment, frustration and loneliness is transcended in a divine necessity and security; that man in his guilt and despair has also a transcendent blessedness and perfection. All particular being depends for its existence and its fullness of meaning on that which is not particular being, but the basis of all being. Thus the paradox emerges that finiteness participates in infinity, contingency in security, the evil in the good, the imperfect in the all-perfect. Our way to the God beyond all predicates is through human experience, of which much predication is possible. Yet the whole gamut of argument in liberal theology which moves from man to God by saying that God must be like the highest we know in man is misplaced, Tillich holds, for it assumes that God is simply a highest being who may be known by analogy. To take this route is to make of God a magnified man, and thus to blaspheme him.

Hence we find ourselves in a paradox. We must find God in our experience, discovering Being as the quality of the unconditioned in all qualities. Yet to attach descriptive terms to this Being is illegitimate, for to do so is to regard as *existential* that which is essential. Religion must speak theonomously if it speaks, and to do so is to speak of the ineffable. It *must* speak, for without a Word there is no mediation of God to man.

Tillich's way out through this paradox is to regard man's phenomenological knowledge of God as symbolic. Such symbolism is not false, but it is inadequate. It becomes false when symbol is taken as literal truth. The one element in our knowledge of God which is literal fact, and not symbol, is God's character as the Unconditioned.

Accordingly, Tillich distinguishes between what he calls the *ontic* and the *ontological* concept of God. The ontic definition of God is: "God is a reality exceeding the ordinary reality with respect to power and value, to which man has personal relationships according to the character of his God." The ontological definition makes God "the Unconditioned of being and of what ought to be, the foundation and the 'beyond' of all that is conditioned." Nearly the entire structure of modern theology, including the whole of nineteenth century liberal theism, is set in the ontic framework. As pointers toward the nature of God and as convenient aids to religious worship and service, the ontic pattern is not erroneous. But as a systematic philosophy of religion, it falls into the error of making symbolism into literal truth, and therefore it obscures the truth. All attempts to answer the unanswerable problems of a philosophy of religion (which in their course create theodicies which are blasphemous) root in this tendency to take the ontic interpretation as if it were ontological fact. As good poetry is poor science, so is good phenomenology poor ontology.

All attempts to prove God's existence by argument fall down from the fact that they proceed from ontic premises. God's existence needs no defense by argument if it is recognized that apart from the presence of Unconditioned Being in all particular being, there would be no existence at all, and therefore nothing for us either to experience or talk about. Questions about the attributes of God—with the corresponding answers which make him good, loving, wise, omnipotent, omniscient or eternal—are not irrelevant since they have to do with the symbols under which man must frame his picture of God, But to suppose that these attributes give an adequate representation of God is to mistake picture for reality. The alternative is, with the mystic, to grasp by intuitive awareness the unconditioned Reality of God, and then—as cautiously as we can—attempt to state in philosophical language that which in its ultimate nature is ineffable.

All our knowledge of God is in symbols. But this is not to say that all our knowledge is unreliable. A sign can be changed and something else substituted: a symbol cannot. The symbols of Hebrew-Christian faith—particularly those symbols which relate to creation, wrath and salvation—are indispensable symbols. God is the Creator, Judge and Redeemer of men, though it is no super-person who creates, judges and redeems, but the ultimate ground of being.

Of all the symbols through which we have knowledge of God though imperfectly, that by which we know him most perfectly is Christ. Christ is the center of history for he is the perfect ontic symbol, the "fullness of the Godhead." The Holy Spirit is the dynamic life principle, the *Geist* of God moving throughout history. Without the Trinity there is no understanding of the manifestation of the Unconditioned within the conditioned, of the Word which was made flesh, the light which shone in darkness.

III

It is difficult for the American mind to envisage what Tillich means by the abyss. It almost inevitably connotes—if not hell—at least a yawning chasm from which one must keep a safe distance. But to fear the abyss is wasted energy, for we are already in it! The abyss is the inexhaustible basis of all being, whether good or evil. The term comes from Jacob Böhme, whom Tillich follows in his mysticism. Sometimes he uses "depth" for the divine inexhaustibility and "abyss" for the possibility of the demonic. But it is an essential element in Tillich's position that good and evil have a common root. Hence, the term abyss applies to both good and evil to connote the bottomless base from which all that exists comes into being.

One of the most suggestive essays in *The Interpretation of History* is that which deals with the demonic. This word is not a new one in American diction, for it has been popularized by Reinhold Niebuhr and is used uncritically by many. It denotes the antithesis of the divine, but also—contrary to popular usage—the antithesis of the satanic. In Tillich's terminology, the divine is the positive creative ground of existence which imparts meaning to life; the satanic is the negative, destructive principle inimical to all meaning. The satanic has a conceptual but not a metaphysical existence, for there is never complete negation of meaning. The demonic is the eternal tension between the form-creating and form-destroying elements of existence. Its metaphysical roots are in the divine, since God is the unconditioned ground of all being. Yet the demonic elements in life are those which move toward the disintegration of meaning rather than toward its creation. (It is necessary to speak of *meaning* rather than of *value*, for Tillich rejects the entire value-philosophy as setting up too sharp an antithesis between value and reality.) The rootage of the demonic in the divine means, phenomenologically, that there is never a clear cleavage to be drawn between them, and metaphysically, that God must have a "dark nature" within him, an aspect of the divine being which the Hebrew prophets grasped when they spoke of a God of wrath.

Illustrations of the demonic are manifold. In primitive art there is ugliness in the distorted representation of the organs of sex and the organs of the will to power (hands, feet, teeth and eyes), yet behind these distortions magnificent vitality is manifest. What is thus portrayed in art is found in life in its entire range. Throughout history one finds holy demonries—the interplay of divine and satanic elements in the religious sanctification of the sex impulse, of acquisitiveness, of the craving for prestige and the will to power. The Christian church as an institution is no exception to this mixing of good with evil under guise of sanctity. Such holy demonries, like Kronus eating his own children, create and at the same time destroy. Viewed in this setting, the stories of demoniac possession in the Gospels become more than a first century fancy—for the demons which wrecked life could nevertheless recognize Christ as the Son of God.

In current society, capitalism and nationalism, the acts of nazi Germany or of Japanese military aggression, might be cited as instances of the demonic. Were they wholly satanic they could not exist, for they make their way by virtue of the fact that they are conserving real values of physical existence or national culture in one group at the expense of the corresponding values in another, exalting within the dominant group a Nietzschean set of values at the expense of the Christian. Demonries never wholly destroy and crush; the insidiousness of their power lies in the fact that at the same time they nourish and destroy, create and crush. Demonry, which is "the form-destroying eruption of the creative basis of things," is clearly more dangerous than a hypothetically satanic eruption would be, for the latter is prevented by its inherent self-destructiveness from coming into being. To cite an illustration for which I do not claim Professor Tillich's authority, the Hitler who considers himself the God-given savior of Germany and Austria, precisely because he is in some respects such a savior is a greater menace than the devil at which Martin Luther is reputed to have thrown the ink-bottle.

It is evident that this theory of the demonic has important historical and ethical implications. It substantiates Reinhold Niebuhr's thesis (constantly reiterated but seldom understood) that sin is so permeating a characteristic of human life that even the most religious person is never wholly free from it, that sin appears in its most insidious form when man cloaks his arrogance and self-will in religious robes and tries to make himself God. But what bearing has the presence of the demonic on the nature of God?

Professor Tillich has not, so far as I know, very clearly answered this question in any of his writings. He does not evade the issue that if God is the unconditioned ground of all being, he is the ground of the demonic. "Form of being and inexhaustibility of being belong together. Their unity in the depth of essential nature is the divine, their separation in existence, the relatively independent eruption of the 'abyss' in things, is the demonic. . . . In the demonic . . . the divine, the unity of bottom and abyss, of form and consumption of form, is still contained." How there can be within the divine a "relatively independent eruption of the abyss" is a crucial point which is not clear to me.

It is, however, clear that Professor Tillich rejects outright the ordinary theodicies which start from ontic presuppositions. Assuming that God is a personal being who wills the good, one is forced into one of three alternatives: (1) to deny the existence of evil, (2) to hold that either by a general providence or by many special providences, God wills the existence of evil that a greater good may come of it, or (3) to make God limited in power, placing some of the world's evil outside of his control. The first is the procedure of Christian Science and some forms of personalistic pantheism, the second of ordinary liberal theism, and the third of the proponents of a finite God. Tillich breaks with all three.

From the ontological standpoint Tillich believes that the dilemma of God's omnipotence and goodness may be avoided, for omnipotence and goodness are themselves only ontic symbols rather than descriptions of the real nature of God. Omnipotence is not a metaphysical attribute of God; it is a name for the empirical fact that in religious experience man's "embarrassment of acting" is paradoxically overcome. God is not good, as another existential being might be considered to be good or evil; rather, God is the Good. Providence is not a matter of miracle or invention in man's behalf; it is a name for the fact that through religious commitment to divine grace one finds *Trotz*—a faith which can be fulfilled "in spite of" anything. Since in Christ the Unconditioned and concrete ontic reality are joined, there is in Christ not only a revelation of the depths of God's nature but also a saving power by which to overcome the abyss of evil.

IV

Professor Brightman's concept of the Given may profitably be compared with this doctrine of the abyss; for it places the source of evil within the divine as Tillich does, but with important differences. The classic statement of its meaning is in *The Problem of God*: "There is in God's very nature something which makes the effort and pain of life necessary. There is within him, in addition to his reason and his active creative will, a passive element which enters into every one of his conscious states, as sensation, instinct and impulse enter into ours, and constitutes a problem for him. This element we call the Given. The evils of life and the delays in the attainment of value, in so far as they come from God and not from human freedom, are thus due to his nature, yet not wholly to his deliberate choice. His will and reason acting on the Given produce the world and achieve value in it."

A more exact definition of God is found in *Personality and Religion*: "God is an eternal conscious personal Spirit, infinite in duration, self-existent, limited only by the eternal reason and content of his own personality and, of course, by such conditions as he voluntarily imposes upon himself."

Both Brightman and Tillich recognize the presence of evil in the world as a destructive force which must be acknowledged, its reality being neither denied nor explained away. In this sense both are religious realists. Both repudiate dualism, finding the roots of evil in God and not in Satan or a self-existent physical universe. Both have a religious world view, or to use Tillich's phrase a "theonomous metaphysics." Both men preach and practice the Christian religion—not simply religion in general.

Yet two may walk together without having agreed! Brightman's view is set squarely in the *ontic* rather than the *ontological* framework. The descriptive adjectives he applies to God, "eternal," "conscious," "personal," "infinite in duration," "limited," are attributes which in Tillich's view cannot be taken as literal descriptions. ("Self-existent" I take to be practically synonymous with "unconditioned.") Professor Brightman denies the distinction between the ontic and the ontological, and therefore claims for these predicates the status of ontological applicability. His God is not only personal, but a *Person*. This to Tillich is to make God a being among other beings, and thus to blaspheme him. To argue from what man *is* to what God *must be* is to overlook the basic fact that the Unconditioned cannot be reached through the categories of the conditioned. As well might one attempt to explain human personality in terms of the structure of the physical organism and its behavior, as to attempt to explain the nature of God in terms of human personality.

A further difference appears in the use made of Hebrew-Christian tradition. Personalism, like the rest of liberal theism when its eyes are open, is too astute to consider such terms as "King," "Judge" and "Father," to be literal descriptions of God. It takes them, however, as symbolic descriptions of a literal person, a God whose actual character is described through them. Tillich regards these terms as necessary, but necessarily inadequate, symbols for what cannot be described. This does not mean that he disregards the biblical foundations of Christian thought; for his philosophy of history is derived mainly from the prophets and, as was noted earlier, he regards Christ as the center of history, the only true meeting-point of the ontic and the ontological.

Tillich's theory of physical nature is dynamic, as the personalistic theory is, but in such a different way that there is scarcely any meeting-ground for comparison. To personalism nature is the eternal activity of God, and therefore its reality consists in its being an aspect of the conscious experience of God. In Tillich's thought, nature is interpreted through the categories of history. These are freedom and fate, paradoxically interrelated. Creation to Tillich is not a matter of God's making something. The ontic approach, he believes, prompts us to ask such unanswerable question[s] as: What was time before time began? Did God create *ex nihilo*? Why did God make this kind of world if he could have made a better one? Yet creation, like providence, may be understood in terms of man's experience. In our strangeness we find a paradoxical unity beyond our world, in our loneliness a paradoxical community, in our uncertainty a paradoxical meaning, in our frustration a paradoxical power to act. This is not to analyze, it is to discover, the God in whom we live.

A final point of difference between Tillich's and Brightman's thought is epistemological, and is therefore primary from the standpoint of method. One cannot linger long in the atmosphere of Union Seminary without hearing much of "paradoxes," "dialectics," and "tensions." While Reinhold Niebuhr is the efficient cause of much of this diction, Tillich is its unmoved mover. At Boston University the keyword to truth is "coherence." Paradox and coherence make strange bedfellows. Eventually they nudge each other out into the cold, for each claims the bed by right of prior possession.

V

My own thought has so long followed an ontic pattern that I cannot readily get a *pou sto* from which to evaluate Tillich's position. I shall attempt, however, to suggest a few points in which I find myself drawn toward or away from his position.

I agree with Tillich in refusing to call God a person. To say that God is *personal* does not seem to me to be blasphemous, to speak of him as *a person* does. When I analyze this distinction, I find its roots in the difference between symbolic and literal truth. To say that God is personal means that we have a partial and fragmentary knowledge of his nature through the categories of human personality. It is to admit that we "see through a glass darkly," though as far as we can see he is like personality. To call him a person is to make a literal statement. If he is a person as we are persons, he is not God. If he is not, why call him a person? The term involves either incoherence or presumption.

On the other hand, I am equally dissatisfied with Tillich's term, the Unconditioned, and with the "cloud of unknowing" which seems to me to surround it. It is too quality-less, and does not even have the affirmative values of the *ens perfectissimum* of the ontological argument. Though we have a useful set of symbols, if God himself does not possess literal attributes which are knowable, how can we know that these symbols are not the construct of our human imaginings, and therefore not simply inadequate but false?

This problem becomes particularly acute with reference to biblical symbolism, since Christian faith is built upon it. It is no refutation of Tillich's position to say that the prophets and Jesus did not call God "the Unconditioned," for they spoke the language of religious experience and not of philosophical analysis. But the crucial question is whether they intended by their symbolism to convey literal truth about the nature of God. I cannot escape the conclusion that they did. Otherwise they would have had no reason to speak. To call God "Creator of the ends of the earth" or "our Father" is meaningless unless God is what creation and fatherhood symbolize. It appears to me illegitimate for Tillich to erect a philosophy of history on prophetism unless the prophetic concept of God is in essential aspects a true concept, as it seems also illegitimate to make Christ the center of history unless we have sufficient factual knowledge about the historical Jesus to assure us of the fitness of ascribing to Christ this centrality.

Not only in regard to God, but man's approach to God, I find myself both attracted and disturbed by Tillich's view. It is not philosophical speculation but the mystic's vision and the claims of practical religious experience which are our primary avenues to God. To discuss theology apart from Christology is, if not futile, at least inadequate. A recognition of the validity of myth, not as fiction, but as symbolism for supra-rational truth, is indispensable. Paradox has its place. Yet its place is easily abused, and when it is invoked to curtail the quest for reasoned answers to our eternal—albeit pedestrian—problems, I suspect it.

My metaphysical position, stated in *The Recovery of Ideals*, is shamelessly ontic. It is monistic in its foundations and fruition, dualistic in a qualified though not ultimate sense in its theory of God's relation to the world. With the personalists I regard nature as the eternal activity of God. But I do not equate it with an aspect of God's consciousness. Both human and physical nature are the product of God's creative will, and in both there is an interweaving of what Tillich calls freedom and fate, though to escape panpsychism I prefer to use the terms spontaneity and order for physical nature. God wills the existence of nature, but not all the juxtapositions of circumstance which arise within the given, uncreated structure of possibilities. God is limited, therefore, both by human wills and the element of chance which emerges within nature and history. There are some circumstances which God cannot prevent, but there are none which cannot be transcended through God's limitless power to enable men to triumph over tragedy.

The theory thus briefly outlined comes out just where Tillich's and Brightman's do—in man's capacity to draw upon the inexhaustible resources of God for personal mastery over the demonic forces which assail him. Whether evil is regarded as emerging from the abyss of the Unconditioned, from the Given within the divine Person, or from recalcitrant factors within a world created by a God whom we symbolize under the guise of personality, the road to its mastery is through the assurance that "He hath made us, and not we ourselves." Any attempt at solution which faces toward the emptiness of cynicism or the presumption of human self-confidence is defeated by life's evidences. Any truly theonomous world view, whether it makes its way by the incisive but sometimes deceptive route of logical coherence or by the more subtle route of paradox, reveals to the searching spirit the inexhaustible depths and the dependable basis of our being.

READING 12

I

That nature is in some sense instrumental to grace has been implicit in the main stream of both Catholic and Protestant thought. If God did not take the initiative, there would be no grace. But if God works through nature and if man through nature lays hold upon grace, there is no radical cleavage between the

From "Nature as the Vehicle of Grace," *Religion in Life* 9 (Winter 1940): 503–12.

two realms. In evangelical terms the issue is, "What must I do to be saved?" The correlate in religious education is how nurture (that is, growth through a right use of nature) may contribute effectively to the Christian life.

The difficulties latent in the problem have been obscured by ambiguity in the term *nature*. Traditional Christian thought has taken the natural to mean sometimes the opposite of the spiritual, sometimes the opposite of the super-natural—and usually both. For philosophy, science and common sense, nature has generally meant physical nature—that which exists but is not mind or spirit. For theology it has not only meant physical nature, but this world in contrast with an ultimate and eternal world. As a result the spiritual and the supernatural have been unconsciously identified. This telescoping of terms was made possible by the fact that God was conceived as a supernatural Spirit and man, made in the divine image, as a spiritual entity higher than nature.

As long as nature is regarded as other than but nevertheless instrumental to spirit and to supernature, the problem of nature as the vehicle of grace is the question of *how* nature (in either sense) can serve the interests of the higher spiritual life. The question of *whether* it can do so need not be raised. However, two approaches now widely current have shifted the basis of procedure, and by doing so have denied that nature is the vehicle of grace.

One of these is the identification of man with nature in a naturalistic monism by which nature is made to mean all there is, man being subsumed within it. This is the route followed by Dewey, Whitehead, Sellars, Boodin, and most of the contemporary naturalists. Such a view is not necessarily antagonistic to spiritual values, and as is evident in the religious naturalism of Wieman, it makes large place for more-than-human cosmic processes which may be both contem-plated and worshiped as God. But it has no place for the supernatural, and there-fore, since grace is conceived as a supernatural intervention in natural processes, no place for grace.

Religious naturalism gets rid of the problem of the relation of nature to super-nature by emphasizing the inseparability of nature and spirit. If man is wholly a part of nature he ought to be a better part of it, but he need have no aspira-tion to be anything more. The exponents of this view (who quite significantly are philosophers, educators, and social scientists rather than theologians) tend graciously to anathematize the theologians for talking about grace. For them the road ahead lies through more knowledge (particularly more scientific knowl-edge), a more thorough-going application of the knowledge we have, a more sensitive imagination, a more consistent and determined attempt to make the right adjustment to social forces. It is an enterprise on which all men of good will can agree, and to the extent to which both agreement and action are achieved, community is enlarged and its values enriched. Such a spiritualized naturalism which is more or less religious, ranging from atheism through humanism to a profound religious mysticism, is the substructure of political and social liberal-ism in America. To its acceptance John Dewey has contributed more than any other individual, and he epitomizes its social significance.

The second approach by which nature ceases to be the vehicle of grace is that of the new orthodoxy. It cannot turn the tables by getting rid of nature as easily as religious naturalism does of grace, for the world is too much with us—both in its fleshly and mundane aspects. Yet the very fact of its hold upon us is the signal for a shift in the point of reference. We cannot save ourselves by a right use of nature. Our fallen state forbids. Though made in the *imago dei,* man's spiritual nature is no avenue to grace, for we bear this image no longer. We are saved only by the grace of a transcendent God through the mediatorial agency of Christ.

Though man is held to be impotent to lay hold upon the grace of God through nature, nature would still be the vehicle of grace if God, taking the initiative, were to make His created world an instrument of man's redemption. If I understand correctly the fundamental difference between Barth and Brunner at this point, it is that Barth will allow no place for general grace, any more than for general revelation, while Brunner affirms that there is *sustaining* but not *saving* grace within the state of nature. If this "sustaining grace" is really grace, then in Brunner's thought nature is its vehicle and creation is an instrument in redemption. Yet he seems to regard sustaining grace only as the regulation of society in the general direction of order and decency, and in no sense as a force efficacious for redemption. If this is all, it is difficult to see why the same result could not be achieved on naturalistic presuppositions, or why it should be called *grace.* John Baillie justly criticizes Brunner's position when he writes, "We gain nothing by admitting the operation of the grace of God in the wider sphere if we then go on to deny that this grace is in any least degree a saving grace. We gain nothing by admitting a continuity between nature and grace if in the next moment we deny all continuity between the grace that saves and the grace that only sustains . . . for, as Doctor Barth says, there is nothing gracious about a grace that sustains with no intent to save."[7]

Thus it turns out that from whichever extreme of contemporary theology we start, nature ceases to be the vehicle of grace. Religious naturalism gets rid of the problem by making nature everything and eliminating grace; the new orthodoxy admits the fact of both nature and grace but denies to nature any efficacy in the attainment of saving grace. If the question as to how nature is the vehicle of grace is a live issue, there must be another route to take. Before attempting to pursue it, it is necessary to define our terms more precisely.

II

Nature is the sum of that reality, physical and mental, individual and social, human and subhuman, which falls within the range of man's objective and verifiable experience. It is not the whole of reality, for values and ideals, past memories and future possibilities, are also real. God is real, and while God is in nature, God is neither the whole of nature, a part of nature, nor a process of nature.

Contemporary naturalism has rendered both philosophy and religion a great service in contending that no clear-cut line can be drawn between the physical and the mental aspects of nature. We are not half body and half mind, but one personality; the world is not half mind and half matter, but one universe. Similarly, the sciences of biology, psychology and sociology have presented data which makes clear the interrelatedness of the individual and the social aspects of personality, and of the interplay of conscious with unconscious forces in both biological and social evolution. These facts of organic relation may be taken as established, though the metaphysical deductions to be drawn from them are, and will remain, in much dispute.

While naturalism is right in placing man within nature, certain assumptions made on this basis, not by all but by many naturalists, are unwarranted. The most important of these are: (1) that *all* nature is amenable to description in terms of categories applicable to physical nature (materialism), (2) that consciousness is reducible to observable bodily behavior (behaviorism), (3) that human choices and human conduct are mechanically, or at least unalterably, determined (determinism), (4) that values are a mere matter of individual preference or at most of social determinism (relativism), (5) that the universe has no cosmic source, goal, or significance (atheism, humanism). These meet in the denial of the uniqueness and distinctive character of personality. If man is only an element in nature, of no more value, significance or capacity than any other part except insofar as he has a somewhat more complex nervous system, then all five of the above assumptions follow. If consistently and generally accepted, such a view would cut the roots from under, not only religion, but every kind of endeavor requiring moral responsibility. But if man is *in* nature yet *more than* nature, as his power to understand, appreciate, criticize and control nature indicates, then the first four of the five assumptions noted above become indefensible.

What of the fifth? Religious naturalism of the Wieman type does not ally itself with materialism, or behaviorism, or mechanistic determinism or a subjective relativism. It attempts to undergird theism by affirming that values are over-individual and cosmic, and that in their progressive integration and mutual support, God is at work. Is the attempt successful?

In my judgment the result is unsatisfactory, and for the same reason that a naturalism which denies the uniqueness of human personality is unsatisfactory with regard to man. If man is simply an element in nature along with other elements he cannot exercise any determinative control; if God is simply a process in nature, even a high and valuable process, He cannot be the source and goal of values—much less the object worthy of supreme loyalty and devotion. Man has to be a person before he can assume his rightful place in nature; God must be personal, else He cannot be the ground of either cosmic order or cosmic values. Professor Wieman, if I understand him correctly, is willing to wrest man from the toils of naturalism, but not God. As I read him, he seems always to be claiming for his type of theism the values of a personal God without being willing to affirm personality in God.

If either through the channel of the historic Christian tradition or of idealistic philosophy, God is thought to be a Personal Being supreme in wisdom, power, and love, the problem takes on a different aspect. We do not need to attach to God all the attributes of human limitation to conceive Him in personal terms, and any analogies drawn from human experience must be used with caution lest

He cease to be the Most High. Yet the relation of God to the world as creator and sustainer of all nature, and as judge and redeemer of that part of nature which is man, is meaningless apart from divine personality. Before nature can be the vehicle of grace, both nature and grace must proceed from the Living God.

But what of grace? While no single meaning can be attached to it, it is a much simpler term than nature. The reason is that everybody talks about nature, while only those who believe in grace (or are irritated by it) take the trouble to use the word.

Grace is the free, loving, personal activity of God for the salvation of undeserving men. All of the adjectives and most of the nouns in this statement require elaboration.

"Free as the grace of God" is a phrase which has survived the encroachments of secularism to appear occasionally even in the diction of the nonreligious. Free of what? The theological systems most concerned to stress the divine initiative tend to decry works as a means of grace, and therefore to give the impression that it is free of human effort. Yet faith and repentance are its preconditions, and these are not passive states. If Paul in rejecting the efficacy of works had meant to identify saving faith with moral passivity, the pastoral exhortations with which his letters abound would be pointless. Grace is not without cost; yet it is free, for God imparts it graciously, spontaneously, naturally, without coercion or constraint.

To say that grace is imparted *in love* is to affirm the basic insights of New Testament Christianity as epitomized in John 3:16, and to reject all propitiation, substitution and governmental theories of the atonement. It connotes the willingness, even the yearning eagerness, of God to forgive the sinner and empower the weak. And grace can be neither free nor loving unless it is *personal.* In a Person-to-person relation only are the conditions fulfilled by which it can be wrought. To say that it is the *activity* of God is to emphasize the dynamic character of the total relationship between God and man, not only in redemption but in creation and providence. To say that men do not deserve it is both to emphasize the divine initiative and to affirm what any sensitive soul must admit upon introspection if he is honest with himself.

The most difficult and most crucial term in the definition is *salvation.* From what, to what, and by what are men saved? From sin, or from finiteness, or both? And if from both, from both together or by a different process for each? To moral victory, to emotional exaltation, or to new insights? To blessedness in this life only or in the next? By a common course for all men? Or was Francis Thompson right when he wrote:

> "There is no expeditious road,
> To pack and label men for God,
> And save them by the barrel-load"?

Upon the answers given to these questions hang most of the problems of theology and of religious experience. The more inclusive the answers, the more likely to be true—up to the point where inclusiveness runs into generality. To be converted means in psychological terms to get a new center of loyalty and devotion, a revaluation of values in which the former self-regarding interests are subordinated, an enhancement of sensitivity of imagination and of power for action in the light of ends projected as the will of God. In theological terms this means that the curse both of sin and finitude is lifted, and man becomes a new creature.

That such regeneration (or at least such change) takes place, and that by it the course of individual lives and of history is altered, is an objective fact. We must ask now whether nature is the instrument by which it occurs and if so, in what manner.

III

The most obvious and perhaps the most important aspect of the question is the relation of creation to redemption. Is the very fact that there is a world, with human selves a part of it, an evidence of divine grace? The answer hinges upon the meaning of grace. I see no good reason to reject the view that creation is the free, loving, personal activity of God. In spite of the complexities of the problem of evil, both the order in nature and the values in human social experience reinforce the affirmations of Hebrew-Christian faith. Not only God, but man, may look upon creation and call it good.

Yet grace is more than free loving personal activity on the part of God. It requires also in some sense man's *salvation*. At this point any attempt to identify creation with redemption breaks down. All men, however miserable, enjoy by virtue of existence more or less of the sustaining power of nature. Our lives are set in a physical, biological, social framework from which the only escape is death, and our reluctance to die gives illogical evidence that this order of nature makes a claim upon us. But if this sustaining power of nature is to be called "sustaining grace," the term grace loses any distinctive meaning. If *to be* is to be saved, then all living creatures are more or less saved, and there is no point in talking about being saved by grace.

The elimination of grace from the vocabulary of religious naturalism is thoroughly consistent with its presuppositions. Less consistently, some other theists try to retain grace (or some equivalent in terms of salvation through growth) and do so on the basis of the identification of God with the curative processes of nature. It will not work. Natural theology will carry us to the point of affirming a God of sustaining care who manifests His goodness in "our creation, preservation and all the blessings of life." But it will not take us to a God of grace.

Reacting from liberalism's tendency to identify the work of an immanent God with natural processes, exponents of the neo-Reformation theology go to the opposite extreme and talk as if nature had nothing to do with salvation. *Development* is anathema, as savoring of human presumption. Christian education is not growth in Christian personality through a right use of nature: it is apprehension of and witness to the revelation of God in Christ. At the Oxford

Conference, difference of opinion on this point was so sharp that the work of the Education section was nearly wrecked by it, and compromise was reached only by stating in the report two alternative views. It would be hard to find a more thoroughgoing denial of the efficacy of nature in the work of Christian education than is implied in the statement, "Her (the Church's) real concern is with regeneration, which can never come about as the result of a process of development but is an act of God."[8] Taken seriously, such a separation of nature from grace undercuts any effort for the amelioration of those physical and social aspects of nature in which men must find their life, and therefore their salvation. It limits the function of the Christian as God's agent in salvation to witness-bearing—and if held to consistently not even this would be in order, for to bear witness requires communication through a physical body.

As in most matters, the truer view lies not in either extreme but in a mediating position which makes room for the truth in each. The problem centers in the nature of God. If God is wholly transcendent, He will either refuse to vouchsafe His grace to men through nature, or will use nature only by a *tour de force* or intervention in which a miracle occurs. Salvation is then limited to the saving work of Christ, and there is no salvation in any degree or manner except through the Christian channel. If God is wholly immanent, either there is no grace, or so general a grace that anybody of sympathetic imagination and some knowledge of natural processes can appropriate it. Evangelism is then repudiated as a form of religious hysteria, and religious education becomes character development with little to distinguish it from the work of the public schools.

If God is a Personal Being, both immanent and transcendent, the creator and sustainer, the judge and redeemer of men, neither of these extremes can follow. As nature is the vehicle of revelation, but only as there is a subjective apprehension of what is objectively revealed, so nature is the vehicle of grace to those who will lay hold upon it, *and not to others.*

The graciousness of nature is instrumental, not intrinsic, to salvation by the grace of God. It requires to be joined with "saving faith" in the God made manifest in Christ before it will have its fullest power. Though the Christian revelation is not the only avenue to grace, without it men are inclined to view nature merely as the sphere of a general beneficence splotched with evil. When nature is seen from the Christian standpoint, it takes on a new character. John Masefield has given a classic description of this experience in "The Everlasting Mercy," where he represents Saul Kane as saying,

> "O glory of the lighted mind!
> How dead I'd been, how dumb, how blind!
> The station brook, to my new eyes,
> Was babbling out of Paradise,
> The waters rushing from the rain
> Were singing Christ has risen again. . . .
> The lights in huntsman's upper story
> Were parts of an eternal glory."

Not only the physical universe with its order and beauty, but the social process with its communication from the past and community in the present, becomes the carrier of God's gracious and saving power. The problem of evil, though never solved, is redeemed by the assurance that nothing can pluck us out of the Father's hand. The intimations of theistic philosophy then become, not substitutes for or foes of Christian faith, but its reinforcement and ally.

The question of the relation of "saving" to "sustaining" grace is on this basis largely one of temporal continuity. No person can retain without diminution the fervor of religious feeling, or the light of religious illumination, which comes at high moments. For most Christians the greater part of life is spent on the plains, not on mountaintops. The continuous nourishing of the religious life through worship and the many "means of grace" is necessary, and the consequent awareness of being sustained by God may be termed "sustaining grace." The true evangelical theology is not "'Tis done! the great transaction's done!" but rather "Moment by moment I'm kept in His love." This is something quite different from saying that without conscious effort or response on man's part, God imparts sustaining grace by way of nature.

By such an approach, Christian education can be both Christian and educative, as it tends not to be in either contemporary naturalism or supernaturalism. Religious naturalism makes ample room for education, and for some important aspects of religious education, but in its stress upon growth of meaning and value it fails to make clear to what or by what in historic Christianity the developing organism is to grow. Religious supernaturalism makes focal the act of regeneration by the grace of God but undercuts the educative process. Fortunately we do not need to choose either alternative.

At several crucial points the procedures of religious education will be altered if it decides to take grace seriously without excluding nature. The first of these is the Bible. Apart from the Bible we should know something of the revelation of God in nature, but we should know nothing of the *grace* of God—of a living, loving, saving deity who in justice and mercy condemns yet forgives His erring children. From present trends we may anticipate a return to the Bible as the center of the church-school curriculum in the next few years. A second is recovery of a sense of sin—a term which has so far got lost in contemporary education that many children grow up without having any connotation to attach to the word. A third is the reality and the importance of conversion—not as a substitute for Christian nurture but as an element in it. The experience may be called commitment or decision or religious awakening rather than conversion, but it cannot be omitted if the Christian is to make the personal appropriation of divine grace which is a vital aspect of its reality. A fourth is clarification of the missions of the Church as the carrier of the Christian gospel, and therefore of the gospel of grace, as mediated through the Christian community.

That nature is the vehicle of the saving and sustaining grace of a God both immanent and transcendent, a Personal Being acting freely in love of undeserving men who must personally appropriate His gift, is the primary tenet of evangelical liberalism. It is not a new concept. But the fact that it is not new is no sign that it is not true! It is closer to the truth than any alternative segment of contemporary thought, and an important field now groping in the dark for a theology might profitably explore its implications.

READING 13

I

This is by all odds the best book Reinhold Niebuhr has written. Though it may not have the popular value of *Moral Man and Immoral Society* in puncturing the illusions which Niebuhr so loves to deflate, it will last longer.

There are various reasons. The obvious reason is that it is the most scholarly of the author's publications, as one of a series in the Gifford Lectures might well be expected to be. It represents the fruits, not only of Dr. Niebuhr's entire structure of thought, but in particular of a decade of theological thinking along a line in which he is the recognized pioneer in America. Though many readers of CHRISTENDOM differ radically from him, few of us have failed to be influenced by him. The most distinguishing feature of this book is that its statements are clear and its mood is not polemic. The comment overheard after a college chapel address by Dr. Niebuhr, "I didn't understand him but he made me mad!" reflects, I suspect, the reaction of more than one of his more mature contemporaries. To read this book is to discover that Niebuhr can write without damning the pacifists, and in a vein which, though critical of liberalism, is for the most part constructive in its approach to the basic issues of Christian faith.

In stating the problem in the first chapter Dr. Niebuhr says, "All modern views of human nature are adaptations, transformations and varying compounds of primarily two distinctive views of man: (a) the view of classical antiquity, that is of the Graeco-Roman world, and (b) the Biblical view" (p. 5). After calling attention to the medieval synthesis of these views and its destruction in the Renaissance and Reformation, he says, "Liberal Protestantism is an effort (on the whole an abortive one) to reunite these two elements." Niebuhr's own thesis is, of course, that the only true basis for a Christian doctrine of man is the Biblical view.

This putting of the problem lays the foundation both for the strength and weakness of the entire argument. Niebuhr rightly emphasizes the importance of a Biblical approach to Christian faith and of the dimension of depth which has too much been omitted from both classic and modern liberal thought. But in so doing he makes, in my judgment, some serious errors in emphasis and therefore distorts an otherwise rich body of truth.

"A Symposium on Reinhold Niebuhr's *Nature and Destiny of Man*," *Christendom* 6 (Fall 1941): 567–70.

It is true that in attempting to synthesize Hellenic and Hebraic thought, liberalism has tipped the scales toward the former. This accounts at least in part for its characteristic optimism with the general omission, as Niebuhr points out, of the note of melancholy found in Greek tragedy. It has come to terms not only with science but with the whole rationalistic mood of the modern world, and thus in some of its expressions has moved a long way toward secularism. It has not banished God outright. But in putting the emphasis on God's immanence in the natural order and on man's discovery of God in his works (rather than on God's self-disclosure), it has diverted attention from the transcendent holiness of the Creator to the divinity that resides in every man. Tacitly adopting the Greek dictum that "knowledge is virtue" and not reckoning adequately with the power of human sin, it has thought to correct the evils of society by social intelligence and determined good will. Along this road lies an arrogance regarding man's powers which, according to the Biblical view, is the root of sin. "Pride goeth before destruction," and in the present chaos we are reaping the fruits of our self-esteem.

While I agree with Dr. Niebuhr in much of his criticism, I believe that his interpretation goes astray at two crucial points. One of these is in an over-identification of religious liberalism with the secularistic liberalism of bourgeois culture. The liberalism (or better, the modernism) of the 1920–30 decade was much more shallow, far more Hellenic and less Biblical, than the chastened liberalism of the present. But it never, to any great extent, took over, as secular liberalism did, the presuppositions of naturalistic metaphysics. Drawing its moral authority from Jesus and its spiritual vision from the revelation of God in Christ, it could not do so. Much of what Niebuhr says was more true of Columbia University than of Union Seminary in the days when liberalism was the dominant mood at Union. In fact, I doubt whether Niebuhr himself as a former liberal leader ever cherished the utopianism regarding man's powers that he now so readily assigns to those holding the liberal position.

A more basic error lies in an almost complete identification of the term *Biblical* with *Hebraic-Pauline*. In the index of Scripture passages which the author has obligingly furnished the reader, there are forty-five citations of passages in the Old Testament, forty-two from the writings of Paul, and only twelve from the Synoptic gospels. In the index of proper names, references to Paul and Augustine far exceed all others, with Luther, Nietzsche, Kierkegaard and Calvin (in the order named) receiving numerous citations. It would, of course, be a mistake to conclude too much about a man's theology by the simple mathematics of enumeration! But the presuppositions of every page, though characterized as Biblical, are the presuppositions of the Hebrew prophets, Genesis, Job and Paul, and only to a slight degree those of the records of the life and words of Jesus. Jesus is mentioned but a few times, and for the most part incidentally. The story of the rich young ruler is cited as illustration of the error of modern liberal theology in holding that there is any essential difference between Jesus' view of human nature and Paul's (p. 288).

With due recognition of the fact that we do not have in the Synoptics a biography of Jesus, I question whether any doctrine of the nature and destiny of man may rightly be called "Biblical" which so largely leaves out of account that part of the Bible which gives the early Christians' recollection and interpretation of Jesus. In him they saw God; from him they learned the supreme worth and dignity of man; out of the impact of his life the Christian movement to serve men was born. In Jesus' view of man there was neither optimism nor pessimism—neither a naive confidence in human nature nor an inordinate emphasis on man's sinful state. There was, on the contrary, a realistic awareness of human limitation and a joyous confidence that any man could be "made whole" through the power of God if one would accept this gift in penitence, faith and love. Such a balanced view of man the Christian Church has maintained through the centuries with aberrations which have been internally corrected by a recurrent return to "the mind of Christ." In failing to give Jesus a more central place in his study, Niebuhr, like Kraemer in *The Christian Message in a Non-Christian World,* seems to me to have a Christology without Christ—that is, to present a structure of Christian soteriology without "the Word made flesh" in an historical figure whose life and words are still relevant to the human enterprise.

Because of these differences in standing-ground, I find implications for Christian democracy and Christian social action stemming from Jesus' view of man which differ at numerous points from the conclusions reached by Dr. Niebuhr. Nevertheless, I am profoundly indebted to this book and its author. The relations of Christian doctrine to current rationalism, romanticism and Marxism; the place of the individual in modern culture; the dual nature of man as *imago dei* and as sinner; the responsibility of man despite the inevitability of sin—these and many other themes are treated with incisiveness, originality and insight. The second volume of the lectures, dealing with "Human Destiny," will be eagerly awaited.

VII

The Faith of a World Church in a World Crisis (1938–40)

SECTION PREFACE

As Harkness's liberalism was remade in the 1930s, one of the key shaping factors was her participation in the ecumenical movement, particularly her attendance at four international ecumenical conferences between the summer of 1937 and the summer of 1939 in Oxford, Madras, Amsterdam, and Geneva. Readings 14–18 (as well as "Spiritual Pilgrimage," reading 1) were written during this period and bear the impact of her ecumenical experiences.

"The Faith of the North American Churches," reading 14, comes from a presentation that Harkness gave in June 1938 in Niagara Falls, New York. North American scholars and church leaders who would be going in December as delegates to the Madras conference had gathered for preliminary discussions. Madras was the first major ecumenical conference where delegates from the United States and Western Europe would not outnumber delegates from what were then called the "younger churches" (i.e., churches which had been established by missionary efforts in the previous generations.) As leaders from these "younger churches" had reflected on their indigenous theologies, American delegates were asking, in preparation for Madras, if there was a distinctively

119

North American theology. Harkness would later write that her self-appointed role in the Madras discussions was to keep the perspective of liberalism before the delegates and not allow the neo-orthodox perspective to go unchallenged.[1]

In preparation for Madras and for the Niagara meeting, North American delegates had surveyed church leaders trying to determine what were "the basic elements in the faith of the North American churches" and asking in particular what beliefs were essential to Christian faith. One of the delegates then developed a composite statement that Harkness thought was too conservative and did not accurately reflect the theology of North American churches or the data that had been gathered. In "The Faith of the North American Churches" Harkness offers a different interpretation of the data and lays out briefly her understanding of the North American theological context.[2]

Soon after returning from the ecumenical conference in Madras and writing in *The Christian Century* about the changes in her theology over the previous decade,[3] Harkness came back to this topic of what is essential for Christian theology—particularly an ecumenical Christian theology. She wrote reading 15, "The Theological Basis of the Missionary Message," for the *International Review of Missions,* a publication of the International Missionary Council, which was one of the predecessors of the World Council of Churches. Harkness, lamenting the fact that churches from the United States and Western Europe generally dominated the theological discussions at the major ecumenical conferences, stressed the need for church leaders outside Western Europe and the United States to help "bring fresh theologies to light." Insisting that the classical Christian creeds were not adequate for new contexts, Harkness argued that the key question was not what has been believed always, everywhere, and by everyone (*semper, ubique, ab omnibus*), but instead, what faith has helped to nourish Christians and their witness throughout Christian history. Harkness went on to lay out some basic "elements" that should be included in any ecumenical Christian theology.

Readings 16–18 come from *The Faith by Which the Church Lives*, a book drafted by Harkness in the fall of 1939, delivered in April 1940 as the Mendenhall Lectures at DePauw University, and published soon thereafter. Harkness sought to "state in outline, the basic and perennial, and therefore the living, convictions of the Christian Church."[4] As she was writing, Harkness moved to Evanston, Illinois, where she joined the faculty of Garrett Evangelical in January 1940. Having taught ethics and philosophy of religion to undergraduates for eighteen years, Harkness was now the professor of applied theology at one of the major seminaries of her Methodist denomination.

In the first reading, taken from the chapter "A World Church in a World Crisis," Harkness describes two forces that were shaping her theology and the life of the church. The first shaping influence was the ecumenical movement, particularly the worldwide conferences that she had attended in 1937–39. At Madras, Harkness helped to draft a statement from which the title of this book was taken—"The Faith by Which the Church Lives." Through these conferences, she had become much more intensely aware of the global nature of the church and of ecumenical efforts to find common theological and missional ground.

The second shaping force described in this reading is the international crisis that led to the outbreak of World War II as Harkness was writing this book. She seeks in *The Faith by Which the Church Lives* to "discover what God is saying through the events of our day."[5] And the events were momentous. In the spring of 1939, Germany had occupied Czechoslovakia, and in September when Harkness had begun working on this book, Germany invaded Poland; Britain and France subsequently declared war on Germany; the United States declared neutrality; and the Soviet Union invaded Poland and then, several months later, attacked Finland. In April 1940 when the lectures were delivered, Germany invaded Denmark and Norway and then, a few weeks following the lectures, annexed France, Belgium, Luxembourg, and the Netherlands. Throughout the fall of 1939 and early 1940, Hitler had continued to place greater restrictions on Jews, enacting curfews, outlawing the use of radios, forming ghettos, and so on. In April and May the Nazis began the deportation of gypsies and closed off the many Jews still in the Lodz Ghetto in Poland.[6]

When Harkness spoke to her audience at the Mendenhall lectures in April of 1940, this global crisis was at the forefront of people's minds. Harkness asked her audience, "What can we who are servants of the Church say to a stricken world?" The answer? "To announce to others without apology or arrogance, that the Christian Church, under God, is the greatest hope of a baffled and needy world. . . . The Christian Church has turned the world upside down to shake human nature from its lethargy, and in these troubled days it is holding the world together."[7] Christians could respond best to the world crisis by proclaiming "the faith by which the church lives." Writing a book on theology, then, was not a retreat from the world crisis but a timely response to it.

Harkness was also shaped by a third force, the ongoing theological debates among different theological camps (many of which were represented at the ecumenical conferences of Oxford, Madras, and Geneva). John Bennett wrote that Harkness had "assimilated . . . the impulses of recent theological trends and their criticisms of liberalism without completely shifting the center of her thought," and that in this book she gave "neither a patched-up form of liberalism nor a surrender to Catholicism or semi-Barthianism, but a fresh start in thinking that grows out of fresh experiences within the life of the Christian church."[8] This is exemplified in the three readings included here from *The Faith by Which the Church Lives*.

In reading 17, "By What Authority," Harkness, working from her awareness of these various theological positions, attempts to find a mediating position on religious authority that is more positive about the external authorities of Scripture and the church than her earlier writings had been[9] and yet is still solidly liberal in its bent. Harkness describes "five main sources of authority": "the Church, the Bible, the world of nature, the Holy Spirit, and the person of Jesus Christ." In addition to these five authorities, she uplifts an overarching authority—the mind of Christ—as a "guiding principle" that unites and directs the five other authorities. By the mind of Christ she means not only the model provided in the Jesus of history and his teachings, but also the Christ of faith dwelling in the heart of the person of faith. Harkness often writes about the mind of Christ as equivalent to the Holy Spirit.[10] In reading 17, as in reading 8, Harkness turns to the Wesleyan tradition of the spiritual and moral senses but takes things a step further than many Wesleyans. The overarching authority is not Scripture but the leading of the Spirit or the mind of Christ.

In reading 18, "Retrospect and Credo," Harkness lays out a brief credo that reflects her liberal heritage as well as her growing appreciation for the traditional language and teachings of the church.

READING 14

[In the previous paragraphs, Harkness had been reflecting on a survey, described in the preface to this section, in which North American church leaders were asked what theological claims were essential to Christian faith.]

. . . The most vital part of the report is that which has to do with distinctive and essential Christian beliefs. . . . [In] three primary issues the study reveals a latitude of judgment which I suspect would not be found in any comparable group of Christians outside of America. These are in regard to the deity of Christ, personal immortality, and the Church. . . . [T]wo-fifths of those who replied placed either the incarnation or the deity of Christ among non-definitive beliefs, one-third so listed personal immortality, and three-fifths the Church. This does *not* mean that in this proportion they personally reject these elements of Christian faith. It does mean that a considerable proportion of American Christians, though they personally believe in the unique divinity of Christ as an essential Christian concept, are not willing to brand as unchristian a Unitarian who thinks differently. Similarly, personal immortality is more widely believed in than held to be a *sine qua non* of discipleship. The Church as an institution possessing divine authority obviously has no such hold upon American as upon European Christianity. The tendency is to regard it, not as the Body of Christ or an extension of the incarnation, but as an essential but nevertheless fallible medium of worship, instruction and fellowship.

From an examination of the data presented by this study certain questions emerge. . . .

1. *What shall we regard as more and less essential?* It is imperative that degrees of essentiality be recognized. Christian belief is not on a "dead level" nor is it all on an equally high level. If we do not recognize this fact, we shall go on falling into one or the other of two undesirable extremes: (1) exclusion from Christian

From "The Faith of the North American Churches," typewritten manuscript of lecture, Niagara Falls, New York, American delegates of the Madras Conference on June 16, 1938, Georgia Harkness Collection, United Library, Garrett Evangelical Theological Seminary.

fellowship on doctrinal grounds, or (2) a spineless tolerance which lacks incisiveness through failure to believe anything in particular. The first has been the besetting sin of the fundamentalists, the second of the liberals. Neither extreme is Christian.

2. *Is there, or can there be, an American theology?* No section of Christendom has so variable a theological climate as ours. Have we anything distinctive—any unity in diversity?

American Christianity, viewed in cross-section, falls into five major groups. At the extreme left is the humanistic wing of Unitarianism. It tapers off into a humanism which is secularlistic rather than Christian; yet there is a brand of the Church here which, though small in number and influence, is indubitably a part of American Christianity.

To the right of this group is the religious naturalism of the Wieman school. It is not widely espoused by either the clergy or laity of the churches, though as a "gadfly" to liberal theism it exerts a challenging influence. My impression is that it has made more headway among college professors and YMCA and YWCA secretaries than among ministers.

The centrum of American theology is liberalism. In spite of premature funeral obsequies, it is likely to remain the basic American theology for some time to come. It dominates the instruction of nearly all the theological seminaries. While liberals probably do not constitute the majority of the membership, liberals are in positions of leadership in most of the denominations. Although theological [liberalism] has made more headway than social liberalism, they are strong allies. The social gospel is not dead, nor is the spirit of free inquiry.

To the right of the center is the new orthodoxy. Its exponents, few in number but great in influence, are liberals or ex-liberals who see the need of a return to the insights of historic Christianity regarding human sin and divine grace. They have been much influenced by Barth, but few, if any, in America are thoroughgoing Barthians. From this group is emerging a valuable corrective to those aspects of liberalism which had gone to seed.

At the extreme right is fundamentalism, numerically strong but small in influence. The spearhead of conflict is the historical approach to the Bible, and the liberal view is gradually making headway against what is still in some areas very determined opposition.

Such variability as this we have within the American scene—a range of outlook which by no means follows denominational lines. Add to it the fact that there is wide disparity between the relatively clear-cut theology of the seminary professor, the more nebulous theology of the parish minister whose most immediate concern is with practical matters, and the almost complete lack of theology which characterizes the religion of most of the laity—and the difficulty of formulating any characteristically American body of belief becomes apparent.

That it is not altogether impossible is attested by the fact that the Committee has in some measure already succeeded in doing it. The more important matter, however, is future procedure. Upon the question of whether we shall put major emphasis on our agreements or our differences hinge vital issues. Among them are participation in the ecumenical movement (witness the discussion already emerging from Utrecht), the application of creedal tests to ministers and missionaries, the basis of our Christian message whether at home or abroad. In my judgment it is neither important nor desirable to have a distinctively American theology, but it is highly important that Americans should have a theology, characterized by unity in diversity and therefore by a union of tolerance with conviction.

3. *In the formulation of our faith, what place shall be given to non-theological movements?* It is essential to recognize that theology always emerges from living social situations and in turn redirects them. It cannot disregard them, for theology which is out of touch with living situations falls on deaf ears and is unable to direct either life or thought.

In America at least four non-theological movements are of much importance. These are the social gospel, a resurgence of interest in worship, personal evangelism, and religious education. Each has its theological presuppositions, more often inchoate than explicit. The social gospel centers in the ethical teaching of Jesus regarding the intrinsic worth of all persons in a Kingdom of love; worship in the exaltation of a transcendent-immanent God; personal evangelism in the reality of sin and the possibility of salvation; religious education in the capacity of spiritual personality for adaptation and growth in Christian ideals. The direction taken by American religious thought, and in turn our missionary message, will depend in considerable measure, first, on which of these implicit theologies is given primacy, and second, on the degree to which elements now in conflict can be brought into a constructive synthesis.

4. *How far can the Christian message converge with secular social movements without losing its distinctiveness?* It is a familiar fact that much which was formerly regarded as the function of the Church has largely passed to secular agencies. Character training is the prerogative of the public schools and the Boy Scouts; troubled souls go to psychiatric clinics for personal redemption; for recreation, hospitalization, relief, action directed toward economic change or world peace, almost every community has its organization.

Whether in America or on the mission field, the Christian must decide where to put his effort. He cannot work in the church and in all these agencies at once. To refuse to work with them is often to refuse to cooperate with those of other faiths for the real advance of the Kingdom. To place one's effort wholly with them is not only to weaken the Church, but to contribute to a flattening of its message to a point where it means nothing distinctively Christian.

To escape this dilemma a more clearly thought out theology is needed. Character education, by whatever agency it is given, is Christian if it is based on a Christian valuation of personality; it is unchristian when its fundamental philosophy is simply training in enlightened self-interest or social conformity. Psychiatry may be a means of personal regeneration; it usually is not, because [it is] based on a false or fragmentary concept of human nature. Work for social amelioration is Christian when it stems from and contributes to a Christian concept of the Kingdom of God. But one must know what these basic Christian concepts are before he can act with discernment.

5. *By what authority shall we proclaim our message?* Without some authority it is impossible to speak with conviction. But authority is not dogmatism or the surrender of inquiry.

In America we cannot speak by authority of the Church. There is no American Church; there is not, to any great extent, a Church-idea among American Christians. Nor can we speak by authority of the Bible. The Bible is respected and studied as a revelation of God, but historical criticism has done its work too thoroughly to permit any considerable body of informed Christians to regard it as *the* revelation.

Our only ultimate source of authority is that which has been the ground of authority throughout Christian history, *the mind of Christ*. We do not have in America any very clear-cut Christology, or any great sense of the need of one. Our Christianity is God-centered in its philosophy, Jesus-centered in its ethics. Our next forward move in theology, in my judgment, will be for someone to write a book on Christology which in terms congenial to American thought will combine the Jesus of the social gospel with the Christ of living faith. When this is done, we shall not have an "American Christ," but we shall be closer to an American apprehension of the mind of Christ for all men.

READING 15

. . . [The missionary] movement began in the early Church before there was any systematic theology. The Church was born in a living experience of Christ and was nourished upon the simple yet potent creed: "Jesus is Lord." Only as it felt the impact of rival systems and cultures did a theology become necessary. In the elaboration of this theology it moved in two directions—toward the enlargement and enrichment of its faith and, at the same time, toward compromise and the corruption of its initial spirit. What we have in our historic creeds is a product of both tendencies, hence the danger of treating these creeds either as inconsequential or as sacrosanct.

These facts ought not to lead to any disparagement of theology. It is important for a Christian to know what he believes and why, whether he tries to be a Christian in London or New York, Shanghai or Tokyo. Unless we know what our Christian message is we shall not know whether to have a Christian movement. Unless we have a clear sense of its relation to non-Christian faiths we shall not know which way to move. Unless we can defend our faith on other than subjective grounds we shall not be able to present it with the conviction that convinces others. We need a great deal more theology, not less, in the missionary

"The Theological Basis of the Missionary Message," *International Review of Missions* 28 (October 1939): 518–26.

outlook and enterprise. But we ought never to suppose that "the Faith by which the Church lives" is a theological structure—much less any of the particular theological structures which are now rival claimants in the field. Nor ought we to suppose that the creeds of the first five centuries, wrought out of particular historical exigencies, can be superimposed upon a very different historical situation and be found fully adequate.

As in the first centuries a combination of a Gospel with a set of circumstances produced the creeds, so must we expect and hope that among the younger Churches the same Gospel in conjunction with other circumstances and in impact upon other cultures may bring fresh theologies to light. God has more truth yet to break forth from His holy word—and we may look for it to break forth in Asia, Africa, South America and the islands of the sea. The vigorous participation of the delegates from the younger Churches at Madras substantiates this hope. That their contributions were much more confidently made in the field of practical programs than of theology suggests, on the one hand, that they were inclined to defer too much to the theological spokesmen from the older Churches, and, on the other, that their contributions to the theology of the future may be all the more vital because these will come out of dynamic life-transforming experience. Only when these contributions are brought forth and integrated with the faith of the older historic streams will there be a truly oecumenical theology. The Madras meeting made an important step in this direction, but the drafting committee that wrote the report on "the Faith by which the Church lives" was overweighted with Europeans and Americans. Perhaps one of the main objectives of the next world missionary conference may well be the explicit elaboration of the theology implicit in the life and work of the younger Churches.

Since I am not myself a member of one of these younger Churches and have never lived among them I cannot presume to say what this theology will be. Instead I shall try to suggest certain elements which I believe any oecumenical theology must possess. I shall not attempt to distinguish between an oecumenical theology and the theological basis of the missionary message, for the two are one. Any world Christianity is by its nature a witness-bearing Christianity. We shall discover it best not by asking what has been believed *semper, ubique, ab omnibus*, but by asking what has been the nourishing, sustaining faith that has driven Christians through the ages to witness to the Gospel of Christ.

In the first place, any oecumenical theology must be Christ-centred. Though the report of the Jerusalem meeting lacked definiteness in explaining the implications of its statement, it put the focus in the right place when it declared: "Our message is Jesus Christ." A philosophy of religion may legitimately erect a structure of religious belief from the evidences of God in nature, history, art, human personality, or the spiritual strivings of men of all faiths. This approach to Christian faith has its uses, and to many for whom the traditional Christian message has become sterile such channels bring fresh draughts of spiritual refreshment. But all such approaches are either sub-Christian or only tangen-

tially Christian. It is impossible to build upon them a full Christian theology
or a life-transforming Christian experience. The missionary movement is not
nourished upon arguments for the existence of God but upon a personal confrontation with Christ.

Secondly, any oecumenical theology must believe that in Jesus Christ we
see the Incarnation of God. This is not, however, to say that the Incarnation
must be understood in terms of the Utrecht statement.[11] The proposed constitution of the World Council of Churches defines the Council as "a fellowship
of Churches which accept our Lord Jesus Christ as God and Saviour." I share
the conviction of many American Christians—and some outside America—
that for the World Council to take over the "Faith and Order" formula as the
creedal basis of oecumenical participation was an exclusive rather than a truly
oecumenical move. The controversy stirred up by it has thus far proved divisive
rather than unitive, and to the degree that the younger Churches wrestle with
the problem of church unity, it is apt there also to thwart rather than hasten
co-operation. If the early Church could preach Christ and win men to Christ
on the basis of the simple formula: "Jesus is Lord," why need we more? But this
we must have as a minimum—a minimum laden with a maximum of meaning—that God was in Christ reconciling the world unto Himself. Jesus is Lord
because in His life and word, His death and resurrection, we see the living God
at work in the world for our redemption.

Thirdly, any oecumenical theology must make room both for the historical
Jesus and the Christ of faith. Any informed Christian will grant the difficulty of
digging through the layers of first-century tradition to get at the historical Jesus.
But we grow faint-hearted too soon if we conclude that we cannot really know
anything about Jesus. If we cannot know anything about Him, then we cannot
know whether in Him was a real incarnation. The miracle of the New Testament is that out from the pages of the Synoptic Gospels, wrapped up though
they are in first-century interpretation, shines a clear, luminous Figure who
through all ages since has captured men's loyalty and devotion. Upon deductive,
if not upon historical, grounds we can be sure that this Jesus was adequate to
become the Christ of the early Church.

The primary danger—and falsity—which many of us see in the type of biblical realism presented in Dr Kraemer's great book, *The Christian Message in a
non-Christian World,* is that at this point it is not realistic enough. It centres too
largely in St Paul, too little in Jesus, for a genuine doctrine of the Incarnation.
Not a system of first-century Christian theology, but a living and dying, completely godlike Person, is the centre of our faith. It is this Person who has been
the motivating centre of the missionary enterprise. Apart from Him, the whole
structure of Christian witness collapses—or at best passes over into a rationalist
or vitalist movement which has no stable historic centre.

We in America have much to learn from Continental theology. Perhaps too
slowly, we are learning to reckon with the profound fact of sin and the redeeming act of God in Christ. It is good for us to find again in the foreground the

Pauline emphasis on justification by faith in the crucified and risen Lord. But let us give fair warning: any theology which tries to take from us the Jesus of history as the central pivot of our faith will not carry many of us with it. Such a theology can be called oecumenical only by the excommunication of dissenters.

In the fourth place, any oecumenical theology must bear witness to the Kingdom. Since our faith centres in Jesus Christ it must also centre in His dominant message to men. Jesus preached pre-eminently the coming of the Kingdom—the righteous rule of God. No enterprise can remain truly Christian which drops out the Kingdom or relegates it to the margin of thought and activity.

There is of course room for latitude of judgment as to what the Kingdom means. The Kingdom is both within and beyond this world. It sets before us both an individual and a social gospel. It is an attainment through God's gift and an eternal quest. As the Madras report on "The Church and the Changing Social Order" succinctly puts it:

> The Kingdom of God is both present and future; both a growth and a final consummation by God. . . . The Kingdom means both acceptance and action, a gift and a task. We work for it and we wait for it.[12]

That there should be a difference in emphasis upon various aspects of this great paradox is the inevitable consequence of the fact of Christian liberty. Such diversity is fruitful if held in Christian charity. Yet certain extremes must be ruled out if we are to be at all faithful to what the New Testament presents. We need to guard against identifying the Kingdom with any current social scheme or system; we need equally to guard against any interpretation so exclusively eschatological as to rob the Kingdom of all social and temporal relevance. Jesus did not preach capitalism or socialism, fascism or political democracy; but He announced principles of our personal worth and responsibility as sons of God, which call us to judge the social order and to be co-workers with God for its redemption.

We have talked too much, particularly in America, about "building the Kingdom of God." Rather, the function of all Christians is to be the good ground in which the seed of God's Kingdom can grow. But never are we called to be acquiescent in the presence of evil. Only as we participate in suffering love for the establishment of God's righteous rule among men do we enter into His Kingdom. Our surest clue to its nature and its insistent, manifold demands is in the witness of our Lord who proclaimed it, and whose life—all of one piece, with His teaching—is its perfect manifestation.

Fifthly, any oecumenical theology must regard the Church as the primary instrument for the advancement of the Kingdom. The Church and the Kingdom are complementary terms; for the Kingdom is the end and goal of the Christian enterprise, the Church its primary means of fulfillment. Much discussion has been elicited in the United States by the publication in *The Christian Century* of an article by Dr E. Stanley Jones entitled, "Where Madras Missed Its Way," which charges the meeting with having put the Church in the focus of its thought at the expense of the Kingdom. My opinion is that we said too little at Madras about the Kingdom but not too much about the Church. In a day when everything else totters, a recovery of confidence in the Church—least shaken of all our major institutions—is an achievement of major importance. It was a true word, deliberately spoken, when the meeting declared its faith: "In all humility and penitence, we are constrained to declare to a baffled and needy world that the Christian Church, under God, is its greatest hope."[13]

As in reference to the Kingdom, neither the oecumenical nor the missionary movement can hope to enlist complete agreement about the nature and function of the Church. To some Christians it is a social institution—an essential medium of Christian worship, instruction and fellowship—but still a human institution impregnated with all the deficiencies of its human membership. To others it is a divine institution—the Body of Christ and the extension of the Incarnation. To the main stream of Christian thought it is both. Though not all Christians would agree, in my judgment the Church is not the only vehicle of God for the redemption of men and the extension of His Kingdom. Throughout all ages God "by divers portions and in divers manners" has spoken to men and has made manifest His works. Not only among Christians outside the Church but in the non-Christian religions we see God at work for man's salvation. Nevertheless, "through the nurture and discipline of the Church, Christian life comes to completion; in glad service within the fellowship of the Church, Christian devotion is perfected."[14] Apart from the historic heritage of which the Church has been the carrier there is no full stability for the Christian enterprise—this, I believe, must be granted before either an oecumenical or a missionary movement can come to birth.

Finally, any oecumenical theology must look to the Bible for its basic faith. From the Bible, "instructor and sustainer of the Christian faith through the ages," we derive our knowledge of Christ and of the personal, righteous, creating, judging, redeeming Deity who was the God and Father of our Lord Jesus Christ. From the Bible we get our insights into the nature of the Kingdom; on the Bible the life of individual believers and of the worshipping community has been fed. From its authority, not dogmatically or literalistically but vitally conceived, we ever draw fresh truth and the stabilizing power of an historically grounded faith. Many types of religious literature, Christian and non-Christian, give us truth about God, but for the Bible there is no substitute. Unique and supreme among all writings, it is what Christianity has long declared it to be—the Word of God.

This brief survey has made no attempt to canvass the whole field of Christian belief. But other doctrines are at the same time more controversial and less basic.

There is a Christian doctrine of men, without which we should have no Christian movement for man's salvation. An oecumenical theology must reckon with it. Yet it is at this point that dogmatism becomes most dangerous. While all Christians agree that man needs God for fullness of life, some lay major emphasis on man's sin and powerlessness to cleanse himself, others on his potential

greatness as the child of God. Hence, some find in conversion and the awareness of forgiveness of sins the crux of the Gospel; to others gradual growth in
a many-sided Christian experience seems the more enduring evangel. It is an
empirical fact that the Gospel has been proclaimed, and highly effective work
has been done, on both bases. To say that either approach must be adopted to
the exclusion of the other is to postpone the day of Christian unity—and by
disunion to cripple the Christian enterprise at its roots. So it is with numerous
other elements in our historic faith.

Not theological agreement but common loyalty to Christ and fellowship in
the Christian task stand at the heart of the missionary movement. The early
Church, unencumbered with superfluous creedal baggage, found its divine
imperative in, "Go ye into all the world and preach the Gospel to every creature." So may we still. The greatness of the Madras meeting lies in its truly marvelous demonstration of the power of faith and fellowship to bridge differences
in belief. Christ when lifted up not only draws all men unto Himself; He draws
men to one another in bonds of faith and hope and love which transcend the
strife of systems.

READING 16

"The Christian Church today is called to live, and to give life, in a world shaken
to its foundations." So runs the opening sentence of the Madras report.

That the world is shaken to its foundations is evident to all. At the close of
the last World War a story, perhaps apocryphal, was told of a certain mountain-
eer who wandered into town on Armistice Day, and from the bells and whistles
learned for the first time that a war had been going on. Such complacency of
isolation has not been granted to us. The radio and the newspapers have seen
to that—and in any barbershop, as in any ministerial gathering, one may hear
speculations, more or less profound, about the probable fate of mankind in these
troubled days. The gist of them all is, "What's the world coming to?" And no
one knows.

What, then, has the Church to say if it is to live and to give life in such a
world? Has it a message for our day?

There are many possible starting-points for an examination of our faith. One
may start from God, or from Christ, or from the Bible, or from the revelation of
God in nature, or from the psychological data of religious experience, or from
the past history of the Church. I have chosen to begin with the Church of our
own time. If we can see what is vital in it *now,* in a shaken world, set in the midst
of a secular culture and under fire from many quarters, we shall be the more
ready to discover its perennial message.

From "A World Church in a World Crisis," *Faith by Which the Church Lives,* 13–43.

1. A world Church

There are many to tell us that the Church is dead or dying; that it is an empty shell from which life has fled; that its buildings, its sermonizing, its rituals, its vestigial remains in our marriage and burial customs, are but relics of departed usefulness.

A good deal of distrust regarding its present efficacy finds expression among the friends of the Church as well as among those indifferent to it. . . . No one knows better than those who love the Church its pettiness, its compromises, its divisive sectarianism, its defeats along many fronts where it is passed by for other social agencies and interests.

Yet it is recorded that our Lord at a high moment said, "On this rock I will build my church, and the gates of hell shall not prevail against it." The floodgates now are wide open. Can the Church resist them?

To this crisis within the Church, as within the world, the ecumenical movement brings assurance of victory and power through the living Body of Christ.

It has been my privilege to attend four ecumenical gatherings: Oxford, Madras, Amsterdam, and the Geneva Conference called to consider the relation of the churches to the international crisis. They have left what I believe will be a permanent impression on me. A cynic is said to have remarked, "I believe in the Church Universal, and regret that it does not exist." I *know* that it exists, for I have four times beheld it in action, experienced the thrill of its fellowship, witnessed the evidence of its victories, felt upborne in my own halting spiritual pilgrimage by its abundant and encompassing sources of power. Such an experience can never be transmitted in words. The most that I can do is to set forth a few impressions.

a. Oxford.

The ecumenical movement is, of course, not new. There were history-making ecumenical conferences in the early Church, which established the major treads of Christian theology, and the modern movement stems primarily from the Edinburgh missionary conference of 1910. Yet as a dominant element in contemporary Christianity something new emerged with the Oxford Conference of July, 1937.

When I think of Oxford . . . I think of unforgettable half-hours of worship in historic Saint Mary's Church, where the Spirit spoke without need of translation; of fellowship in the University halls and over the teacups; of brisk theological clashes—almost wrangles at times—in the dingy upper room of Saint Mary's, where the Education section met; of the Town Hall, where clergy and laity, youth and elder statesmen, men and women of the Christian world observed each other's odd haberdashery and listened to addresses in three languages; of the managerial skill of the veteran presiding officer, Dr. John R. Mott, who kept counseling us to use the tedious translation periods for meditation and prayer.

My mind goes to a thrilling moment one evening when the vote was taken to unite with Faith and Order to form a World Council of Churches, and the great Communion service on the last Sunday morning in Saint Mary's Church, at which all baptized Christians, forgetting past denominational schisms, met together at the table of our one Lord.

As I look back upon Oxford it seems a good deal of a miracle. The sessions were exhausting; many of the speeches were dull; the section meetings were full of sharp division between liberalism and continental theology. We were not there to discuss theology, but there was no avoiding it. So many diverse views, not only theological but practical, were presented that agreement seemed impossible. What could the reports say that would be worth saying? Yet when the reports were brought in, they spoke great truth! They were almost unanimously adopted, for they said what all believed. They were not watered down to the dead level of compromise; they were lifted to the high level of Christian unity. "Unity in diversity" was no longer a shibboleth, but a reality, and the key to the mystery was in the word of Christ, "And I, if I be lifted up, will draw all men unto me."

There is no space here in which to outline these findings. . . . [The official reports] affirm what the conference demonstrated—that the Church is a supra-national, supra-racial, supra-class fellowship. They are characterized by a mood of humility and repentance, by vigorous grappling with a wide range of social issues, by confidence of victory over evil through the power of Christ. The forces shaking the world were recognized for what they are—cataclysmic, even demonic. But these forces are not beyond the reach of the gospel which the Church of Christ proclaims.

The Oxford Conference made over my conception of the Church. The little worshiping community at the corner of Main and Church became part of a world-embracing fellowship. In a deepened consciousness of the historical as well as the contemporary in the great fellowship of Christian believers, the archaic phrase, "the communion of saints," came alive. I felt a fresh confidence in the power of the Church to span all man-made barriers and withstand the floods of evil that threaten to engulf us. I found myself with a new awareness of the meaning of the Church as the living Body of Christ, a continuing community that can no more be destroyed than can Christ himself. More important, perhaps, than any of these impressions, was a deepened realization of the meaning of the words we often sing too lightly:

> "The Church's one foundation
> Is Jesus Christ her Lord."

b. Madras.

Then, a year and a half later, in December, 1938, came the Madras Conference of the International Missionary Council. Madras had many of the same features as Oxford, and deepened the impressions of the earlier gathering. Yet it was distinctive and unique. The Oxford Conference was signally deficient at a crucial point, namely, that all but about thirty of its voting delegates were from North America or Europe. In this respect it fell short of being truly ecumenical. Madras was set up on the basis of having an equal representation from the younger and older churches. This participation of Christians from Asia, Africa, South America, and the islands of the sea—the fruits of missionary effort—gave to the Conference a remarkable fellowship and an amazing vitality.

In many respects the atmosphere was like that of Oxford. There was the same sense of being one in Christ regardless of external differences in dress or speech or culture, of Christianity's deep roots, of the unassailable power of the Church to conquer evil through Christ. Yet the setting was very different. Instead of a medieval university town, sedately clothed with age and dignity, its meeting-place was the little village of Tambaram, fifteen miles from Madras, and its buildings were those of a modern Christian college erected to serve the awakening life of India. This is typical of other differences. At Madras there were more variations in racial complexion, more weird costumes (which, after a day, no one bothered to notice), fewer badges of ecclesiastical eminence, fewer great minds, and, if one may venture to judge, more great-hearted, self-effacing, victorious souls. I have never been in any other group so completely free from race consciousness and from barriers such as those of age, sex, and position, which often keep even Christian bodies from being truly democratic. . . . Madras epitomized the great democracy of the family of God.

I said above that my Oxford impressions of the power of the Church and of its deep rootage in Christ were re-enforced. These need not be restated. But certain new insights emerged.

The most poignant was the revitalization of faith in the missionary enterprise. I have always believed in missions. But at Madras the connection between the money-raising efforts of our little local churches and the genuine world service of the Church came to life. The delegates from the younger churches, in spite of a language handicap (for all sessions were conducted in English), made their contributions without self-consciousness and without bombast, with good humor and earnestness, and withal, with *power*. In what they said and in what they were, one could read "living epistles" of the power of Christ to transform lives and to fashion social environments toward happy, hopeful, friendly living. Christmas in Tambaram was memorable, for at the morning service we heard as "glad tidings of great joy to all the people" testimonies to the victory of Christ around the world. This typified the witness of the Conference as a whole. In their many communities those who have found Christ through Christian missions are leaders, not only in specifically Christian work, but as teachers, nurses, social workers, physicians, judges, legislators, and other agents of social advancement. Their influence is far in excess of their numerical proportion. . . .

A second dominant impression from Madras was the degree of vitality and optimism that characterizes the Christianity of the Orient in contrast with our tiredness. Where the Christian message is fresh, vigorous, and life-transforming it spends its energy, not in trying to save itself from being engulfed by the secular environment, but in saving human souls. The result is its own renewal and increase. A case in point is the amazing greatness of spirit, calmness of outlook, and freedom from bitterness manifest by the Chinese delegation. East of Suez Christianity ceases to be effete. The apocalyptic pessimism of continental Europe and the discouraged liberalism of America are foreign to the mood of the younger churches. Should war and secularism get the victory in the West, Christianity as an evangel would come to us again through the virile forces of the East.

A third impression was of the power of Christian faith to span differences in belief. There were deep-seated, radical theological differences. As a member of the drafting committee of the two sections where this cleavage was most acute . . . I had plenty of occasion to witness and experience them. There were Barthians, fundamentalists, and liberals at Madras. Some were enthusiastic about the Pauline theology of [some participants]; others felt disturbed at the minor place it accords to the Jesus of the Synoptic Gospels and his teachings. When one group puts its major emphasis on following Christ's way of life, and another says that "to follow Christ's way of life" is a meaningless and untranslatable phrase which—if it means anything—is blasphemous, one wonders if there are not two faiths present. . . . [So it was with discussions of] man's essential greatness as a child of God versus his innate sinfulness and depravity; and with the Kingdom in which we can be coworkers with God upon earth versus the eschatological hope. . . .

Yet again a miracle happened. The report stating the faith by which the Church lives is neither liberal, fundamentalist, nor Barthian. It speaks great truth, to which all could assent, regarding God, man, salvation through Christ, the Kingdom, the Church, the Bible, and our call to action in the light of this faith. It follows the deep main stream of historic Christianity. One would have said agreement was impossible. Yet in love and charity, and without compromise of conviction, agreement was achieved. Once more it was evident that Christ when lifted up draws all men to himself above the strife of systems.

c. Amsterdam.

I shall speak more briefly of the Amsterdam World Conference of Christian Youth in July, 1939. It is a significant fact that it could be held at all in a time of such tension and disturbance. . . . In discussion the young people were earnest and thoughtful, without cocksureness but with a sense of certainty about the Christian faith. If anything they were too certain, for they gave the impression at times of being unwilling to consider rival views because, being Christians, they had all the answers.[15]

What did they take from the Conference? According to such testimony as I have gathered, they discovered the Bible, many of them for first time; they had their lives spiritually challenged and enriched by varied forms of worship and by contact with their fellow Christians; they found a sense of togetherness in the power of the Church to span all divisive cultural barriers; they were rudely awakened to the divisions within the Church by the necessity of holding four different Communion services.

d. Geneva.

Oxford, Madras, and Amsterdam were great world gatherings. The Geneva Conference of July, 1939, was of a different order. It was a meeting of a small board of strategy, a group of thirty-four from eleven countries summoned by the Provisional Committee of the World Council of Churches to consider the relation of the churches to the international crisis. It owed its origin mainly to the proposal of President Albert W. Palmer before the meeting of the Federal Council of Churches that the churches should take the lead in trying to induce the heads of states to confer for the settlement of disputes in advance of war. . . .

Not much could be done about President Palmer's proposal, for psychologically the war was already far advanced in July, 1939. Suspicion ran high, and to most of the Europeans it seemed that any suggestion of a conference would be interpreted as "weakness and another Munich." Enveloped in war clouds as we were, with delegates sitting side by side from countries already at war or in mobilization against each other, with reasons or rationalizations to justify war already established, with members present whose military equipment was ready to be put on at a moment's notice, it is a wonder that the group held together. We met in the very room where in 1921 a similar group broke up over the war-guilt issue. Yet our group held together, bound by the unity of Christian faith, and produced a report which if taken seriously by the churches would be the Magna Charta of a new international order.

I shall attempt only a few observations on the content of the report. Its first section, which deals with presuppositions, demonstrates that theological differences between continental and American thought are far less divisive than they were at Oxford two years earlier. While the continental Christian never lets one forget that there is a radical difference between the redeemed individual (who can be Christian) and the unredeemed state (which cannot), there is not the tendency we formerly found to derive from this distinction an attitude of social quietism. The group came to an agreement on certain basic principles of Christian morality, applicable to states as well as to individuals, which are affirmed to include "the equal dignity of all men, respect for human life, acknowledgment of the solidarity for good and evil of all nations and races of the earth, respect for the plighted word, and the recognition that power of any kind, political or economic, must be coextensive with responsibility."

The second section deals with the international order. . . . It states succinctly the long-range and immediate causes of the present disorder [and] lays down the basic principles of action necessary to secure justice and order in the international community. Being drafted mainly by advocates of collective security, this part of the report could easily have become a collective-security manifesto. It is to the credit of the group that they were willing to rest the maintenance of order upon the collective will of the community, our differences as to method being covered by the single sentence, "As to the use of force in this connection we are not agreed." A strong assertion is made that changes in the interest of justice lay as much claim upon the collective will as does the protection of the nations from violence. . . .

The third section deals with the tasks of the churches and of individual Christians. Its significance lies in the fact that it constitutes a blueprint for action—not in the form of rules, but in the enunciation of principles and suggested procedures which if followed would keep the Church from ever again becoming the sword-bearing arm of the State. In adopting it, the Provisional Committee of the World Council of Churches commits no church to a program, but it goes on record as opposing the travesties upon religion which masqueraded as religion in the last war. . . .

There are other pointed statements in the report—about the maintenance of bonds of unity in the ecumenical Church, about refusal to give the State the supreme loyalty due only to God, about preaching and praying as Christians, about refusing to be agencies for the spreading of national propaganda or the dissemination of hatred, about working for a just peace, about caring materially and spiritually for the victims of war, about cultivating mutual understanding, forgiveness and trust, about accepting our responsibility for the sin of war. The statement ends with a call to prayer and a triumphant affirmation of the power of God to work out his will even in the midst of conflict.

2. The Church in the international crisis

These conferences have passed into history. Turmoil surrounds us. What can we who are servants of the Church say to a stricken world?

In the first place we must realize for ourselves, and must announce to others without apology or arrogance, that the Christian Church, under God, is the greatest hope of a baffled and needy world.[16] It is the only functioning international organism, international because it is supra-national. It spans all racial and national lines and its evangel enables those of enemy States to meet one another in love. While the nations build and let loose armaments for mutual destruction, the Church goes on spreading brotherhood and healing. While the nations darken the minds of their people with propaganda tinctured with hate, the Church spreads education and light, and endeavors by its glad tidings of great joy to bring peace on earth, good will among men. Least shaken of all our major institutions, it grows daily in unity and power.

Among many uncertainties, of this we may be sure—that the power of Christ and his Church will be adequate to withstand any torrent that may come pouring forth from the gates of hell. Kingdoms may rise and fall, but like the saving remnant in Israel of old, a little nucleus will carry on the torch of living faith as long as there are men upon earth. In the book of Acts it is recorded that some scoffers said of those in the early Church, "These Christians turn the world upside down!" In the epistle to Diognetus written in the second century, the author says that Christians "hold the world together."[17] Both words are true. The Christian Church has turned the world upside down to shake human nature from its lethargy, and in these troubled days it is holding the world together.

I have made no attempt to analyze the state of the world, for all are familiar with it. Suffice it to say that the world is shaken by profound disturbances which are primarily psychological, economic, and political in character. The Christian gospel, if it means anything, is a message of salvation *in* the world and not *from* it. It is not a social panacea, but it "speaks to our condition" no matter what that condition is. What does it say in the presence of these disturbances?

For our psychological instability it offers peace and power. "Let not your heart be troubled . . ." "Be of good cheer; I have overcome the world." "Come unto me, all ye that labor and are heavy laden . . ." "I can do all things through Christ . . ." "I have learned in whatsoever state I am, therein to be content." These promises and these affirmations are timeless and spaceless. Through all ages and around the world they have brought to men assurance and victory through the power of the living Christ. They are doing it still. Whatever dispute there may be about the social implications of the gospel, its message to the inner life is self-validating and incontrovertible. Only he who views it from without, as a casual onlooker, can deny its reality. In the Christian's experience of cleansing, renewal, and power lies the perennial source of the faith by which the Church lives.

To our economic life the gospel offers no blueprint. Neither capitalism nor socialism can be identified with the Kingdom of God. Any reconstructed society we might devise would fall short of Jesus' ideal of the Kingdom, for any human society would be corrupted by human frailty. Yet the gospel has a message of power and incisiveness to our economic life. It speaks for justice to the oppressed and for the equal dignity of all men as sons of God. Its warnings of the perils of riches, if taken seriously, contain enough dynamite to remake the structure of society. Though we are more callous to unchristian relations in economic matters than in any other aspect of our living, the gospel continues to stir consciences to an uneasy awareness. Much has been said truly of an unholy alliance of the Church with capitalism; yet I know of no group more alive to the evils of capitalism and more anxious to correct these evils constructively than are the ministers of the Christian Church. In those areas where Christian missionaries are at work, even the most skeptical critic can scarcely fail to be convinced of the fruitfulness of this effort when confronted by tangible evidences of rural reconstruction, and other forms of economic change.

In the field of political ideologies the major rivals of democracy are Communism and Fascism. From a Christian standpoint the complexity of the problem, which makes snap judgments unfitting, lies in the fact that both Communism and Fascism at some points converge with, and at others diverge from, the demands of the Christian gospel.

Communism in too many respects makes common cause with the social message of Christianity to permit us to dismiss it lightly. Godless though it may be, it expresses something of the will of God. Communism as a program for social reconstruction has a concern for the underprivileged, a demand for the equitable distribution of wealth and opportunity, an insistence on racial and sex equality, which should challenge our complacency and call us to penitence for inaction. Yet I hasten to say—lest the Dies Committee get me—that I could never be a Communist! In its orthodox Marxist form it breaks with the gospel by its materialistic view of man and his destiny, by its revolutionary strategy, by its lack of regard for the sacredness of individual personality. So radical are these affinities and these divergences that to some, as in China today, Christianity and Communism seem quite capable of a united front; to others, as in Germany before the Soviet pact and among the Red-baiters of our country, they are foes between which there can be no peace. Atheistic, materialistic, dictatorial, and often ruthless, it nevertheless came into existence as a prophetic protest against the injustices of a class-ridden society, and it will remain with us until some more constructive force—perhaps the Christian Church—eradicates the evils which brought it into being.

Fascism is at present the primary political menace. Like Communism, it has an economic root, and their agreements are greater than their differences. It stems from the struggle to survive, and it is not by accident that its most virulent expressions are in the nations lacking colonies and adequate internal resources. Fascism is autocratic, but powerfully efficient, and so strong in man is the craving for security that a citizen, assured that his State is adequate to guarantee to him his economic needs, will willingly do without much for the sake of having more. It is part of the Christian enterprise to work for such a condition of economic justice that Fascism and Communism will not need to rebuke us, as they do now, for our lethargy.

Yet deeper than the economic root of Fascism is its sense of community. Its soul is in a narrowly limited, deliberately cultivated, powerfully binding sense of togetherness. The more the Fascist states are outlawed by the democracies, the more close-knit and dangerous becomes this unity of race and blood and soil. We may condemn it if we like, for some of its fruits are hideous; we may take up arms against it; we may not deny its reality or its power. . . . Those who think that external coercion will push the Fascist states to inner disruption reason without due awareness of this communal loyalty which, above all else, gives Fascism its being and its strength.

This sense of community is not in itself an evil. Churches exist to provide it for those who are bound together by a common loyalty to Christ, and had Christians not proved recreant to manifesting this fellowship concretely in a world community, Fascism need not have arisen. But in Fascism this sense of community is intense but limited, and boundaries are set beyond which fellowship and respect for persons as persons have no claims. Hence the persecution of Jews and dissenters. To maintain this intense but limited fellowship, the State is exalted to the order of deity, and intolerance receives divine sanction.

Against all such half-gods and half-goods, the message of the gospel is unequivocal. "Thou shalt love the Lord thy God [not an economic class, not a nation] with all thy heart." "Thou shalt love thy neighbor [not a proletarian, not an Aryan neighbor] as thyself." The application of this gospel is far from simple and unequivocal. In no social group have we adequately achieved it. We must judge and we must act, but let us judge in charity and act in repentance.

I do not propose to speak at length upon the game of death now in progress in Europe. The issues are complex, and upon them Christians have a right to differ. For myself I must say that I believe profoundly it is our duty to stay out of this war—not in selfish isolation, but the better to serve a stricken world. This we must do without self-righteousness, recognizing our common sin. My judgment about the present issues has been stated succinctly by Dr. Harry Emerson Fosdick: "The democracies could have saved democracy in Germany if they had really cared for democracy as much as they now say they do. But they did not, and we in America would not even join a world organization to help. This world disaster is the work of us all. Hitler made the war, but we, all of us, helped make Hitler. Not hatred, but humility becomes us well."

The fundamental ground on which I believe it to be our Christian duty to preserve neutrality is the fact, spoken by our Lord and written on the signposts of history, that we cannot by Satan cast out Satan. There are things worth fighting for—truth, liberty, love, justice, the preservation of human life. But the things worth fighting for are the things we destroy when we try to preserve them by mass destruction. As we cannot gather grapes from thistles or figs from thorns, so we cannot gather truth from organized deception, liberty from dictatorship, justice from annihilation, love from hate, life from wholesale slaughter.

The democratic ideal of the intrinsic worth of all persons is of supreme importance; political democracy is merely a roughly successful means to this end. The democracy of the gospel, rooted in Jesus' ideal of the brotherhood of all men as sons of God, is one that war is far more likely to thwart than to preserve. To the preservation of such democracy, Christian leaders are unequivocally obligated. Though opinions may differ as to procedure in the political and social scene, certain indispensable tasks of the churches are noted in the Geneva report:

> The churches and all Christian people should strive to make concrete our Lord's injunction, 'Love your enemies.' The true Christian spirit of forgiveness does not arise from a condoning of evil but from the knowledge that we ourselves have been forgiven. To cultivate good will toward all, not only to those within but also to those without the Christian fellowship; to spread the spirit of forgiveness and trust; to increase the habit of charitable judgment; to widen knowledge and understanding—of the causes of conflict—these things help to remove the psychological roots of war and are characteristic fruits of the spirit of Christ.

Finally, what is our major responsibility within our churches in these days? It is certainly not to seal ourselves hermetically in a vacuum, and to think by inculcating spiritual peace to turn our backs on a world at war. But neither is it to make our churches into agencies for the spread of hate. It is, as the Geneva report puts it, "to preach and pray like Christians." Whether in war or in peace, this means, if the Spirit of the Lord is upon us, "to preach good tidings to the poor, to proclaim release to the captives and recovering of sight to the blind, to set at liberty them that are bruised, to proclaim the acceptable year of the Lord." Whatever our specific efforts in behalf of peace, we shall best serve a war-torn world in these desperate clays if we refuse to be desperate. And we cannot despair if we continue to announce the gospel of Christ. No one of us alone can bring peace to the world, but the Christian churches jointly can preserve an area of fellowship and good will wherein the seeds of peace can grow again. The most important thing any of us can do in this world crisis is to keep on doing our work, wherever we can and as well as we can, assured that above the battle the Lord God omnipotent reigneth.

READING 17

. . . [L]et us not forget that we stand in a glorious heritage of those who have known and loved Christ, who in love and wisdom have served their generation and have made us their legatees. There have been, and there now are in every land, a great company of those who have spoken with authority. Because they have witnessed, the world is different. We must inquire now the basis of their faith, the grounds wherein they found assurance to speak. Unless we know in what direction to look for truth, we shall not know when we have found it.

How Shall We Know?

Whatever the demands of the scientific spirit to maintain an attitude of tentativeness, science, philosophy, religion and the everyday business of living unite in the desire to *know*. Ignorance breeds superstition, and the tyranny of uninformed minds, says science; therefore, if one would know the truth about anything, observe the data, form an hypothesis, deduce what would follow if the hypothesis were true, verify it by further observation under controlled conditions. Fragmentary knowledge inclines to dogmatism, says philosophy; therefore, if one would know the whole truth, be the spectator of all time and all existence, bring not only facts but meanings under scrutiny, and make a coherent synthesis.

"O that I knew where I might find him!" cries the seeking religious spirit, and the answer is the response of faith to what is believed to be revealed by God for man's salvation. And in the turmoil of our ordinary living, everybody wants something solid to stand on—something he *knows* he can be sure of—else "doubts assail and fears annoy," and neuroses and conflicts get the better of us.

This is but to say that man, at all times, in all states, in all pursuits, is bound to seek an authority. It is the widespread loss of authority in personal living and in social relations that is mainly responsible for the chaos of our day.

From "By What Authority," *Faith by Which the Church Lives*, 51–73.

To speak with disparagement of an authoritarian religion is to speak with ambiguity. Doubtless there are right kinds and wrong kinds of authority, but there can be no religion without some authority. All we can have without authority are leaps in the dark that fail to arrive at solid footing, guesses that neither inform nor sustain. These are not religion, for religion exists to bind man back to God with a tie that holds.

Within historic Christianity there have been, and in current Christian thought there still are, five main sources of authority. These are the Church, the Bible, the world of nature, the Holy Spirit, and the person of Jesus Christ. These are not in most instances mutually exclusive, but they represent distinct and divergent emphases. Christian thought, without wholly dropping any, has swung in sequence from one to another of them. For centuries it was an authoritarian Church, with its priesthood and sacraments, that held Christianity and the social order together. Then came the Protestant Reformation, which substituted an authoritative Book for an authoritative Church. The Reformation theology, with its doctrine of *sola Scriptura, sola gratia, sola fide,* was powerful but obdurate in the teeth of scientific fact, and it was bound to be challenged by the rationalism of the Enlightenment period. Yet Christian faith could not die, and deism, with its defense of a spiritual universe "by the natural light of reason," became the refuge of many minds. Meanwhile the Friends, with their doctrine of the inner light, and other exponents of mystical religion, were saying what Christians of all ages had declared in their moments of illumination, that spiritual truth must be spiritually discerned. Then with an increase in study of the New Testament, particularly of the Synoptic Gospels, there came in the latter nineteenth and early twentieth centuries a deepened appreciation of the life and teachings of the historical Jesus. The man of Nazareth, teacher, prophet, leader and Lord, became the assurance of our certainty of the God to whom he drew all men.

We stand now in the fruitful and provocative situation of having a vigorous revival of all the earlier forms of authority, together with an embattled but still lively defense of the last. While it is, of course, impossible to step out of time to get perspective, I doubt whether there has been since the germinative period of the early Church a more interesting theological era.

The Church, long since discarded by Protestantism as authority in matters of truth, though retained as a medium of instruction in truth otherwise obtained, is surging up again in the Protestant mind. The ecumenical Church is not only drawing us together for more concerted action, but is revealing our theological likenesses and differences and helping to clarify our basis of authority. There emerges the conviction that the Church as a divinely established fellowship is not only the custodian of the Christian gospel, but its matrix for growth. The Church is the worshiping Christian community, and the community determines the heritage of truth from the past and the direction in which to look for fresh discoveries.

The Bible is the alleged authority of the highly influential stream of thought we variously called crisis theology, or dialectical theology, or continental theology, or Reformation theology, or neo-orthodoxy, or (too superficially) Bar-thianism. A renewed emphasis on the Bible as the primary basis of our faith was clearly apparent at Madras and Amsterdam, and even in our American colleges, with their more or less impregnable walls of sophistication, the study of the Bible is once more becoming respectable.

Liberalism is under fire. Its affirmation, on grounds compatible with science, of the God discernible in nature and its high appreciation of the life and teach-ings of Jesus seem to many an inadequate basis of faith. Yet if one may judge by *The Christian Century*'s series of thirty-five testimonies as to "How My Mind Has Changed," liberalism in America at least is "bandaged but unbowed."[18] Mean-while mysticism, more timeless by nature than any of these other approaches, con-tinues in bold disregard of theological controversy to quicken many to worship, and to find in the light of the Spirit guidance to live in serenity and serve in love.

Any of these approaches may be perverted or it may be used with power. The full richness of the gospel message requires that all be employed, and used without the narrowness that has too often made them snares instead of guides. I shall try to suggest briefly what happens when we use them awry.

Shall we believe simply "What Mother Church believes"? To do so is to save a deal of thinking. There is spiritual as well as ecclesiastical power in the kind of unquestioned obedience and unquestioning faith that result, but the way is wide open to autocracy and superstition. Since Protestants are prone to think of illus-trations innumerable from the Roman Church, let me suggest that to do obei-sance before the Apostles' Creed is in effect to make the Church of an earlier day the arbiter of our faith. The creeds of Christendom are halting and on the whole surprisingly successful attempts, as far as they go, to state what makes Christianity Christian. As yardsticks by which to measure the boundless reaches of our faith or as molds within which to confine it, they are dangerously deceptive.

As for the Bible, most people, at least most people sufficiently informed to be ministers of the gospel, recognize the dangers inherent in the proof-text method. It is a truism that one can prove anything one likes from the Bible. In the last Presidential election, there was plastered in every New York subway train as a party slogan the affirmation, "You shall know the truth, and the truth shall make you free." One doubts whether during the Christian era there has ever been a notion, wise or foolish, that has not been defended by someone on the authority of this great word! A more recent example is an attack on American neutrality re-enforced by the text, "He that is not with me is against me." Such misappli-cation offends our sense of the fitness of things. Yet it is a curious fact that we recognize the danger of quoting out of context much more clearly when other people do it. What minister is there who has not made up a sermon according to his own ideas and then picked a text to justify it?

The revolt against fundamentalism has centered upon the other great pitfall of reliance on the authority of the Bible, namely, the disregard of historical and scientific fact that ensues from belief in its literal inspiration. The battle is not yet won. Like the poor, literalism is always with us. Young people still come to college from your churches—at least, from some churches—wondering whether they can believe in Genesis and evolution. There is no more contemporaneous book in the Bible than Revelation—dealing as it does with the persecution of those who refuse to bow the knee to Caesar, and a crown of life to him that overcometh through the power of Christ. Literalize it—or worse yet, allegorize it—and you get weird nonsense. From Genesis to Revelation the Bible has been cheapened, perverted, flattened out to a dull dead level by those who find their authority in the letter and not the spirit.

Distressed and perhaps disgusted at the sorry substitute for truth that Biblical literalism gives, many have turned to the observable, humanly accessible processes of nature, and have found in a spiritual interpretation of scientific fact their basis of authority. I am not speaking now of the atheism or naturalistic humanism that has so widely dominated our culture as a result of the victory of science over revelation. I refer to the naturalistic theism that looks to no revelation from heaven, but finds God in the ordered regularities of the heavens and in the social process, to the sincere religious faith that has no place for quaint Old Testament tales, but sees "every common bush aflame with God." Such faith in its concept of deity has no place for the more-than-natural, but it has a large place for the more-than-human. It is a long way from humanism or atheism. It merits high respect. Emerging in many forms since John Locke and the other English deists wrote of "the reasonableness of Christianity," the rejection of supernaturalism today finds its ablest and most persuasive exponent in the philosophy of Henry Nelson Wieman.

I shall not linger long to try to refute religious naturalism in this form or in any other. I have suggested elsewhere some grounds of its inadequacy.[19] The problem of the relation of natural to revealed theology is large enough to be the theme of a *Summa Theologica*. . . . One may find in physical and human nature much evidence of a Creator who works with orderliness and with long purposes. One may read out of the social chaos that follows evildoing the evidence of a God of moral judgment. One may find in the fact of our social dependence and relatedness the urge toward community as a religious imperative. But I do not find, save in the Bible, the assurance of a God who is Father and Redeemer—of a living, loving, saving Deity who in grace and mercy condemns, yet forgives, his sinning children and empowers them to new life.

There is reason for this, for revelation and redemption with which the Bible deals are Person-to-person relationships. They have meaning only in terms of personal confrontation with a personal God. If there is no revelation, or only such general revelation as is discernible through nature, there is only such salvation as man can discover for himself through a right use of nature. This is much, but not enough. Without a living God who takes the initiative in revealing himself in love and saving men from sin, there can be religion—good religion. But it is not the religion of Christian faith. It is primarily this lack of authority for the central assumptions of the Christian gospel of redemption that makes deficient any philosophy of religion that excludes the more-than-natural.

We said that another source of authority was the mystic's vision, or, to speak more generally, the inner leading of the Holy Spirit. Belief in the guidance of the Holy Spirit has, of course, not been limited to mysticism. John Calvin was anything but a mystic, yet he believed that the power to interpret the Scriptures lay with those, like himself, to whom the Spirit spoke. Current neo-Calvinism follows the same pattern. Exponents of the Reformation theology, eschewing mysticism as savoring too much of a monism that would deny the ultimate difference between man and God, will tell you that their sole authority in matters of faith is the Word of God. Yet there is always implicit the assumption that God has spoken this word to them, and has revealed to them by faith truth that is hidden from those who think differently. This is what makes argument so difficult and, for the most part, futile.

I do not wish to oversimplify by treating together two points of view as disparate as those of the Quaker mystic and the Barthian. They are as far apart in their conceptions of the nature of man and of deity as they are in their social programs. The one asserts that there is within man a divine seed or ground which must be nourished and that through communion with God in a quest for true unity the cloven and chaotic character of man's world is healed. The other maintains that there is an infinite qualitative difference between the holy God and sinful man, and that only through an unmerited act of divine grace can the sinner find salvation. Yet far apart as these positions are, the extremes meet in the assumption that God reveals his truth through the Spirit to those who seek in faith.

This assertion of the need of guidance by the Holy Spirit is basic to Christianity. As an expression of our need of being willing to be led if we would find our truest leading, it is an indispensable expression of man's dependence. Without it, prayer would be empty verbiage. The things of the Spirit of God must be spiritually discerned.

Yet when this reliance on the Spirit makes revelation or intuition a substitute for reason, view it with suspicion! It runs into the excesses of the "guidance" with which the critics of the Oxford groups have acquainted us. It makes for a hallowing of our subconscious impulses. It fosters a sleek assurance that we are the children of light while others sit in darkness. In theology it begs the question by eliminating the rational grounds on which its judgments might be challenged; in action it too often makes Christians "the butting rams of the Holy Ghost." Much mystery is hid from us, but of this we can be sure—that what we think the Spirit reveals as truth is not the truth unless it can meet the tests of our experience. God never contradicts himself.

What of the fifth source of authority, the life and teachings of Jesus? Here has lain the main source of liberalism's strength. To any moot question of creedal authority, to any crude ethical concept in the Bible it could speak an emancipating word: "Test it by the witness of our Lord. If it conforms to the pattern of his life and to what he taught of God, accept it. If not, cast it out without regret." To the revelation of God in nature it has said, "Let us prize it and learn more of it, for it speaks truly of deity, but let us make the moral message of Jesus the center of our faith." To those who have thought to find in the testimony of the Holy Spirit their road to truth it has shown that subjective judgment about holy things gives us gods many and lords many, but in "the God and Father of our Lord Jesus Christ" is unshakable rootage of faith.

While liberalism was in its theological heyday, we thought that the battle with obscurantism was well on the way to being won. We might go forward indefinitely, but never, it seemed, could we retreat from a type of faith that made room for both science and religion, that called men to worship the God Jesus worshiped and to live as Jesus lived, that challenged the evils of an unchristian society and called us to action on the basis of his teachings, that linked faith in God with faith in man, and asserted man's infinite possibilities as coworker with God. It seemed a settled conclusion that the second coming of Christ would occur, not apocalyptically as the early Church expected, but in the gradual advance of the indwelling spirit of Christ in the lives of his followers. Premillennialism was largely relegated to the Pentecostal sects. If we would fulfill our calling as Christians, the object of our thinking, our acting and our praying must be for us, as for Jesus, not to fit our souls for the sky, but to serve the present age by bringing to all men the more abundant life. If we would do this, we would be helping to build the Kingdom of God upon earth.

All this seemed to be established theologically. It awaited only acceptance in action. Such liberalism as I have described was, and is, a cleansing and emancipating force for many Christians. Note that I am not discussing the "straw-man" liberalism that is said to have believed in automatic progress, to have preached only moral platitudes, and to have regarded Jesus merely as a great good man. This kind may have existed but it was never the main stream of liberal thought.

Largely within the past decade a reversal of current has taken place. Many Christians are now ready to tell us, not on the basis of Biblical ignorance, but of highly elaborate Biblical criticism, that we really know very little about the historical Jesus; that it is to the early Church and especially to the writings of Paul that we must look for the Biblical basis of Christianity; that it is not the life and teachings of Jesus, but the death and resurrection of Christ that are the focus of our faith. On the basis of this Pauline Christology, effort directed not to social change but to personal regeneration becomes our major calling, while to work for a new social order on the authority of Jesus is to fall into "activism" and "moralism." Once more we hear talk of the return of Christ in glory to establish his Kingdom—this time not from the depressed classes, theologically speaking, but from the most eminent European theologians, and one has to fight at ecumenical gatherings for a recognition of the coming of the Kingdom on earth. To "build the Kingdom" is anathema. To suggest that Jesus treated men as if they were not wholly impotent and sinful, or to say that man in his essential greatness is akin to God, is to precipitate the charge of humanism and to call forth a counter-affirmation about man's righteousness being as "filthy rags."

All this seems curious, after we thought we had got the truth established by the authority of Jesus. But here it is. It is not limited to Europe. At the Madras

Conference I heard an American delegate declare that Paul understood the gospel better than our Lord, for he had witnessed the crucifixion and the resurrection while Jesus had not. Here is a statement worth pondering. If it is true, it shifts radically the basis of authority.

The Mind of Christ

In the midst of these crosscurrents, we have three alternatives: First, we might choose one of these bases of Christian authority to the exclusion of the rest. This has been done; it can be done again. But the route is lined with the pitfalls of the past. Second, we might conceivably find a new basis of faith. But if we do, we shall hardly keep within the bounds of historic Christianity. Such discontinuity would mean a new religion, such as humanism under the impact of science, or Communism and Fascism under changed political conditions. The third alternative is to make a synthesis of these approaches under some guiding principle that can unite them all. This is what an evangelical liberalism, at its best, attempts to do. It can be done.

The guiding principle to be applied to each of these bases of authority is the mind of Christ. Under greatly varying conditions this has always been the touchstone of Christian faith. When the Church has wandered off the main track into the arid wastes of ecclesiastical controversy, into the bogs of fruitless speculation, or into the red-light district of a jazz evangelism, the mind of Christ has again and again recalled us to the meaning of the gospel. Where it has been, no effort to proclaim the gospel could be unloving in its motive or sterile in its fruits.

By the mind of Christ I do not mean solely the personality and mood of the man of Nazareth. It is true that the Church was born, and Christianity as the faith of the Church, in a first-century conviction of the living presence of a crucified and risen Redeemer. It was when those "who knew him after the flesh knew him no more" that a faith came into being which was to transform the world. This faith was linked with the only partially understood but never doubted assurance that through the death of Christ God had acted in love for man's salvation, that through the resurrection of Christ God had won in time an eternal victory over sin and death.

I believe these insights of the early Church to be true. We are no nearer than was Paul to explaining how it could come about. With him we must at times give up the attempt to explain and simply cry out, "Thanks be to God for his unspeakable gift!" Yet the fact of a living and abiding spiritual Christ as the free gift of God for man's salvation is one of the bedrock foundations of our faith. Any concept of Christ which leaves it out becomes decimated and enfeebled.

Yet the indwelling spiritual Christ is not the only foundation of our faith. Without an historical Jesus there would have been no continuing Christ. Had there not been a Man who was tempted in all points as we are, yet without sin, we should not know the reality of a God-given victory over sin. Had there not been a Man who lived in love and lifted sinners from their sin through love, we should not know the reality of an all-merciful, forgiving God. Let us admit, as far as we find it necessary, the inaccuracy and inadequacy of the gospel records, and the fact remains that the early Church would not have drawn the picture it did if it had not been convinced of the reality back of the picture. Out from the pages of the Synoptic Gospels, clouded over as they are with the dust of first-century Jewish-Christian thought, shines a luminous human figure. In this portrait we discern the face of God. Those who think to build a faith on Christ without Jesus leave out that which makes the incarnation real. What I have been saying is that the mind of Christ includes both the historical Jesus and the Christ of faith, and if we do not have both, we do not have the Word made flesh. In Jesus Christ God spoke: in him, in so far as we can read his message aright, is our ultimate authority.

If we put the incarnation at the center, not only of the gospel of redemption but of the quest for Christian truth, other approaches take on new meaning and become once more dependable guides.

It is clear that the Church can never be a safe authority so long as it is simply a human institution, one more social group among many. Every social group has in it good people and bad, wise men and foolish, and there is no guarantee that the counsels of the good and the wise will prevail. This is why it is dangerous to regard the pronouncement of any existing church, whether in creed, legislation, or conference appointment, as having divine authority.

But if the Church is more than a social group; if it is a worshiping fellowship of those who seek to have the mind of Christ, then the mind of Christ affords a regulative principle by which to judge its action. Any human member of it will fail, and all its members together will sin and fall short of the glory of God, yet still through the miasma of our human frailty will shine the glory of God in the face of Jesus Christ. Christ's true Church, like Christ himself, exists in time yet beyond all time. Because it is more than a human institution, it cannot fail to resist the floods of evil from the gates of hell; because it is more than a human institution it will continue to conserve our Christian heritage and point men forward toward new truth.

So too with the Bible. The Bible can profitably be studied as great literature, or as a valuable collection of sociological data, or as a more or less accurate historical record of an exceedingly tenacious people. There are other less profitable ways to study it. And there is a more profitable way. The Bible is not all of one level. But it is all of one piece. Through many varied types of literature written over many centuries, it has one great theme—the obligation of man to God and of God to man. More than once this obligation was crudely conceived, for man's own vindictiveness and passion have a way of getting mixed with his idea of holy things. If we would sort out the humanly crude from the divinely pure in the message of the Bible, we have an authoritative measure—the mind of Christ. We may fail in our use of it—but the measure is not corrupted by our misuse.

If we read the Bible with eyes to see and ears to hear, we shall find the message of a creating, judging, redeeming God growing in power throughout the record to culminate in the living witness of Christ. Read in faith, the Bible is the Word of God. Read otherwise, it may seem what Aldous Huxley calls it, "a remarkable compendium of Bronze-Age literature."[20] Some parts of the Bible have more of the voice of God than others, though on the whole it was a true insight based on living religious experience that determined the selection of the canon. If we read the Bible, not uncritically nor hypercritically, but in a mood to hear what God speaks and to judge all by the mind of Christ, we shall be nourished afresh and shall find great truth.

The relation of the God and Father of our Lord Jesus Christ to the God of natural phenomena is less obvious. I have already said what I believe to be crucial—that a purely natural theology is bound to be deficient because it leaves out the God of redemption. This is to say that it leaves out the incarnation, or so reinterprets it as to devitalize it.[21]

It makes a difference which way you move. Begin with nature, and it does not take you to the mind of Christ. There is order, beauty and nourishing power to be discerned in both physical and human nature, but there is also cruelty and a vast indifference. There is little in nature to suggest a God of suffering love who cares for each of his human children. Who of us, confronted by the fact of the illimitable distances in the heavens and of our own littleness, has not felt with the psalmist: "When I consider thy heavens, the work of thy fingers, The moon and the stars, which thou hast ordained; What is man, that thou art mindful of him?"

Reverse the process, begin with the insights of Christian faith, and nature takes on a new aspect. Neither its physical immensities nor its human masses are remote from the Father's hand. It does not seem unfitting that a God who loves all men and who cares for each should send his rain alike on the just and the unjust. Not only do the heavens declare the glory of God; man takes on new dignity as God's child. A little lower than God, he is crowned with glory and honor. Our task, then, is to use nature for the enhancement of human good.

If we have the mind of Christ, we shall seek the guidance of the Holy Spirit; for, like our Lord, we must have leading and light through fellowship with the Father. There is no guarantee that we shall not make mistakes, for we have our heavenly treasure in earthen vessels. We must use our own eyes to discern the signs of the times, even while we endeavor to see with the eye of faith. We must put our insights to the test of reason and the demands of Christlike living. To fail to do so is to corrupt the truth. Yet the most serious error we could make would be to suppose that we could discover all we need to know by our own unaided seeing. If we would find the truth, the true light which lighteth every man that cometh into the world must shine upon us.

I do not know where we shall come out from among the tangled hedgerows and byways of present-day theology. Its future is almost as unpredictable as is the future of Western civilization. But the outlook is much less dark. As society has become more chaotic, Christian faith has been deepened and clarified. The grounds of Christian authority are now both more varied and more stable than they have been for a long time. I anticipate, though I do not know, that we may look for an increasing vitality in Christian theology through the interpenetration of diverse modes of thought. We must await the future with open minds. But as we wait we can be assured, if we are Christians, that God has revealed himself in Jesus Christ and has called us out of darkness into his marvelous light.

READING 18

It is fitting that I should bring together in conclusion what I have been trying to say throughout. These convictions will be stated, not as a summary but as a credo, for the Church does not live by an assembling of dogmas but by an affirmation of faith. And while I state my own faith, I believe it to be also the faith by which the Church lives.

I believe in God—a Being supreme in wisdom, power, and goodness who controls the universe and presides over human destinies. Though any symbol drawn from human personality is inadequate to describe the fullness of his nature, God is best conceived in terms of personality. Creative power, moral judgment and redemptive love meet in Jesus' symbol of divine fatherhood.

I believe in man—child of eternity in time, a creature fashioned in God's image yet unable to be master of himself. Though man is endowed with the gift of moral freedom, his use of it is limited by weakness and corrupted by sin. To the receptive and the penitent, God in gracious love offers forgiveness and power.

I believe in Jesus Christ—friend and teacher, Lord and Saviour, the incarnation of God. In him is both the supreme revelation of God and the supreme gift of God for man's salvation. God has not left himself without a witness among any people, and this presence is to be discerned through nature, through history, through beauty, through human personality, through the spiritual insights of men of all faiths. Yet in Christ alone is God fully manifest. God has not left us to strive in utter feebleness; he empowers us through our natural endowment and our social heritage to aspire toward the good life and in some measure to achieve it. Yet in Christ alone is the grace of God fully laid hold upon. No man may live without sin; whosoever will may find victory through Christ.

I believe in the Kingdom—the righteous rule of God within the family of God. It is both a divine gift and a human task. It is an invisible and eternal goal; yet its reality is visible in time, manifest in redeemed individuals and in communities transformed by love. It comes upon earth as brotherhood increases; it will come beyond earth as God admits us to a more perfect fellowship with himself.

I believe in the Church—the living body of the indwelling Christ, the worshiping Christian fellowship, the conserver of the gospel and its growing-point in history. It is related to the Kingdom as means to end, and it is the indispensable, though it is not the only, agency for the advancement of the Kingdom. As a visible structure the Church has in many respects fallen short of Christ's true

"Retrospect and Credo," *Faith by Which the Church Lives*, 158–61.

Church. Yet even within the visible Church with all its imperfections we see in the fact of the world Christian community a sign of the coming of the Kingdom.

I believe in the duty of the Christian to bear witness to his faith. The ways in which to do it are infinitely various, and each must find his way. We must do this in a union of tolerance with conviction, of courage with tact, of reticence with boldness, of initiative with willingness to be led. Both prayer and action, both reason and revelation must steadily correct and clarify our witness.

Finally, *I believe in the limitless resources of God for every situation.* This is a day in which to be serious. But it is not a day in which to give up. The Christian heritage of truth and brotherhood is in jeopardy and only divine power in conjunction with the wisest human effort can preserve it. Yet we know it will not be lost. Both within and beyond this world, the riches of God revealed in Christ will deliver us from evil. The Church has a mission and the capacity to perform it, for the Church has a faith by which it lives.

VIII

Fighting for Peace (1941–42)

SECTION PREFACE

On December 10, 1941, three days following the Japanese attack on Pearl Harbor, as the nation was preparing for a war that had just been officially declared, an editor at *Time* magazine sent Harkness a telegram testing her pacifist convictions. "Are [you] still as opposed to war as you were in June and feel that you cannot bless sanction or support war[?]" Harkness wired her reply the same day: "My pacifist convictions remain unchanged. They are based on the Christian gospel, not on news reports, and were formed in full awareness that the United States might become a belligerent. . . ."[1]

Harkness became a pacifist long before the war. In 1924 she joined the "American Seminar" and traveled through Western Europe with a group of pastors, scholars, and other professionals to learn about the conditions of post–World War I Europe. The trip, Harkness later reflected, "opened my eyes to the realities of war and made me a pacifist."[2] Reinhold Niebuhr had also become a pacifist on one of these tours in the 1920s. But by the early 1930s, Niebuhr was moving away from his pacifist commitment. Harkness, reflecting later on this change in Niebuhr's position, wrote, "I believe that Niebuhr-then was closer to the truth than the Niebuhr-now."[3] In large part because of her pacifist commitments, she went to see Mahatma Gandhi when she was in India in December of 1938 and wrote later of talking with Gandhi and spending the night in his ashram with the pacifist and social reformer Muriel Lester.[4]

In June 1939 Harkness joined Emil Brunner and John Foster Dulles for the Geneva Conference. About three dozen Christian religious and political leaders from around the world gathered, at the invitation of the provisional committee of the World Council of Churches, in the hope that they might come up with a plan to take to heads of state in order to avoid war. World War II began less than two months later.

Unlike many of the liberal pacifists of the 1920s, Harkness remained a pacifist throughout World War II, writing about pacifism and speaking about it at national meetings, and she continued to oppose war throughout her life. In 1966 her former student George McGovern placed in the Congressional Record her article opposing the Vietnam War.[5] For Harkness, pacifism was not only a position to be fought for but also a way of being in the world. An opponent of pacifism once said of Harkness, "She is the only pacifist I ever met who was pacific in argument."[6]

The final readings here are three of the many articles Harkness wrote in support of pacifism in midst of World War II.[7] The first is from August 6, 1941, four months before the bombing of Pearl Harbor. Things were going badly for the Allies. France had fallen the year before, as had Yugoslavia and Greece earlier in 1941. German planes had been bombing British cities, and Hitler's ground troops were now focused on the Soviet Union. The United States had not yet entered the war but had begun in July to freeze Japanese assets in the United States, and in his Independence Day radio address, Roosevelt warned of the consequences of doing nothing: "I tell the American people solemnly that the United States will never survive as a happy and fertile oasis of liberty surrounded by a cruel desert of dictatorship."[8]

In an article from June 1941, Reinhold Niebuhr had criticized the Christian idealists who argued for "peace through mediation" in what Niebuhr called "this final hour of America's decision." They were not only wrong politically, but also theologically. Their idealist illusions were "the final fruit of a theological movement that thinks that the Kingdom of God is a simple extension of human history and that men may progress . . . if they have become sufficiently courageous, pure, and selfless. All such illusions finally end in disaster."[9]

Harkness wrote "The Christian's Dilemma" in direct response to Niebuhr's article. If, as Niebuhr had charged, the idealists were guilty of "bad politics" derived from "bad religion," then not only pacifist political claims but also the theological underpinnings must be explained. In this article Harkness examines the theological foundations—some shared and some diverging—of those supporting and those opposing the war. As in previous readings, one sees here Harkness's conviction that doing theology can, in itself, be a form of political activity.

The final two readings were published in back-to-back issues of *The Christian Century* in November 1942 when the world crisis was particularly brutal. In the few months before their publication, the Battle of Stalingrad, which would ultimately claim as many as one and a half million lives, had begun and was still raging; the United States had begun heavy bombing of European cities; and Jews were being gassed in Auschwitz. Although Stalingrad proved to be a turning point in the war, from the perspective of the fall of 1942, things still looked bad for the Allies.

In this bleak context, Harkness was as stalwart in her pacifism as ever. Indeed the brutality of that time was a key part of her argument. "The crux of the problem now confronting the churches is that under present conditions, the merciless bombing and starving of civilian populations may be requisite to military victory. Unless one is prepared to say that God wills the canceling of all humanitarian scruples until the war is won, one can hardly identify military triumph with the divine will." This argument and others were quite controversial at the time. For example, Harkness called for church leaders to help Christians in the United States see their complicity in the war and move toward repentance and humility. She insisted that peace would be possible only when nations were willing to give up "absolute national sovereignty."

The most striking feature of both articles is the hopeful note on which they end. In the fall of 1942, it was not at all clear how the war would turn out, and the casualties—both civilian and military—were very high. Even in this bleak moment, Harkness pointed toward the coming Kingdom of God and the human part in helping to bring it about. She wrote, "Though earthly systems crash in ruins and anguish engulf the earth, we can know that God reigns, and that he works with men to make the kingdoms of this world become the Kingdom of our Lord." And again, "Though the world is in flames the authentic work of the churches must go on. Only as this goes forward, not contracted but expanded because of the national emergency, can we hope to see beyond the battle a new world fashioned in the image of the family of God."

READING 19

A paradoxical situation prevails in our churches. On the one hand, there is ground for rejoicing that within the church, in spite of differences of opinion, there continues to be a potent moral and spiritual leadership. There is now in the church more fellowship among those of divergent political opinions, more spiritual steadiness in the face of nationalistic hysteria, more determination to work creatively for a just and enduring peace, than in any other of our social institutions. There is hope in the fact that there is apparently far greater resoluteness at these points now than was characteristic of the churches of twenty-five years ago.

"The Christian's Dilemma," *Christian Century* 58 (Aug. 6, 1941): 977–79.

On the other hand, many persons are confused because the leaders of the church do not agree as to America's duty, or the individual Christian's duty, in the present crisis. Christian leaders, equally sincere and greatly trusted, are passionately urging opposite courses. It is not surprising that the man on the street, whether churchgoer or onlooker, often fails to find in the church any clear guide to action.

Basic theological presuppositions have more to do with the problem than is commonly realized. Among Christian leaders who understand their faith and who take it seriously there are some important agreements. Non-theological factors being given due allowance, it is these agreements in faith that are binding us together and giving the church its moral effectiveness. There are also certain fundamental differences in theological emphasis which go far toward explaining differences of alignment in international policy. To understand these foundations should help us to work together more effectively and to maintain tolerance at those points where our decisions must differ. It is the purpose of this article to outline some of these differences and agreements. After surveying the Christian pacifist and non-pacifist presuppositions I shall suggest some bases of united action.

I

Christian pacifism grows best in the soil of social-gospel liberalism, where the central ethical emphasis is drawn, not from the Old Testament or from Paul, but from Jesus. This helps to explain why there is more pacifism among the great preachers of America than among the theologians. In Union and Princeton seminaries, where the prevailing political climate is that of interventionism, the dominant theological mood is the new orthodoxy with a strongly Hebraic-Pauline-Augustinian note. On the other hand, most of our outstanding preachers were reared in liberalism and, though their liberalism has been chastened and deepened in recent years, they are still liberals. Whether this is stigma or compliment depends on the point of view! To mention Fosdick, Buttrick, Tittle, Palmer . . . Halford Luccock, E. Stanley Jones—and others whose names will as readily occur to the reader—is both to call the roll of America's leading pacifist preachers and to name some of our most forthright crusaders for a liberal social gospel. It is, of course, impossible to equate liberalism with pacifism, since such stalwart liberals as Henry Sloane Coffin and Henry P. Van Dusen are in the ranks of the interventionists.

If pacifists are for the most part liberals, even though not all the liberals are pacifists, what are the basic postulates which give pacifism a growing point?

The familiar charges brought against Christian pacifism by its critics are that it is "perfectionist," "utopian" and "idealistic"; that it is based on a false and sentimental optimism about human nature; that it misunderstands or at least misapplies the ethics of Jesus; that it has a wrong conception of the Kingdom of God and of man's relation to it; that in exalting the love of God it gives too little place to the God of judgment. In a recent statement, Reinhold Niebuhr brings together most of these charges when he writes:

It is the fruit of a "religious idealism" which never gauged the tragic factors of human sin in human history adequately. It was an idealism ostensibly devoted to the "truth," but yet unwilling to face the truth about men. . . . This is the final fruit of a theological movement which thinks that the Kingdom of God is a simple extension of human history and that men may progress from the one to the other at any time if they have become sufficiently courageous, pure and selfless. All such illusions finally end in disaster. Communist utopianism ends in the sorry realities of Stalinism and this liberal-Christian utopianism ends by giving the dubious politics of "America First" the sanctity of the Sermon on the Mount.[10]

Since my purpose is not polemic I shall not attempt to answer these charges. Dr. Niebuhr will doubtless tell us whether his brand of interventionism can find a better bedfellow in "the sorry realities of Stalinism" than in the "liberal-Christian utopianism" which he so vigorously renounces. While these charges as they are commonly set forth are a caricature of the Christian pacifist position, they stem from certain vital emphases.

Christian pacifism roots primarily in four theological convictions: a doctrine of God, a doctrine of man, a moral attitude toward Jesus, and a conception of man's responsibility with reference to the Kingdom of God. Each of these is a great subject, the outlines of which can only be suggested here.

1. God is the Father of all men. His character is Christlike. His primary method of dealing with men is redemptive love. He dwells both within and beyond history. His cause may be temporarily thwarted but it cannot be defeated. Each of these convictions for the Christian pacifist has important consequences for action.

If God is the Father of all men, he is the Father of the enemies of our state as well as of our compatriots. Their wrongs ought to be rectified and their sufferings relieved instead of their being slain. If God's character is Christ-like, then one will not participate in war as the will of God unless one believes that Christ could have done so. If God deals with men by the method of redemptive love, not only our ends but our means for the restraint of evil must be prompted by love. If God is both within and beyond the human scene, he cannot be indifferent to the human struggle and, however deferred the victory, good must in the long run triumph. Knowing that God is on the side, not of the heaviest battalions but of justice and love, we can labor for peace by such ways of peace as are available, and leave with God the outcome.

2. The Christian pacifist's doctrine of man is by no means as naive about human sin as it is sometimes represented to be. It is precisely because the pacifist knows men to be sinful and life to be full of conflict that he sees no good to be gained by the colossal sin and conflict of war. On the other hand, he sees in every man the image of God, however much defaced by sin, and he cannot therefore adopt a devil theory of history. He sees in every war a conflict, not between an all-good and an all-bad state, but between states composed of men who are sons of God and who, like ourselves, are mixtures of good and evil. With this perspective he may—and must—judge some men and movements to be more evil than

others and in need of restraint for the common good. But since he sees in every man the divine image he cannot judge any man to merit death for the sin of his national affiliation.

3. All Christian pacifism worthy of the name stems from the revelation of God in Jesus Christ. Pacifism's affiliation with liberalism and the social gospel is evident in the high estimate it places on the words and deeds of the Jesus of history. The Synoptic Gospels are its major authority and source. Yet regarding the non-resistance enjoined by Jesus there is no single point of view. Some pacifists literalize the injunctions of the Sermon on the Mount while others do not. Some are disturbed by the incident of the money-changers, while others see no close analogy between this relatively mild and harmless use of force and the total destructiveness of modern war. Those are on safest ground who do not deny that Jesus in at least one instance used physical coercion and that he said nothing specific about war.

If one believes that Jesus regarded persons—all persons—as of supreme worth, this is bedrock for the pacifist position. Add to it the fact that Jesus himself chose the way of the cross instead of military force in a situation tense with nationalism, and one finds more potent testimony in this fact than in any specific word about non-resistance. The charter of the Christian pacifist's obligation to a positive ministry of reconciliation was stated in classic terms by Paul: "God was in Christ, reconciling the world unto himself, not imputing their trespasses unto them; and hath committed unto us the word of reconciliation."

4. With reference to the Kingdom, there is both wide variation among pacifists and close agreement between pacifists and non-pacifists. That it is not impossible for pacifism and apocalypticism to form a working partnership is demonstrated by Jehovah's Witnesses, to say nothing of the early Christians. On the other hand, there are probably as many non-pacifists as pacifists who talk about "building the Kingdom."

The central focus of the matter lies in man's responsibility for the Kingdom and the means to be used in the exercise of this responsibility. As the Madras report declared, the Kingdom is "both present and future; both a growth and a final consummation by God. It is our task and our hope. . . . We work for it and we wait for it." To most Christian pacifists, this means active responsibility for helping to create those conditions of economic justice, international cooperation and personal understanding through which God can progressively establish his Kingdom. This does not mean perfectionism or utopianism or a doctrine of automatic progress. It does not make the Kingdom "a simple extension of history" or assume that we shall ever have a sinless political or social order. It does mean a hope and an effort born of the conviction that God will use man's labor to bring the Kingdom nearer to fulfillment on earth if man will seek to use God's methods. But not otherwise. Specifically, this means the faith that war is not ineradicable, but that it can be eradicated only by means consonant with God's governance of his Kingdom in justice and love.

II

At many points the non-pacifist understanding of the Christian faith converges with the pacifist. However, important differences in emphasis cause different conclusions to be drawn. I shall mention some of these matters with reference again to God, man, Jesus, the Kingdom.

1. God is Creator, Judge, Redeemer, and the Lord of history. He is a God of mercy as well as of justice; he saves and redeems unworthy men by his grace when in our sin we forsake his paths. Thus far the pacifist and non-pacifist can walk together. The non-pacifist believes that the pacifist inadequately reckons with the sovereign righteousness of God. God is the righteous Ruler before whom evil men and movements are weighed in the balance, and he does not draw back from using even dire catastrophe to enact his will. Some non-pacifists argue that because God uses force to bring to pass his judgments, men may and must do likewise. All hold that men must be his instruments, even at the cost of the sternest measures, to check tyranny and defeat evil enterprises.

2. Man is a sinner and must ever, even at his highest moments, stand under judgment. Since men are evil, all political systems are infested with evil. So far, pacifist and non-pacifist agree. Divergence arises when the non-pacifist affirms that war, if fought for a good end, may be the lesser of two evil courses. To refuse to take this course is to lapse into political irresponsibility and do incalculable harm to persons whose freedom ought to be defended.

3. Positions vary widely as to the moral absolutes of Jesus. Explanations in terms of an "interim ethic" are less commonly advanced than the view that Jesus was concerned only with the individual, in whose relations non-resistance, though never perfectly attained, is at least a feasible possibility. The pacifist is charged with illicitly transforming "non-resistance," which Jesus enjoins upon individuals but not upon states, into "non-violent resistance," which he enjoins upon nobody. Frederick C. Grant, in *The Gospel of the Kingdom,* makes Jesus' pacifism depend not on a universal spiritual principle but on his intellectual discernment of the futility of resistance under the circumstances of his time. The familiar argument that Jesus was himself not a pacifist because he said, "I came not to bring peace but a sword," and used a whip on the money-changers, is seldom adduced by the more competent non-pacifist scholars.

4. With reference to the Kingdom, the non-pacifist position strikes in at two different angles. On the one hand, there are those who hold that Jesus' primary concern was with an otherworldly Kingdom. His Kingdom has its foregleams upon earth, not in a transformed society but in the souls of redeemed individuals who in repentance and faith receive forgiveness by God's grace. This position, which dominates Continental theology, provides little soil for pacifism to grow in, for it tends to turn over to the state the management of the social order. It correlates closely with the doctrine of "the orders," long familiar in Lutheran thought and now being widely adduced by non-Lutherans. According to this position the state is an order ordained of God, and therefore it is a

God-given duty, not as a Christian but as a citizen, to go to war when the state so ordains.

On the other hand, interventionism, like pacifism, springs from the soil of American social-gospel liberalism. Man must act with God to help bring in the Kingdom and establish justice upon earth. And he must act by any means available. The non-pacifist, differing radically from the pacifist at this point, holds that there are no specifically Christian means. It is always better to act in peace than in war if one can, but in some circumstances, so this argument runs, war is the only instrument by which men may move toward a more just society. To participate in a just war and to give oneself sacrificially to its high ends then becomes the first duty of the Christian.

III

In a welter of such diverse opinion, is there any common ground? It is my conviction that there is, and that we must increasingly discover and act upon it.

First, we can agree upon the evil and unchristian character of war. This does not mean that we shall all agree to be pacifists. It does mean that all Christians can endorse the Oxford Conference statement, unanimously adopted, that "war is a peculiar manifestation of the power of sin in the world; and is a defiance of the righteousness of God as revealed in Jesus Christ and him crucified." This paragraph is the only one italicized in full in the Oxford report. It may seem on the face of it not to be worth much, since Christians keep on fighting each other in good conscience. Yet it means a great deal for the most inclusive body in Christendom to declare officially that war is sin. This judgment has been passed many times by individuals and by individual churches; it was never before spoken with the united voice of the church.

Whether as the result of Oxford or of the cumulative peace effort of the past twenty years, this judgment has been bearing fruit. Even among those Christians who believe most ardently that American intervention is necessary to save democracy, there is an almost unanimous judgment that war, though it may check evil, cannot create good. The disposition to look beyond the battle to lay now the foundations of a just and durable peace is altogether Christian and almost wholly new. Only as Christians unitedly keep this perspective can anything constructive come out of the present holocaust.

Second, we can agree to avoid the extremes of a Utopian optimism and of a defeatist pessimism. The world will not be free of sin as long as there are men in it, and as we judge evil to be present we must always ourselves in humility and penitence stand under judgment. But there need not be so much evil as there is. To adopt one of Reinhold Niebuhr's most constructive phrases, love is always an "impossible possibility"; and if we emphasize its possibilities as grounded in the nature of God, there is no upper limit set to its achievements. All that is most vital in the Christian's faith in the eternal and living God—a God of Christlike love whose purposes are long and whose victories are sure—corroborates this hope.

Third, we can avoid both acquiescence in evil and ruthlessness in the attempt to overcome it. No space need be taken to demonstrate that Christian pacifism is not an irresponsible tolerance of colossal wrongs. It is not a "sit-down strike" in the presence of tyranny. Those non-pacifists who know us best do not make this charge. On the other hand, it needs to be pointed out that among those non-pacifists who see with clearest vision, there is an endeavor to prevent war from becoming mere retaliation and barbarism. Those who read the *British Christian Newsletter* cannot fail to be moved by the greatness of spirit of Dr. J. H. Oldham and his collaborators, who, though not pacifists, have argued repeatedly against reprisals, the bombing of civilian populations, and the loss of Christian understanding and fellowship through war. Should our country become a belligerent, it is devoutly to be hoped that our churches will have leaders equally empowered by Christian insights to see "above the battle."

Fourth, Christians can agree on the duty of absolute loyalty to God alone. Whatever our differences as to moral decision arising from this loyalty, the obligation to obey God rather than men remains unequivocal. The Christian's primary devotion is to the God who is above all gods.

Finally, we must—and can—maintain our faith in God and our faith in one another. In the Christian gospel the two are indissolubly connected. We sever them at our peril. If we love not our brother whom we have—or have not—seen, how shall we love God? And how shall we find in God our refuge and strength? The Christian church exists to bring to men in a living fellowship the power of the living God. The Christian gospel is the gospel of Jesus Christ our common Lord. Before him we can stand in differences of opinion but not in dissensions of spirit. In him our dilemmas of thought are resolved in love.

READING 20

Any attempt to answer the question raised by the title of this article is dangerous. The danger does not lie primarily in the risk of misunderstanding and resentment, though these may be expected in these days of tension. It lies rather in the possibility of "absolutizing the relative," of reading into the mind of the Almighty and All-wise what must be at best a fallible human judgment. Yet the importance of the question exceeds its danger. Only as the Christian gains such light as may be had from pursuing the inquiry, "What is God doing?" is he in a position to answer the ever pressing question, "What must I do?"

Numerous suggestive treatments of the question have appeared in *The Christian Century*. My only reason for adding another is that I have not found in them what I believe needs to be said regarding the relations of cause to purpose in God's activity. When one asks the question, "Why does God permit it?"— whether one is talking about totalitarian war or Mr. Jones' rheumatism—one may mean either of two things. One may mean, "What elements in the physical and social situation existing in God's world have brought this to pass?" Or one

"What Is God Doing in This War?" *Christian Century* 59 (Nov. 4, 1942): 1346–48.

may mean, "What good end is God endeavoring to achieve, through, or in spite of, this situation?" The answers to these two questions will not be identical. Yet each question impinges on the other.

I

Let us first try to clear the ground somewhat by asking what God is *not* doing in this war.

1. God is not changing his nature, or altering his dependable way of working with men, to deliver those on either side of the conflict from disaster. The God of Christian faith is one whose nature is Christlike, whose supreme attribute is love, whose supreme purpose is that all men shall live unselfishly and deal justly with one another. God has endowed us with moral freedom and placed us in an interrelated society. God works with men and calls upon men to work together to establish his Kingdom on earth. Only as men meet the conditions consistent with God's nature and purpose can his Kingdom come and his will be done on earth. God does not alter his nature or his conditions to avert human catastrophe.

This means that God is not delivering man from the consequence of past events. When for a generation the life of individuals and states had been organized primarily on the basis of personal and national self-interest, social irresponsibility, greed and conflict, the only thing a God of love who works consistently could do was to let causes bring effects and global war break forth.

We do well to pray for "peace in our time." But we must not expect that peace in our time will come through a miracle that suspends the conditions within which our lives are set. In the dark days of May 1940, a French commander cried out for a miracle to deliver France. France fell. In those same dark days what is often called the miracle of Dunkirk took place. But . . . one might well ask why there needed to be a Dunkirk at all. Whether in specific events or in the total world situation, we must expect that deliverance from disaster will come through conformity to God's physical and moral order, and that it will not come in any other way.

2. God is not guaranteeing the triumph of the better cause through military victory. There is a perennial tendency to sing and to believe:

> Then conquer we must
> When our cause it is just.

Yet if conquest is understood in a political sense, history does not substantiate this assurance. Israel sinned but Assyria sinned more, and Israel fell. There was injustice in the Rome of the fifth century A.D. but probably more injustice— certainly less spiritual culture—in the barbarian hordes which sacked Rome and destroyed the *Pax Romana*. One reason why most Americans are not very well informed on the Mexican War of 1847 is that it is so hard to identify conquest with justice on that occasion. History records conspicuous and epoch-making instances of the victory of the juster cause, but it will not do to neglect the negative instances. Insofar as it is possible in retrospect to pass an objective judgment it does not look as if the right cause has always won.

This suspicion is supported by a glance at the factors on which the outcome of every military conflict depends. When nations engage in war, which side wins? If either, the victory depends on five factors: (1) superior manpower, (2) superior equipment, (3) superior stamina, (4) superior strategy, (5) superior ruthlessness. To the first four it is not difficult to give divine sanction. The call to sacrifice life and to give material possessions for a great cause is in harmony with the way of the cross; the assurance of divine support affords staying power; wisdom from God may well be asked in any enterprise. It is, however, at the point of superior ruthlessness that the Christian conscience, whether pacifist or not, balks at making a link with the will of God. The crux of the problem now confronting the churches is that under present conditions, the merciless bombing and starving of civilian populations may be requisite to military victory. Unless one is prepared to say that God wills the canceling of all humanitarian scruples until the war is won, one can hardly identify military triumph with the divine will.

II

At the risk of some repetition it is now necessary to try to say what God is doing in this war.

1. God works for good by remaining true to his chosen and orderly ways. There is a dependable system of nature within which both God and man can achieve ends. Through this world system with its infinitely complex physical and social relations God acts for the increase of values upon earth. Recognition of this God-given world order, not as an imprisonment to personality but as a medium for the expression of high purposes in God and man, is a major contribution of modern religious thought which is not likely to be set aside by contemporary events or winds of doctrine. In a more scientific frame of reference it accords with the great refrain of the Genesis epic of creation, "And God saw that it was good."

On the persistence of this orderly structure of nature man's earthly security and happiness depend. Imagine the terror that would seize men's minds if there came to be any great likelihood that the force of gravitation might for a few seconds be suspended! But the correlate to this security is the fact that when a bomb drops it falls toward the center of the earth, no matter how many innocent civilians may be in its path. God has ordained in the order of nature that human bodies require food to remain alive, and has placed in the earth resources enough for all. When access to food is denied, human beings starve. Fire to warm our bodies is a boon; fire that is spread by incendiary bombs brings devastation and death. Here there is "no variableness, neither shadow of turning."

III

We cannot have it both ways. Either God must remain true to his chosen and orderly ways of working or he must occasionally interrupt them. The evidence is that he maintains them. To suppose that God maintains an inflexible system simply for the sake of the system would make him a moral monster, unworthy of any man's worship. But, on the contrary, it is a bedrock conviction of Christian faith that persons are the supreme object of God's love—that what he does he does for love of persons and with a purpose that justifies the cost.

What God's total purpose is no human mind can attempt to say. Yet he has not left himself without a witness, and insofar as we can read the mind of God in the life and words of Christ we can believe that it is for peace, good will and all that makes for "the abundant life." To the achievement of this end, the system of ordered nature contributes when it is used by men in harmony with God's purposes. When it is used for contrary ends, disaster ensues. We are now living in a day of which the word of the Psalmist may be spoken, "Come, behold the works of the Lord, what desolations he hath made in the earth." If we have not yet come to a time to which the next words are applicable, "He maketh wars to cease unto the end of the earth," it is because we have not yet done those things by which wars can be made to cease.

2. In this war God is judging men for the misuse of his gifts and the thwarting of his holy and righteous purposes. Through this judgment upon us for our sins he is trying to teach us his ways and win us to redemption.

With the familiar argument that the war is judgment I am in general agreement. It is wholesome evidence of progress since the First World War that we hear much more of the political consequences of personal and national sin and that the call to repentance is more frequently and more sincerely sounded. Only through repentance can there be the self-criticism and reorientation of life essential to a just and lasting peace. Only through a deeper recognition of the meaning of divine judgment can we escape the pitfalls of an overblithe optimism in good times and faith-destroying bitterness in evil days.

However, with the idea of war as divine judgment as it is often stated, I have some disagreements. To say, as the editor of *The Christian Century* does, that war is hell and in the divine judgment we are condemned to fight, is to overlook the fact that hell had various meanings. To be in hell may mean to suffer the deserved penalty of sin, or to be removed from the presence of God, or to be cut off irrevocably from a chance to obey God in moral freedom. War is hell in the first sense but not in the second or third. God does not take his Holy Spirit from us even in war, nor bar the door to any further obedience to his will. I agree with Richard Niebuhr that the war may more correctly be called purgatory than hell.

IV

Again, one hears the judgment of God identified with automatic punishment for the breaking of God's laws. There is danger here of substituting deism for Christian faith. Punishment for sin in a moral order, though inevitable, is not impersonal. God always deals with persons as persons and not in any mechanical fashion. When men break the laws of God and are broken upon them, God permits consequences to persons that he does not will. Yet there is no situation, however dark, in which men are forsaken by God. The disaster which is the consequence of sin is sheer, unmitigated disaster—neither judgment nor an avenue to grace—unless the sufferer recognizes both the moral demands and the loving-kindness of the living God. Christian faith must illumine the sufferings of our time or they will turn out to be, not redemptive judgment, but only the path to a deeper hell.

Furthermore, punishment and judgment are not synonyms. Punishment may be meted out in vindictiveness or it may be given in love for corrective ends. Punishment for wrongdoing, whether imposed by God or man, would be not judgment but vengeance if its purpose were not redemptive love. There is altogether too much tendency in current discussion to identify a God of judgment with a God of wrath. From this it is a short step to the claim of God's sanction for our wrath against our enemies.

In saying that the war is a judgment upon us for our sins the issues are blurred by the ambiguity of "us." Judgment on whom? Each individual? Or the United States? Or the United Nations? Or all the belligerents in the present war? Or the human race? Doubtless the statement may correctly be made in all of these senses. But not in the same sense or to the same degree. Although every human being is guilty of sins (at least of sins of omission) which in our corporate life have contributed to the war, the guilt is by no means equal. To deny that there are degrees of guilt is to cancel moral distinctions and to undercut the foundations of Christian ethics. It is fruitful for each of us to recognize that his sin has helped to bring on the present world catastrophe. Such perspective induces humility and corrects self-righteousness. But it is neither fruitful nor true to attribute all the sufferings of others to divine judgment.

The penalties of war are not distributed in proportion to the guilt. Nor can all of them be viewed as vicariously redemptive suffering. As Virgil Aldrich reminded us in *The Christian Century* of August 5: "A simple God-fearing peasant who knows only his acre of land, and nurses the living things on it, and wants only to be left in peace . . . is by no means 'crucified' for a Christian cause or a 'vicarious sufferer' for humanity, when a bomb out of the blue blows him and his family to bits." To call this situation the judgment of God upon the peasant is a travesty upon the meaning of judgment. To call it vicarious suffering is to obscure the fact that vicarious suffering to be redemptive must be voluntarily assumed. It seems more appropriate to say simply that the peasant is the victim of circumstances which he did not make, and which God permits but does not will. God's holy purpose to create a community of love upon earth has been thwarted by the complacent irresponsibility and evil deeds of persons far removed from this peasant's life. He, like millions of other relatively innocent persons, is paying the price of living in an interrelated world in which men sin.

3. God delivers us from evil. I have said that God is not altering either his own nature or his world to avert disaster, and that he is not underwriting military victory. I have said that God is maintaining his dependable world order for a good purpose in which he calls us to cooperate, and that when men persist in sin, not only the most guilty but the most innocent must suffer. This I believe. But to leave the matter here would be to omit the primary gift of Christian faith.

V

God does not leave men to suffer alone. No God worthy of respect, to say nothing of devotion, could withdraw in celestial isolation from the anguish of our day. God suffers in human pain whether man's agony arises from the thwarting or the doing of God's holy will. He who cares most suffers most, and God cares supremely. In God's loving concern for every war-torn body and soul, the divine purpose is at work. Here we may rightly look for evidence of God's overarching providence and the ultimate triumph of his righteousness.

God delivers us from evil through giving inner stability, comfort, courage, poise, and peace to all who in humility and trust commit their lives to his care. The Christian can endure anything when he is sure of God. God gives such power to sincere and humble Christians on both sides of national conflict. Fortunately for our human blindness, our national life does not have to be purged of all sin and error before we can say, "In God we trust."

God delivers us from evil through summoning man to act in ways consistent with his will and purpose. God makes moral distinctions. The God of Jesus has a love inclusive enough to embrace both the just and the unjust. But God docs not condone injustice, and he calls us to work with him for its removal. God wins victories in the affairs of nations as of individuals, and wins them by his chosen ways of justice, love and truth.

God delivers us from evil through vicarious self-giving. What he has done in the redemption of the world through the cross he calls upon us to do if we would be true disciples of his Son. There is no vicarious element in the unredeemed and unredemptive misery of millions of men who are today caught in the toils of war. There is high self-giving and the promise of a new world in those who suffer that the will of God may be done on earth as it is done in heaven.

God delivers us from evil by using any gift of life that is brought in love. In every war, however mistaken or futile or unchristian the enterprise as a whole, there is heroism, sacrifice and the laying down of life in lavish devotion. This ought not to be lightly esteemed. God delivers us from evil by bringing to nought the devices of evil men, by making his wisdom to prevail over the errors of our blinded judgment, but weaving into his pattern of enduring spiritual values every good gift that is offered in integrity of spirit.

God delivers us from evil by creating among Christians a worldwide community in which he is lifted up above all lesser gods. In the fellowship of the church of Christ which spans all humanly divisive lines of class, color, race, and nation, we are today witnessing in some measure the manifestation of God's Kingdom upon earth. In such foregleams of a new day we can find light and take courage.

Finally, God delivers us from evil by the assurance that whatever men may do, his purpose for a new-world must ultimately prevail. When men have done their best—or their worst—in the present conflict, God will be living and loving and laboring still. Though earthly systems crash in ruins and anguish engulf the earth, we can know that God reigns, and that he works with men to make the kingdoms of this world become the Kingdom of our Lord and of his Christ. In this confidence that "the Lord God Omnipotent reigneth" is our peace.

READING 21

In a previous article I tried to suggest what God is doing in this war, I stated my conviction that God is neither changing his orderly ways of working to avert disaster nor guaranteeing military victory, but that within a dependable natural and moral order he is working for good, judging us for our sins and delivering us from evil. Among the ways in which God delivers us from evil is the creation of a world-wide Christian community in whose inclusive fellowship are to be discerned some intimations of the meaning of the Kingdom of God upon earth. We must now inquire more specifically what the churches may do to promote peace in the midst of the present world catastrophe.

There is now no lack of knowledge of what is required for a just and lasting peace. In the studies which the church has fostered in Great Britain and in this country, and in numerous others made under secular auspices, such as the report of the Carnegie Endowment's Commission to Study the Organization of Peace, there is remarkable agreement. Without foreknowledge of future events it is impossible for anyone to say in precise detail what political action may be required. Yet the principles are clear and have been many times enunciated by thoughtful minds.

Requirements of a Lasting Peace

The requirements of a just and lasting peace may be reduced to six. These are (1) the belief that peace is possible; (2) provision for peaceful change; (3) surrender of absolute national sovereignty and the formation of a political organism for international cooperation; (4) economic security for all; (5) understanding and practice of the democratic way of life; (6) an international ethos, or spiritual undergirding, of a new international order.

Space is lacking to elaborate why these are essential, but the outlines are clear. Unless one believes that peace is at least relatively possible, a prejudgment of futility will cut the nerve of effort. Unless provision is made for peaceful change, there is bound to be change by violent means, for the world will not stand still. Unless there is surrender of absolute national sovereignty in such matters of international concern as tariffs, raw materials and markets, colonies, currency and immigration, it is certain that national self-interest—whether in outright aggression or in the subtler forms of imperialism—will produce future wars.

Unless the hungry peoples of the world are fed and see adequate security for the future, unrest will burst forth in civil and international strife. Unless at home and abroad there is a preservation of the essential freedoms of the common man, there can be no peace except the uncertain equilibrium which is maintained by autocratic power. Unless the peoples of an interrelated world are knit together by spiritual kinship and a common recognition of moral responsibilities, even the best ship of state will founder on the reef of stubborn human wills and selfish human desires.

To the meeting of these requirements for a just and lasting peace the churches have a great and, indeed, an indispensable contribution to make. They can make this contribution only if, refusing to yield to the pressure of the moment to become a sword-bearing arm of the state, they hold before their members the timeless message of the Christian gospel. I shall attempt now to indicate wherein the spiritual contribution of the churches has political relevance in each of these six areas.

Basic Faith Needed

1. The creation of a peaceful world requires the faith that peace is possible. There is not much in the empirical situation to justify this faith. The slogan of a generation ago, "A war to end war," rings hollow under the conditions of today's world. The other five conditions just mentioned require changes so far-reaching that it is easy to say they are impossible of fulfillment and dismiss them as wishful thinking.

Only through faith in God and his unfaltering purpose does one find ground for hope. Faith in the possibility of peace means faith in the living God. It means faith in the Lord of history who *can* and who *does* change human nature, and who in spite of the thwarting of his purposes by human indifference and sin carries steadily forward his will for peace and justice upon earth. It means faith in the God who is above and beyond all history, for the song of the angels on the first Christmas morning has relevance in history only because it comes from a realm beyond our human frailty. Here, surely, is a note which the churches can proclaim directly and unequivocally.

Repentance as a Factor in Peace

2. A peaceful postwar world requires provision for peaceful change. The machinery for such change must, for the most part, be left to statesmen and to the experts in political science. However, there is a basic requirement without which any political structure will be futile. This is the capacity for self-criticism on the part of the people. The mood of self-criticism is an obligation resting upon all, but it is a prime responsibility for those exposed to the temptations inherent in power. As Lord Acton put it, "All power is corrupting."

In religious terms, the self-criticism essential to peaceful change means repentance. It means repentance for personal and national sins, a lively concern for the welfare of all peoples—including those in enemy states—and the elimination of vindictiveness in the making of settlements. It is not to condone what has happened in Germany and Japan to point out again what was clear to most of us before the tensions of war arose; namely, that after the last war the lack of such self-criticism and concern for the common good on the part of the victors was a fertile source of those festering sores among the vanquished which, coming to a head in ruthless aggression, have now spread poison through the world.

It is the business of the churches to call sinners to repentance and to lift up, even in wartime, the vision of a world community to judge our self-seeking and partisan claims. This cannot be done in a vacuum. Our preaching of peace will be largely vain unless the people are made to see the extent to which their own sins of complacent irresponsibility and desire for possessions, prestige and power have contributed—and if uncurbed will continue to contribute—to the outbreak of war. This must be done with courage, in friendliness and with tact. But it must be done. If churches do not bring citizens to the mood of humility and self-searching essential to peaceful change, what other agency will?

God's Sovereignty and the State

3. A peaceful postwar world requires international cooperation. In a world united by God in creation and knit together by men through commerce, inter-communication and culture, national isolation is a fatal anachronism which can have no other outcome than war.

Among those who give thoughtful consideration to a new world order there is virtually unanimous agreement that there can be no lasting peace without the surrender of absolute national sovereignty and the establishment of a function-ing international organization. There are problems here of great complexity. But the one crucial factor is that which today lies at the root of international anarchy; namely, lack of a sense of responsibility for all men in a world society. Were there a general will to world cooperation, the procedures for it could be evolved. As long as nations are concerned only with the welfare of their own citizens, or at most with that of the citizens of nations temporarily allied, the struggle for supremacy will continue to set the stage for world catastrophe on an ever larger scale.

Here again religion impinges on politics. Recognition of the sovereignty of the God revealed in Jesus Christ has a direct bearing on the problem of absolute national sovereignty. Taken seriously it means, in the first place, an object of loy-alty and devotion above all rival earthly claims, and a voice that speaks in judg-ment against the worship of any national state as deity. It means, furthermore, that if God is the Father of all men, profoundly important obligations of sonship and brotherhood are laid upon us which cannot stop at any national boundaries.

Many people are willing to assent to the proposition that international coop-eration is essential to peace. But how is the surrender of absolute national sover-eignty to be brought about when it requires, in the immediate foreground, the surrender of markets protected by high tariff walls, the surrender of easy access to raw materials through the exploitation of colonies, and therefore a consider-able surrender of dividends and wages and the comforts they purchase? It is easy to demonstrate that all this costs much less than war. But the demonstration fails to lead to action. Only a religious motivation is adequate. The social scientists can provide plans for a "brave new world," but the world in its cautious steps toward internationalism will be neither brave, new nor peaceful unless the churches alter the motives and the vision of men.

Jesus and Economic Greed

4. The need of economic security for all, if all are to live in peace, is a point almost too obvious to require mention. But mention is essential, for lack of economic security is the corrupt core from which has spread most of the present anguish of the world. To adapt Lincoln's familiar word, a world cannot remain half hungry and half fed. When it tries to, war inevitably ensues.

There are many questions, including that of war itself, on which no clear word of Jesus is recorded. However, on the evil and destructive character of economic greed his position is unequivocal. His call to discipleship was on more than one occasion a call to mercy and justice in the use of this world's goods. We shall have neither a Christian nor a peaceful world until Christians pass beyond the injunction to philanthropy—great and necessary though this virtue is—to a more forthright challenging of the roots of economic injustice in business practices. Until this is done, and done on a scale wide enough to affect action in the total economic structure of life, we shall not have that juster distribution of goods by which the primary occasion of wars can be averted.

The church is not the only agency urging such redistribution of goods. The labor movement exists for this end, and there are capitalists and intellectuals outside the church who have social vision. But I do not see any group except religious leaders, with a small minority of Christian laymen, who are combining radical challenge of existing inequalities with a vital concern for the good of all classes. Without such a concern above the divisions of class self-interest, not justice but only more bitterness and violence are often the fruits of economic challenge. Again, it looks as though, if we are to have the basic social and economic changes essential to peace, the churches may have to initiate the movement and see it through.

Whence Comes Democracy?

5. A peaceful world requires faith in and practice of the democratic way of life. It is essential to understand, interpret and extend Christian democracy. This requires recognition of points of agreement and difference between the existing political structure and the Christian ideal.

Political democracy roots partly in a Christian vision of the intrinsic worth and dignity of all men as sons of God; partly in a Stoic concept of a natural law of human rights to be observed in a just society; partly in the practical compromises and adjustments of an extremely complex social order in which millions of men of competing interests try to live together without open conflict. It is only as the first element vivifies the second and dominates the third that any true democracy is possible.

It is, therefore, incumbent upon the churches constantly to protest against infringements of democracy in the form of race and class discrimination and the setting aside of civil liberties. In war, even more than in peace, it is necessary to keep the searchlight of the Christian gospel directed upon our civic life, and to guard against any identification of conditions as they are in America with things as they would be in a truly Christian democracy governed by the ideal of the sonship and supreme worth of every soul before God. Such criticism can be made without national disloyalty if it is actuated both by love of country and by a higher love of the God whose will it is that all men dwell together in peace and justice. The church can render immense service to the state in the preservation and extension of the Four Freedoms. But only if its perspective is centered in God and his total human family can it be a true defender of these freedoms.

Bonds of Brotherhood

6. The sixth requirement—that of an international spiritual community as the foundation of international order—requires no extensive comment. It has been implicit throughout all that has been said in this article. It means an international fellowship of prayer, missions, the ecumenical church, preaching, evangelism, religious education, the Christian home, the many agencies of every local congregation. There is not one of these channels that is not potentially the builder of a new society based on understanding, good will and justice. There is no Christian anywhere who cannot make his contribution to cementing the bonds of brotherhood. On these foundations, but on these alone, can a just and lasting peace be built.

Though the world is in flames the authentic work of the churches must go on. Only as this goes forward, not contracted but expanded because of the national emergency, can we hope to see beyond the battle a new world fashioned in the image of the family of God.

Notes

Preface and Acknowledgments

1. "The Task of Theology," *Religion in Life* 31 (Winter 1961–1962): 71. Coffin was the uncle of another well-known defender of the liberal tradition, peace activist and pastor of Riverside Church in New York City, William Sloane Coffin Jr.
2. For a fascinating account of the crisis of the late 1920s, see John Kenneth Galbraith, *The Great Crash of 1929* (New York: Houghton Mifflin, 1997).
3. For parallels between the 1929 crash and the events in fall 2008, see, for example, Paul Farhi, "The Crash October 29, 1929: Stocks Had Reached an All-Time High," *Washington Post* (Oct. 29, 2008): C01; and "Parallels Seen as 1929 Crash Anniversary Nears," Associated Press Newswire (Oct. 27, 2008).
4. Paul Krugman, "Franklin Delano Obama," *New York Times* (Nov. 10, 2008): A29.

Introduction: Liberalism as "the Centrum of American Theology"

1. Robert Bruce Mullin, "A Passion for Progress," review of *The Making of American Liberal Theology: Imagining Progressive Religion, 1805–1900,* by Gary Dorrien, *Christian Century* 119 (July 31, 2002): 36.
2. Harkness did not separate theology and theological ethics. Even writing about technical philosophical or theological issues not ordinarily related to ethics, Harkness normally drew an explicit connection between the topic at hand and the moral life. That is certainly true for the readings in this collection. Ethics or moral theology was for Harkness inseparable from theology. I use the term *theology* in this collection as encompassing moral theology.
3. Georgia Harkness, "The Faith of the North American Churches," typewritten manuscript of lecture given at Niagara Falls, New York, to American delegates of the Madras Conference on June 16, 1938, Georgia Harkness Collection, United Library, Garrett Evangelical Theological Seminary.
4. John Bennett, "After Liberalism—What?" *Christian Century* 50 (Nov. 8, 1933): 1403.
5. Henry Van Dusen, "The Sickness of Liberal Religion," *The Plain Man Seeks for God* (New York: Charles Scribner's Sons, 1933), 24–25.
6. Georgia Harkness, "A Spiritual Pilgrimage," *Christian Century* 56 (March 15, 1939): 349.
7. Gary Dorrien, "American Liberal Theology: Crisis, Irony, Decline, Renewal, Ambiguity," *Cross Currents* 55 (Winter 2006): 456.
8. Mullin, "Passion for Progress," 36.

9. Gary Dorrien, *The Making of American Liberal Theology: Imagining Progressive Religion, 1805–1900* (Louisville, KY: Westminster John Knox, 2001), xv.

10. Harkness, "Divine Sovereignty and Human Freedom," in *Personalism in Theology: A Symposium in Honor of Albert Cornelius Knudson*, ed. Edgar Brightman (Boston: Boston University Press, 1943), 149.

11. Harkness, *Our Christian Hope* (New York: Abingdon, 1964), 11–24.

12. James Burtness, review of *Christian Ethics* by Georgia Harkness, *Lutheran Quarterly* 10 (Fall 1958): 74–75.

13. Waldo Beach, review of *Christian Ethics* by Georgia Harkness, *Interpretation* 12 (January 1958): 108.

14. Charles Kean, review of *The Modern Rival of Christian Faith* by Georgia Harkness, *Journal of Religion* 33 (1953): 77.

15. "Spiritual Pilgrimage," 349.

16. See, for example, "Spiritual Pilgrimage"; "Divine Sovereignty and Human Freedom," 149; and *Understanding the Christian Faith* (New York: Abingdon, 1947), 96 and 97.

17. Harkness, *The Recovery of Ideals* (New York: Charles Scribner's Sons, 1937), 90, 93, and 97.

18. Throughout this collection, both in my comments and in Harkness's texts there are references to World War II and the events leading up to it. A good background resource is Peter Calvocoressi, Guy Wint, and John Pritchard, *The Penguin History of the Second World War* (New York: Penguin Press, 1999).

19. In some of the readings and section prefaces in this collection, there are references to these ecumenical conferences and to the missions movement. For historical background and critical analysis, see Dana L. Robert, ed., *Converting Colonialism: Visions and Realities in Mission History* (Grand Rapids: Eerdmans, 2008); T. V. Philip, *Edinburgh to Salvador: Twentieth Century Ecumenical Missiology* (Delhi: CSS and ISPCK, 1999); Alice Conklin and Ian Christopher Fletcher, *European Imperialisms 1830–1930* (Boston: Houghton Mifflin, 1999); and S. Wesley Ariarajah, *Gospel and Culture: An Ongoing Discussion Within the Ecumenical Movement* (Geneva: WCC, 1994).

20. Henry Van Dusen, *The Vindication of Liberal Theology: A Tract for the Times* (New York: Charles Scribner's Sons, 1963), 21–48; and Gary Dorrien, *The Making of American Liberal Theology: Idealism, Realism, and Modernity, 1900–1950* (Louisville, KY: Westminster John Knox, 2003), 10–20.

21. Van Dusen, *Vindication of Liberal Theology*, 21–22.

22. Ibid., 54.

23. "The Quality of Our Lives," *Christian Century* (May 11, 1960): 568. These late comments of Niebuhr's are widely quoted. See, for example, Van Dusen, *Vindication of Liberal Theology*, 54; Larry Rasmussen, *Reinhold Niebuhr: Theologian of Public Life* (Minneapolis: Fortress, 1991), 22; and Dorrien, *The Making of American Liberal Theology: Idealism, Realism, and Modernity, 1900–1950*, 479–80.

24. Letter from Reinhold Niebuhr to John Bennett (March 13, 1943). Quoted in Richard Wightman Fox, *Reinhold Niebuhr: A Biography* (Ithaca, NY: Cornell University Press, 1997), 214; and Dorrien, *The Making of American Liberal Theology: Idealism, Realism, and Modernity, 1900–1950*, 551.

25. This twofold classification has been widely used. See, for example, Kenneth Cauthen, *The Impact of American Religious Liberalism* (New York: Harper & Row, 1962); and Van Dusen, *Vindication of Liberal Theology*. For other typologies of theological liberalism, see William Dean, *American Religious Empiricism* (Albany: State University of New York Press, 1986), 5–12; and Dorrien, *The Making of American Liberal Theology: Idealism, Realism, and Modernity,*

1900–1950, especially 10–20. Dorrien also offers, in these same pages, an assessment of the various typologies including cautions about the evangelical liberal and modernist liberal typology.

26. Harkness, Harry Emerson Fosdick, Henry Van Dusen, and Henry Sloan Coffin were among those who thought of themselves as evangelical liberals.

I. Georgia Harkness: The Making and Remaking of a Liberal

1. "Where Is He?" *Time* 32 (Dec. 26, 1938): 28.
2. For studies of Georgia Harkness and her work, see Rosemary Keller, *Georgia Harkness: For Such a Time as This* (Nashville: Abingdon, 1992); Paula Elizabeth Gilbert, "Choice of the Greater Good: The Christian Witness of Georgia Harkness" (Ph.D. dissertation, Duke University, 1984); Martha Scott, "The Theology and Social Thought of Georgia Harkness" (Ph.D. dissertation, Garrett Evangelical Theological Seminary, 1984); Dianne Carpenter, "Georgia Harkness's Distinctive Personalist Synthesis" (Ph.D. dissertation, Boston University, 1988); Mary Elizabeth Moore, "To Search and to Witness: Theological Agenda of Georgia Harkness," *Quarterly Review* 13, no. 3 (1993): 3–23; Dianne Carpenter and Rolaine Franz, "Georgia Harkness as a Personalist Theologian," in *The Boston Personalist Tradition in Philosophy, Social Ethics and Philosophy*, ed. Paul Deats and Carol Robb (Macon, GA: Mercer University Press, 1986), 159–87; Helen Johnson, "Georgia Harkness: She Made Theology Understandable," *United Methodists Today* 1 (October 1974): 55–58; Margaret Frakes, "Theology Is Her Province," *Christian Century* 69 (Sept. 24, 1952): 1088–91; Dorrien, *Making of American Liberal Theology: Idealism, Realism, and Modernity, 1900–1950*, 390–414; Rebekah Miles, "Georgia Harkness," in *Makers of Christian Theology in America*, ed. Mark Toulouse and James Duke (Nashville: Abingdon, 1997); Rebekah Miles, "Georgia Harkness: The 'Famed Woman Theologian' and 'Glorious Champion' of Women's Clergy Rights," *The Circuit Rider* 30 (May/June 2006): 13–14; Rosemary Keller, "'When the Subject Is Female': The Impact of Gender on Revisioning American Religious History," in *Religious Diversity and American Religious History: Studies in Traditions and Cultures*, ed. Walter H. Conser Jr. and Sumner B. Twiss (Athens: University of Georgia Press, 1997), 102–27; Dorothy Bass, "Georgia Elma Harkness," in *Notable American Women: The Modern Period*, ed. Barbara Sicherman and Carol Hurd Green (Cambridge, MA: Belknap Press of Harvard University Press, 1980), 312–14; and Marianne H. Micks, "Georgia Harkness: Chastened Liberal" *Theology Today* 53 (October 1996): 311–19.
3. Keller, *Georgia Harkness*, 160; and Dorrien, *Making of American Liberal Theology: Idealism, Realism, and Modernity, 1900–1950*, 404.
4. The primary source of accounts of Harkness's early life is her autobiography, "Days of My Years," unpublished autobiography, written for the Pacific Coast Theological Group in 1955, Georgia Harkness Collection, United Library, Garrett Evangelical Theological Seminary.
5. Ibid., 9 and 13.
6. I did this genealogical research drawing on the information that Harkness knew about her paternal great-grandparents and then, using standard Internet genealogical resources, followed the line back into the seventeenth century.
7. Some scholars claim that Nathaniel Hawthorne's character Rev. Arthur Dimmesdale of *The Scarlet Letter* was modeled after Hannah's clergyman father, Stephen Batchellor, a rogue of colonial Massachusetts. See Frederick Newberry's "A Red Hot 'A' and a Lusting Divine: Sources for the Scarlet Letter," *New England Quarterly* 60 (June 1987): 256–64.

8. Harkness descended directly from Provided Southwick, as did another Quaker of Harkness's era, Hannah Milhous Nixon, mother to Richard Nixon. From brother Daniel's line came Jennie Jerome, possible originator of the Manhattan cocktail and certain mother of Winston Churchill.

9. *Grace Abounding* (Nashville: Abingdon, 1969), 40.

10. "Days of My Years," 16.

11. Ibid., 18.

12. *The Church and the Immigrant* (New York: George Doran, 1921), 90–97 and 101.

13. For an early, classic study of the "new immigration" near the time of Harkness's birth, see Jacob A. Riis, *How the Other Half Lives: Studies Among the Tenements of New York* (New York: Scribner's Sons, 1890).

14. "Days of My Years," 18.

15. Reading 3, "Personality, Human and Divine," 35.

16. See reading 10, "How God is Limited," 90.

17. Henry Nelson Wieman and Bernard Eugene Meland, *American Philosophies of Religion* (Chicago: Willett Clark, 1936), 134.

18. This book was finished after her death by her colleague Charles Kraft, *Biblical Backgrounds of the Middle East Conflict* (Nashville: Abingdon, 1976).

19. Charles E. Morris, *The Progressive Democracy of James M. Cox* (1920; repr. Whitefish, MI: Kessinger Publishing, 2004).

20. See Eric Foner, "He's the Worst Ever," *Washington Post* (Dec. 3, 2006): B1; and, for a different point of view, Michael Lind, "He's Only Fifth Worst," *Washington Post* (Dec. 3, 2006): B1.

21. "Days of My Years," 21.

22. Keller, *Georgia Harkness*, 162–63.

23. *The Resources of Religion* (New York: Henry Holt, 1936), viii.

24. "Days of My Years," 23 (my italics).

25. Ibid., 24.

26. Ibid., 21.

27. Keller offers the most detailed account of these events and the relevant letters and interviews; see Keller, *Georgia Harkness*, 236–45.

28. Interview of Mary Dunham (Aug. 19, 1990), Ithaca, New York, 11. Georgia Harkness Collection, United Library, Garrett Evangelical Theological Seminary. This account is also included in Keller's book *Georgia Harkness*, although Keller's version of this quotation is more mild than the actual wording in the transcript, which is what I have used here. See Keller, *Georgia Harkness*, 241.

29. Keller, *Georgia Harkness*, 240.

30. Ibid., 244.

31. Harkness, *The Modern Rival of Christian Faith: An Analysis of Secularism* (New York: Abingdon, 1952), 5.

32. "Days of My Years," 29.

II. "A Spiritual Pilgrimage": How Harkness's Mind Changed

1. "A Spiritual Pilgrimage," *Christian Century* 56 (March 15, 1939): 348–51.

2. Harkness, "Days of My Years," 25.

III. *Conflicts in Religious Thought* (1929)

Editor's Preface notes

1. *Conflicts in Religious Thought* (New York: Henry Holt, 1929).

2. Other Americans of the time were enduring poverty and brutal working conditions.
3. *Conflicts in Religious Thought*, 11.
4. See reading 1, "Spiritual Pilgrimage," 22.
5. See reading 17, "By What Authority," 140–49.
6. Hocking had included Harkness's essay on the evidences of God in a reader that was developed to be used with a book he had coauthored, *Preface to Philosophy* (New York: Macmillan, 1947).
7. *Conflicts in Religious Thought*, 9.

Reading 2 Original Author Notes

8. This of course is only one of the reasons for the Anglo-Catholic movement. Many are attracted by the value of the Catholic ritual for religious experience, and others by the desire to cooperate in a movement toward church union.

Reading 4 Original Author Notes

9. Borden P. Bowne, *Theism*, p. 53. Professor Bowne (1847–1910) was the principal founder of the American personalistic school of thought, which makes personality the primary reality. The argument from interaction forms the most distinctive feature of the philosophy of Lotze, under whom Bowne studied.
10. See Henderson, *The Fitness of the Environment*.
11. Cf. Ch. VII, Sec. 1, for a fuller treatment of the difference. [Ed. note: This is Harkness's original footnote, and it refers to a part of chap. 7 not included here.]
12. Borden P. Bowne, *Theory of Thought and Knowledge*, Pt. II, Ch. II.
13. This analogy is borrowed from Fosdick, *The Assurance of Immortality*, p. 83.
14. The term is not used here in the same sense in which Leibniz used it. He denied interaction among the "monads," or elements of the universe.
15. *Op. cit.*, p. 24. Cf. also A. S. Eddington, *The Nature of the Physical World*, p. 294, "It is a consequence of the advent of the quantum theory that *physics is no longer pledged to a scheme of deterministic law.*"
16. The leading exponent of this view, Hans Driesch, has given this life force the name of *entelechy*, a term borrowed from Aristotle and meaning literally "having a purpose within." Bergson calls it the *Élan Vital.*
17. *Science and the Modern World*, p. 157.
18. John Fiske, *Through Nature to God*, p. 189.
19. L. P. Jacks, *Religious Perplexities*, p. 19.
20. H. E. Fosdick, *The Meaning of Faith*, p. 12.

IV. *The Resources of Religion (1936)*

Editor's Preface Notes

1. *The Resources of Religion* (New York: Henry Holt, 1936).
2. Ibid., vii.
3. For a review of the New Deal and larger political changes standing behind it, see David Plotke, *Building a Democratic Political Order: Reshaping American Liberalism in the 1930s and 1940s* (New York: Cambridge University Press, 1996).
4. "Germany and the War-Peace," *Zion's Herald* 103 (Jan. 7, 1925): 11–12. See also "Germany's Place in the Shadow," *Christian Advocate* 100 (Jan. 22, 1925): 111.
5. *Resources of Religion*, viii–ix.

Reading 5 Original Author Notes

6. A young negro condemned to serve eighteen to twenty years on the Georgia chain gang for the crime (!) of leading a thousand hungry people of Atlanta, black and white, to the State House to ask for relief. He was convicted of inciting to sedition on an ancient statute originally intended to prevent slaves from rebelling against their masters. The law has been declared unconstitutional but at the time this goes to press the case is still unsettled.
7. See Niebuhr, *An Interpretation of Christian Ethics,* pp. 72ff.
8. Sin has been defined by Reinhold Niebuhr (in a class lecture) as "Nature's will to live transmuted into spirit's will to power." Cf. also *An Interpretation of Christian Ethics,* p. 76.
9. By redeemed individuals I do not mean exclusively those who have passed through a conscious process of religious conversion.
10. It probably need not be said that I do not refer to being an "'umble" person after the manner of Uriah Heep.
11. Cf. Charles Webber, "A Minister in a Strike," *Christian Century,* May 13, 1931; also "Clergymen Invade Industry," *The World Tomorrow,* August, 1932.
12. The proposal to build a military air base on Grand Isle, in Lake Champlain, is a ridiculous but tragic evidence that war hysteria is gaining force.
13. Henry Van Dusen, *God in These Times,* 161.
14. Cf. Professor Whitehead's *Adventures of Ideas,* Ch. V.
15. Robert Browning, *Bishop Blougram's Apology.*
16. The complexity of the problem is further indicated by the fact that this organization was obliged in 1932 to take a poll of its members to determine whether its renunciation of violence was to pertain to the class struggle as well as to international war. Ninety percent voting affirmatively, the organization remains pacifist.
17. I do not wish to be dogmatic in including this as a necessary step toward peace, since many sincere, intelligent Christians disagree on the ground that pacifism cannot be effective in the arena of political realities. I must, however, state my conviction that when pacifism does not become "passivism" it is an effective strategy, and the only ultimately effective one.
18. Suggested by an address given by Reinhold Niebuhr.
19. A vivid phrase of Bertrand Russell's, the closing words of *A Free Man's Worship.*

Reading 6 Original Author Notes

20. Cf. Whitehead, *Adventures of Ideas,* Part I.
21. *Op. cit.,* p. 19 f.
22. *The Protestant Ethic and the Spirit of Capitalism,* p. 181.
23. H. Richard Niebuhr, *The Church Against the World,* p. 128.
24. Robert L. Calhoun, *God and the Common Life,* p. 30.
25. *Church, Community and State: A World Issue,* p. 9.
26. As I write, the press announces that Hans Kerrl, head of the Reich Church Ministry, has declared an amnesty for all pastors expelled from their pulpits during the régime of Reich Bishop Mueller. That no real hope of religious liberty can be expected from this action is evident from Kerrl's widely publicized statement: "National Socialism is positive Christianity—love of your neighbor. Your neighbor is in the first place not a Hottentot, but a German—your racial comrade. Out of your blood affinity demonstrate first your love, and then we shall believe that later your love can spread to others. When you march

with the State, then we await the moment when your churches will again come to life." (*New York Times,* Oct. 30, 1935.)

27. *Church, Community and State: A World Issue,* p. 10.
28. Harold Gray's *Character: Bad* gives a vivid picture not only of experiences in Fort Leavenworth but of the events and movement of his thought leading up to this incarceration.
29. Cf. editorial in *The Christian Century,* April 12, 1933. Further evidence of this weird incongruity is presented in an article by Jerome Davis, "If Not Dr. Macintosh, Who?" in *The Christian Century,* March 8, 1933.
30. Cf. Walter Denny: *The Career and Significance of Jesus,* for an excellent treatment of the place of nationalism in the events which led to the crucifixion of Jesus.

V. *The Recovery of Ideals (1937)*

Editor's Preface Notes

1. *The Recovery of Ideals* (New York: Charles Scribner's Sons, 1937).
2. Ibid., 11.
3. Ibid., 3.
4. Ibid., 29.
5. Ibid., 46.
6. Ibid., 88.
7. Ibid., 93 and 97.
8. Brightman, "Personalism as a Philosophy of Religion," *Crozer Quarterly* 5 (October 1929): 385. For more on Brightman's "Given," see reading 7, "The Abyss and the Given."
9. *Recovery of Ideals,* viii.

Reading 7 Original Author Notes

10. I do not deny revelation. But revelation is meaningless apart from a knowledge of man's capacity to receive it.
11. Both motive and consequences need to be taken into account in judging any such interest. The subjective and objective factors in a moral decision are not identical, but an artificial separation is dangerous.
12. This recognition of the permeating character of our moral egotism is most incisive in the prophetic element of Hebrew-Christian faith. But even in so aristocratic a mental climate as that reflected by Plato, there is an implicit recognition of it. The Socratic-Platonic doctrine that virtue is knowledge roots in the fact that nobody will admit having willfully and maliciously done evil. *Cf.* F. J. E. Woodbridge, *The Son of Apollo,* pp. 134 ff.
13. *Op. cit.,* Chap. III.
14. There are, of course, many other impulses characteristic of human nature. Pugnacity may belong here as much as the three explicitly mentioned. However, these are the most elemental. Pugnacity and jealousy often appear when one of these is thwarted.

Reading 8 Original Author Notes

15. "God Is More Than We Can Think," *Christendom,* Spring, 1936.
16. I believe that Professor Wieman is more of a supernaturalist than he will call himself. The word of Professor Roy Wood Sellars, quoted in *American Philosophies of Religion,* p. 264, seems to me at this point to speak the exact truth. "Upon this I

think all naturalists are agreed [he writes in *The New Humanist*] that between naturalism and theism it is a case of either-or." For Professors Wieman and Meland to include such theists as Robert L. Calhoun and William K. Wright, along with themselves, among the naturalists seems to me to denature naturalism.

Reading 9 Original Author Notes

17. *Op. cit.,* 29, 30. Jowett's translation.
18. *Process and Reality,* p. 532.
19. From the Greek ποιητής.
20. This view is stated more fully in my *Conflicts in Religious Thought*, Chap. IX. Since that was written I have changed my position somewhat.

Reading 10 Original Author Notes

21. Ideas and ideals are real, but not as separate types. They are combinations of event and form: that is, psychological events and universal structures of meaning.
22. Professor Whitehead calls them *eternal objects* and declares that we must "seek the forms in the facts." Cf. *Process and Reality,* p. 30.
23. It is at this point that Christian cosmology diverges most sharply from that of Plato.
24. *Form* is the necessary condition of any orderly creation: the specific *forms* which enter into the process of creation might be other than they are.
25. I choose Berkeley's famous example, not because I agree with his view, but because in certain important respects I do not.
26. William P. Montague, "Philosophy as Vision," *International Journal of Ethics,* October, 1933.

VI. Theology and Theological Ethics in Conversation and Crisis (1938–41)

Editor's Preface Notes

1. "The Abyss and the Given," *Christendom* 3 (Winter 1938): 508–20.
2. See reading 11, "The Abyss and the Given," 101; and *The Foundations of Christian Knowledge* (New York: Abingdon, 1955), 67.
3. Martha Scott, "The Theology and Social Thought of Georgia Harkness" (Ph.D. dissertation, Garrett Evangelical Theological Seminary, 1984), 40–41.
4. See, for example, *Conflicts in Religious Thought*, 45 and 175; *Recovery of Ideals*, especially 146–50; and *Resources of Religion*, 142, 176, and 192.
5. See Robert Calhoun, "A Symposium on Reinhold Niebuhr's *The Nature and Destiny of Man*," *Christendom* 6 (Fall 1941): 573–76; as well as Richard Fox, *Reinhold Niebuhr: A Biography* (New York: Pantheon, 1985), 203; and Dorrien, *Making of American Liberal Theology: Idealism, Realism, and Modernity, 1900–1950*, 549–51.
6. Harkness, "A Symposium on Reinhold Niebuhr's *Nature and Destiny of Man*," *Christendom* 6 (Fall 1941): 567–70.

Reading 12 Original Author Notes

7. *Our Knowledge of God,* p. 101. Baillie's citation from Barth is from *Nein!,* p. 20 f.
8. Oxford Conference Report, Section IV, 2 (f).

VII. The Faith of a World Church in a World Crisis (1938–40)

Editor's Preface Notes

1. Harkness, "Days of My Years," 25.
2. "The Faith of the North American Churches," Meeting of North American Delegates to the Madras Conference, Niagara Falls, NY, June 1938.
3. See reading 1, "Spiritual Pilgrimage."
4. *The Faith by Which the Church Lives* (New York: Abingdon, 1940), 9.
5. Ibid., 12.
6. For background information, see Calvocoressi et al., *Penguin History of the Second World War.*
7. *Faith by Which the Church Lives,* 33–34.
8. John C. Bennett, "Review of *The Faith by Which the Church Lives*," *Journal of Religion* 21, no. 1 (1941): 104.
9. See reading 2, "Shall We Walk by Faith?"
10. Because Harkness was a self-identified modalist, she did not need to distinguish logically between the mind of Christ and the Holy Spirit. See *The Fellowship of the Holy Spirit* (Nashville: Abingdon, 1966), 115–20, especially 69 and 119.

Reading 15 Original Author Notes

11. Editor's note: At an ecumenical conference in Utrecht in 1938, delegates voted on a theological statement to be included in the constitution of the nascent World Council of Churches. The final statement was controversial for some members because it referred to Jesus Christ as "Savior and God." Some delegates objected to the direct identification of Jesus with God, but the language was maintained.
12. *The World Mission of the Church,* p. 126 (American edition, p. 106).
13. *The World Mission of the Church,* p. 19 (American edition, p. 16).
14. *The World Mission of the Church,* p. 18 (American edition, p. 15).

Reading 16 Original Author Notes

15. This was not the case with the youth from America, who in some instances were nonplussed to discover that affirmation rather than inquiry might characterize the mood of intelligent Christians.
16. *The World Mission of the Church,* p. 16.
17. *Ante-Nicene Fathers,* Vol. I, p. 27. John Bennett in *Social Salvation,* p. 116, lifted this phrase from oblivion.

Reading 17 Original Author Notes

18. From the title of the article by Robert L. Calhoun.
19. In *The Recovery of Ideals,* Chap. XI. The difficulties in Professor Wieman's thought which are there stated still seem to me crucial, though his article in *The Christian Century* on "How My Mind Has Changed" shows more attempt to include in his system the concepts of historic Christianity than do any of his earlier writings.
20. *Ends and Means,* p. 276. Huxley's reference is to the Old Testament.
21. Students in college have often told me that they were intellectually convinced of the existence of God on philosophical grounds, but that the whole idea left

them unmoved. There may be various reasons, but the central one is that God hat not reached them by the main route of Christian faith.

VIII. Fighting for Peace (1941–42)

Editor's Preface Notes

1. Western Union telegram, from *Time* magazine to Georgia Harkness (Dec. 10, 1941), Georgia Harkness Collection, United Library, Garrett Theological Seminary. Garrett Evangelical Theological Seminary. Quoted in Gilbert, *Choice of the Greater Good,* 90.
2. "Days of My Years," 20.
3. Ibid., 21.
4. Ibid., 25.
5. "The Churches and Vietnam," *Christian Century* 83 (Jan. 26, 1966): 111–13.
6. Margaret Frakes, "Theology Is Her Province," 1091.
7. "The Christian's Dilemma," *Christian Century* 58 (Aug. 6, 1941): 977–79; "What Is God Doing in This War?" *Christian Century* 59 (Nov. 4, 1942): 1346–48; and "The Churches in This War," *Christian Century* 59 (Nov. 18, 1942): 1418–20.
8. "Address by President Franklin D. Roosevelt on July 4, 1941," found at http://gurukul.american.edu/heintze/Roosevelt1.htm
9. Niebuhr, "Pacifism and 'America First,'" *Love and Justice: Selections from the Shorter Writings of Reinhold Niebuhr,* ed. D. B. Robertson (1957; repr. Louisville, KY: Westminster/John Knox, 1992), 290 and 292. Originally published in *Christianity and Crisis* 1 (June 16, 1941).

Reading 19

10. Editor's Note: This quotation is from "Pacifism and 'America First'," *Christianity and Crisis* 1 (June 16, 1941).

Bibliography

Books by Georgia Harkness,
Arranged Chronologically

The Church and the Immigrant. New York: George Doran, 1921.
Conflicts in Religious Thought. New York: Henry Holt, 1929.
John Calvin: The Man and His Ethics. New York: Henry Holt, 1931.
Holy Flame. Boston: Bruce Humphries, 1935.
The Resources of Religion. New York: Henry Holt, 1936.
The Recovery of Ideals. New York: Charles Scribner's Sons, 1937.
Religious Living. New York: Association Press, 1937.
The Faith by Which the Church Lives. New York: Abingdon, 1940.
The Glory of God: Poems and Prayers for Devotional Use. New York: Abingdon, 1943.
The Dark Night of the Soul. New York: Abingdon, 1945.
Understanding the Christian Faith. New York: Abingdon, 1947.
Prayer and the Common Life. New York: Abingdon, 1948.
The Gospel and Our World. New York: Abingdon, 1949.
Through Christ Our Lord: A Devotional Manual. New York: Abingdon, 1950.
The Modern Rival of Christian Faith: An Analysis of Secularism. New York: Abingdon,
    1952.
O Worship the Lord. New York: National Council of Churches in the U.S.A., 1952.
Be Still and Know. New York: Abingdon, 1953.
Sources of Western Morality: From Primitive Society Through the Beginnings of Christianity.
    New York: Charles Scribner's Sons, 1954.
Toward Understanding the Bible. New York: Charles Scribner's Sons, 1954.
The Foundations of Christian Knowledge. New York: Abingdon, 1955.
Christian Ethics. New York: Abingdon, 1957.
The Bible Speaks to Daily Needs. New York: Abingdon, 1959.
The Providence of God. New York: Abingdon, 1960.
Beliefs that Count. New York: Abingdon, 1961.
The Church and Its Laity. New York: Abingdon, 1962.
Our Christian Hope. New York: Abingdon, 1964.
What Christians Believe. Nashville: Abingdon, 1965.
The Fellowship of the Holy Spirit. Nashville: Abingdon, 1966.
A Devotional Treasury from the Early Church. Nashville: Abingdon, 1968.
Disciplines of the Christian Life. Richmond: John Knox, 1969.

Grace Abounding. Nashville: Abingdon, 1969.
Stability Amid Change. Nashville: Abingdon, 1969.
The Ministry of Reconciliation. Nashville: Abingdon, 1971.
Women in Church and Society: A Historical and Theological Inquiry. Nashville: Abingdon, 1972.
The Methodist Church in Social Thought and Action. Nashville: Abingdon, 1972.
Mysticism: Its Meaning and Message. Nashville: Abingdon, 1973.
Understanding the Kingdom of God. Nashville: Abingdon, 1974.
Posthumously with Charles Kraft, *Biblical Backgrounds of the Middle East Conflict.* Nashville: Abingdon, 1976.

Index

Adams, James Luther, 19, 100
American Theological Society, 8
Amsterdam Ecumenical Conference.
  See ecumenical conferences

Bainton, Roland, 14, 100
Barthian theology, 5, 19, 21, 101, 110, 123,
  134, 144
Barth, Karl, 5, 19, 47, 110, 123
  See also Barthian theology
Bennett, John, 1, 5, 19, 121
Boston University, xiii, 10–11, 27, 107
  See also personalism.
Boston University School of Religious
  Education and Social Service, 10
Bowne, Bordon Parker, 11–12, 28, 37, 175n9
Brightman, Edgar, 11–12, 27, 28, 69, 70, 89,
  99, 105–108
  See also personalism
Brunner, Emil, 5, 110, 152

Calhoun, Robert, 14, 100, 177–178n16
capitalism
  economic imperialism and paganism, a
    product of, 59, 62, 64
  excesses of, 8, 48, 54, 137
  oppositional to Christian faith, 62–64
  relation to nationalism, 67, 104
Christ. *See under* Jesus
church, the
  Christ's, 132, 147, 149
  custodian and means for growth of the
    gospel and the Kingdom, 24, 60, 115,
    128–29, 149–50
  ecumenical, worldwide, 3, 15, 24–25, 121,
    130–140, 164

general statements, 24–25, 149
  as hope for healing and peace, 136, 139–40
  North American, 122–125
  responsibility of, 147, 149, 159, 166–67,
    169
  and state, 65–66
  unity within, 24, 127, 130, 136
Coffin, Henry Sloan, xi, 154, 171n1
coherence. *See* truth; synoptic method
communism, 8, 137–38, 146, 155
  Harkness suspected of, 17, 138
conservative evangelicalism, 2
continental theology, 15, 18, 20–22, 99, 101,
  127–28, 132, 135, 157
Coolidge, Calvin, xiii, 13, 67
Cornell University, 9–10
cross, the
  the centrality of, 3
  the meaning of, 21, 98, 164
  the way of, 55, 57, 68, 156, 161
  See also Jesus

Darwin, Charles, 80
  See also evolution
democracy, 4, 10, 12, 25, 62, 100, 118, 128,
  133, 137, 139, 158, 168–69
demonic, the. *See under* evil
depression, the. *See* economic crises and
  depression
discrimination, xiii, 8, 17–18, 169
Dorrien, Gary, 2, 5, 172n24

economic crises and depression, xiii–xiv, 3, 8,
  13–14, 18, 20, 26, 28, 30, 46–47, 58,
  69, 76
  See also stock market crash of 1929

183